swedish breads
and pastries

swedish breads and pastries

Jan Hedh

photography by Klas Andersson

Skyhorse Publishing

Skyhorse Publishing books may be purchased in bulk at special discounts for sales promotion, corporate gifts, fund-raising, or educational purposes. Special editions can also be created to specifications. For details, contact the Special Sales Department, Skyhorse Publishing, 555 Eighth Avenue, Suite 903, New York, NY 10018 or info@skyhorsepublishing.com.

www.skyhorsepublishing.com

10 9 8 7 6 5 4 3 2 1

Library of Congress Cataloging-in-Publication Data is available on file.
ISBN: 978-1-61608-051-8

Printed in China

Foreword

Freshly baked bread for breakfast, lunch, and dinner ought to be a basic human right, but today we don't have bakeries on every corner like I did growing up in Malmö. Now most people buy their bread in supermarkets, where they heat up par-baked doughs for loaves, buns, and pastries. This is all done by staff with no training in the subject or knowledge of how the bread should taste, nor whether it should be baked dark or light. Their Danish pastries (*Wienerbröd/Viennoiserie*) are usually fermented in baking cabinets so hot that half of the margarine runs out of the pastries instead of staying inside of them. French rolls are simply thrown in boxes, inflated by various baking products and always lack the crispy crust, beautiful crackle on the surface, and airy middle that they should have. When I was an apprentice, we used to compete to see who could make rolls and buns that would crackle the most. The buns were so round at the bottom that they would almost spin when you pulled them out of the oven with a baking rod.

At Olof Viktor's Bakery in Glemminge, the bakers are praised for their Danish pastries, which are made with real butter and vanilla cream from actual vanilla beans, not the cold-stirred muck full of modified starch, vanilla-flavored sugars, and other hocus-pocus ingredients that have nothing to do with properly cooked custard. However, one naturally cannot spend too much time only making French rolls when also trying to keep the cost down to a nickel apiece. When something is that cheap, there is almost always something wrong with it.

Back in the day, we used to have several good pastry shops and bakeries in Sweden. In Gothenburg there was Bräutigam's Pastry Shop on Kungsportsavenyn, famous for its nice pralines and marzipan. Bråst was also an excellent pastry shop, I remember. Oscar Berg's Hovkonditori and Filips Hovkonditori in Regeringsgatan were the finest pastry shops in Stockholm, and OGO on Kungsgatan was known across the country as well. There were many famous pastry shops outside of the big cities, too. Fahlman's in Helsingborg is still there, to my great delight. Back then, they also had a branch in Lund. Lennart's in Eksjö, Spencer's in Borås, Holmgren's in Kalmar, Juhlin's in Skövde, Zander Kellerman's in Ystad, Berg's in Värnamo, Börje's in Växjö, Lundagård's Hovkonditori and Tage Håkansson's in Lund, Danielsson's in Örebro, Dackås in Hudiksvall and Palm's in Sundsvall—there are countless classic pastry shops, but I couldn't very well list them all here.

In Malmö, Swedberg's Bakery and Sundets Bröd were the best bread bakers in town, at least according to my parents. Swedberg's was famous for its six-part braided French bread and its Laputa bread. We would buy crumpets and water rolls (water-based French rolls) from one of the home bakeries, which were often run by women. We would get the dark rye bread, *kavring*, at Mellbybagaren's, a master at making *hårdkavring*— a dark, dense rye bread from Skåne—who also held a diploma from the Gastronomic Academy.

When I was in school, we used to have coffee at Kronprinsen and sometimes at Prinsen and Gondolen. Each had their specialties: almond cookies, cream buns, pastries and cakes, ice cream, frozen pudding, meringue sundaes . . . My mother used to get pralines and chocolate-dipped preserved orange peels at Gunnar's Konditori. At Fridhems-skonditoriet we would get Parisian waffles and *Kirschbollar* (brandy truffles), wreath-shaped pastries for special occasions and toffee rolls filled with chocolate butter cream. At Hollandia there were always Napoleon pastries, Zola pastries, crispy freshly baked Danishes (*Wienerbröd*), and apple pastries made with butter dough in their café. We would also have coffee at Residens Schweizerei, where Kurt Andersson was head pastry chef, and their pastries were always of the finest quality. Kurt was a specialist at presenting, and his Christmas decorations, including beautiful cocoa paintings and marzipan figures, were greatly admired when I was a boy.

At Blekingsborg's Konditori, where I was an apprentice, we primarily made French bread, Brioche buns, Berliner doughnuts, wheat dough, Karlsbader dough, Danish dough, butter dough, scalded Skåne bread (*skånska skållade bröd*), and *hålkakor* (hole-cakes—a round loaf with a hole in the middle). This pastry shop's specialty was cream puffs (*skumbullar*), which we made several times a week. We would always dip them in tempered dark chocolate and then roll them in grated coconut.

When I started as an apprentice, 45 years ago, the bakeries made bread, whereas a pastry chef (aside from making pastries) rarely baked any bread in his shop other than French rolls. These days, the trades of bread baking and pastry making have bled into one another: the pastry shops are now baking bread, while most bakeries have disappeared altogether and been replaced by generic stores selling bread full of preservatives and additives.

It has now been 7 years since we started Olof Viktor's Bakery in Glemminge, and there is a neverending stream of customers who wish to buy real brick-oven baked bread that tastes like it did in the old days. Save us from bread in plastic bags! Bread tastes proper when it's fresh. It is not supposed to be soggy and soft, but have a thick, flavorful crust and be somewhat tough and elastic inside.

At Olof Viktor's, everything revolves around the firewood brick oven. No electric oven could ever yield the same flavor and aroma. The clever baker Erik Olofson was the first in Sweden to use a firewood brick oven, at Rosendal in Djurgården in Stockholm. Today he runs a fine bakery in an old mill in Gotland, and he was the one who taught us to light the fire in the oven.

When I got my baker's and pastry chef certificate, brick-oven baking was not mandatory, but rather a lost art in our country. Nowadays, more and more brick-oven bakeries are opening, and interest has increased tremendously among home bakers.

At Olof Viktor's, we retain old baking traditions and knowledge of the trade, and the only machines we use are kneading machines for heavy doughs. We use only butter; for us, margarine does not exist. We almost always start with pre-doughs, sourdoughs, and scaldings before we begin baking. We knead the dough the next day and let it rest, after which we shape the loaves and let them rise slowly overnight. Early the following morning, we bake the bread directly on a baking stone in the firewood brick oven, our pride. At 6 a.m., most of the breads are ready for sale in the store and on their way to customers in Malmö, Höllviken, and Helsingborg. This profession is for early risers . . .

In this second book of mine about bread, I have included many more whole wheat breads than in the previous, and a few more original flours like Emmer, Kamut, and spelt wholemeal. It also contains pastries and some savory dishes that come with the territory. Follow the recipes carefully and use scales for weight indications whenever possible—using deciliters or cups will yield less accurate results! Use a thermometer to ensure the temperatures' precision. Keep in mind that flour is perishable and does not improve with storage. Old and dry flour absorbs more water than fresh flour. Also, put a baking stone in the oven and you will discover what lovely breads you are able to make yourself.

I wish you the best of luck with the breads and pastries in this book, which I dedicate to the memory of my dear mother Kerstin, who taught me what bread and food should really taste like.

Jan Hedh
Malmö, August 2009

Bread is a historically important part of the human existence. It originates from Mesopotamia by the Eufrates and Tigris rivers, where wheat and barley were grown about 9,000 years ago. The earliest breads, made from grain, were flat, as barley does not contain enough gluten to rise. The following elements are all involved in the making of bread: Seeds are sown and grown, heat from the sun and rain ripen the seeds, and, finally, fire is required for the baking of the bread. Without heat—from either a firewood or electric oven—no bread!

Brick-oven baked bread

At Olof Viktor's Bakery in Glemminge, we see long lines of bread lovers who appreciate the taste of bread made in a firewood oven—nothing compares to this bread. These days, each and every baker claims to be using a brick oven. However, using a firewood oven—starting with 75 kilograms (165 pounds) of firewood, kindling, and then letting it burn out—is completely different from simply plugging into a wall. Several hours later, you sweep out the embers and the oven is ready for use. When you put the leavened bread into the oven with a baker's peel and feel the smell of the fire, you are truly baking. Anything else is a simulation that could never create quite the same aroma or flavor.

I remember a conversation with the French baker Poilâne after having inspected his new brick-oven bakery in London, shortly before he crashed his plane into the English Channel. In order to acquire a permit for building a brick oven in central London, he first had to ask both the Queen and Lord Mayor for permission. To him, however, using any other oven for baking was completely unthinkable. Since he passed away, his daughter has been running the bakery in London and in Paris. They deliver bread every day across the world from their Paris headquarters. They make only one kind of levain bread, though their brand is strong in the industry.

Home bakers need not despair over the lack of these professional resources, however. One can actually simulate a firewood oven more than passably by putting a baking stone, roughly 2–3 centimeters (1 inch) thick, in a regular oven. These stones have recently become fashionable in assorted kitchenware stores, much like other baking tools and fermentation buckets—baking has once again become "hot"! Preheat the stone, or at least a tray, low in the oven at 250°C (482°F). When putting bread in the oven directly onto a preheated stone or tray, it rises immediately instead of waiting for the base to heat up.

Golden rules of baking

First of all: Keep your tools handy. Use a good digital scale, if possible, to measure all ingredients carefully. Volume measurements are never as accurate.

Whether the dough should be kneaded by hand or using a machine is constantly debated. I prefer a machine, since it is laborious to knead the dough by hand long enough for the gluten to develop, and the results are rarely as good. Use a highly precise digital oven thermometer to ensure that your oven is showing the right temperature. You can also use it to measure the dough temperature and bread that is finished baking.

There is a great variety of rolling pins of different materials and designs: wood, marble, or teflon, from small and simple models to large professional rolling pins with ball bearings. Wooden rolling pins are the most versatile.

Flouring the table surface prevents the dough from sticking to it and makes it easier to roll out the dough. Sometimes sifting is necessary, especially when mixing in leaveners such as baking powder, bicarbonate of soda, cloudberry salt, etc.

At Olof Viktor's Bakery, where Maria Olsson is the manager and runs the production, pre-doughs and scaldings are made on the first day. The dough is kneaded the next day and left to rest. It is then divided into loaves and left to rest for a minimum of 16 hours in the refrigerator. This method enhances the bread's aroma. The long rising time allows the flour to absorb the water properly, and the sourdough to pick up all of the aroma from the grains. The cold leavening provides the bread with the right amount of acidity and even improves the baking ability of the dough.

During its first rest, the dough benefits most from staying in a lightly oiled plastic container covered with a lid, not a baking cloth. Use a container that holds up to 10 liters (2.6 gallons).

I prefer leavening the bread in a floured bucket or on a floured cloth, in which case the cloth is pulled up slightly between the loaves so that they rise upward rather than sideways. This is especially important when working with loose dough. Oftentimes, I also leave the bread on a floured wooden plate using nothing more than the heat in the room to speed up the process.

When buttering pans for breads and soft cakes, use soft butter, not melted. Unsalted butter is generally fresher than salted. Too much butter can make the dough collapse, whereas too little could cause the bread to get stuck in the pan.

Tip for buttering pans: Mix 1,000 grams (6½ cups + 2 tablespoons) of soft butter with 200 grams (1¼ cups) of sifted potato flour. Margarine, naturally, is forbidden!

Traditionally, a badger brush is used to brush the dough with egg, icings, etc.

When baking at home, I usually spray a little water into the oven with a squirt bottle to wet the surface of the bread while baking; the damp heat helps the bread to expand more easily and become light and airy. Baking bread without any steam dries out the surface and keeps it from expanding the way it should. In the old days, bakeries were sometimes referred to as steam bakeries. It was also customary to stroke—for example, French bread—with a brush dipped in water after the loaf was taken out of the oven in order for it to crackle nicely.

Always let the bread cool on a metal oven rack to quicken the cooling process.

Hygiene is, of course, a very serious matter. I recommend taking off both wristwatches and rings while baking, as flour has a tendency to reach into small spaces.

Baker's Swedish

Anrörning The same as scalding (see below), except with a smaller amount of flour, which holds the bread together better.

Baka av (Bake off) Baking in the oven.

Blötläggning (Soaking) Soaking whole grains, cut rye, or wheat and coarse grains until they swell.

Bortgörning (Combining) Mixing all of the ingredients, including any potential pre-doughs, into one dough.

Bräcka av (Breaching/Breaking off) Breaking off/dividing the dough into buns and loaves.

Degrand (Dough brim) Refers to a condensation of dough inside of the bread, usually at the bottom of the loaf. This is most common for whole grain breads made from rye flour or sifted rye. It can happen for a variety of reasons: flour too rich in diastisis; too much sugar, syrup, or malt; unripe or cold dough; or too–low oven temperature.

Direkt degföring (Direct dough making) Making dough without using any kind of pre-dough.

Dofta (Dust) Dusting flour over the dough or baking table.

Elasticitet (Elasticity) The dough's ability to stretch.

Fördeg (Pre-dough) See page 32.

Grönt bröd (Green bread) Burnt bread.

Indirekt degföring (Indirect dough making) Starting by making a pre-dough.

Jäsningstid (Rising time) When the dough is resting and ripening before getting shaped into buns and loaves.

Knåda (Knead) Working the dough until it is elastic.

Kvalma (Steam up) Spraying steam into the oven.

Langa ut Rolling the dough out into one long piece.

Poolish See page 32.

Rask (Quick) A fermentation cabinet keeping the temperature at 37°C (98.6°F) and humidity level at 70–80% to speed up the rising process.

Raskdeg (Quick-dough) A pre-dough that is later added to the main dough for quickening the fermentation process.

Raskning (Rising) When the bread is rising.

Riva (Tearing) Shaping the dough into round buns by using both hands.

Sammanskuvat bröd (Bread squeezed tightly together) Bread put closely together in the oven.

Skållning (Scalding) Boiling water and pouring it over whole grain flour. This makes for small, moist loaves.

Skuva (Dialect/slang for squeezing together) Putting bread in the oven.

Slagstake (Baking rod) A baker's peel the same length as the depth of the oven. Used for placing loaves of bread inside the oven.

Slå upp (Open) Shaping the dough into loaves.

Spröa Letting bread that has fermented in a *rask* cabinet develop a dry crust prior to brushing it with an egg.

Strykning (Stroking) Brushing the bread with an egg before baking in the oven to create a glossy surface, or afterward, when the bread is finished, with sugar icing or a glaze.

Styv deg (Stiff dough) Hard dough.

Stålrand (Steel rim) A dark brim in the bottom of the bread, which indicates that the flour is rancid or that the rye flour has a low falling number.

Stötning (Pressing) Pressing air out of the dough during the fermentation process to make the dough more elastic and to remove impurities.

Surdeg (Sourdough) See page 25.

Sätta av (Putting away/down) Putting loaves onto a tray, onto a leavening board, or into bread frames.

Tillslag (Addition) Refers to the baking fluid (and its temperature) to be poured over the flour for a dough.

Trågare Refers to the first baker to arrive at the bakery who prepares all the doughs.

Uppslagning (Shaping) Shaping loaves and buns.

Vek deg (Loose dough) Soft or loose dough.

Verk Refers to the seam in the dough at the bottom of shaped loaves.

Vilska A tool made of bound rye straw that, in the old days, was used for glazing loaves of bread still hot from the oven.

Ältning (**Repetition**) Kneading of the dough.

Äril Refers to the bottom of the oven, which is usually made of either stone, iron, or concrete.

Överraskat (**Over-fermented**) Bread that is over-fermented.

A bit of kitchen French

Since France is the stronghold of all bread (and gastronomy), I will from time to time refer to some technical terms in French. There are also many great books in French about bread, and this little glossary might make it easier to understand them.

Abaisser To roll out dough.

Apricoter To brush a pastry with cooked apricot jam.

Beurrer To butter something.

Crème d'amande Almond cream for filling something, such as croissants.

Cuire à blanc To pre-bake a pie shell with peas to keep it flat.

Détailler To divide the dough into pieces.

Détrempe The base for a French butter dough.

Dorer To brush—for example, brioche bread—with a beaten egg and a pinch of salt.

Fariner To flour something—for instance, a baking surface.

Foncer To dress the inside of a mold with dough.

Fouetter To whisk egg yolks and sugar lightly, adding flour as a thickening base for making, for instance, vanilla cream.

Fraiser To ply a short dough with the palm of your hand until it is smooth.

Glacer To glaze bread with water glaze or a fondant.

La mère "Mother" (see pages 27 and 28).

Macérer To soak ingredients—for example, raisins or orange peels—before mixing them into a dough.

Pâte feuilletée inversée A French butter dough.

Pâte sucrée Short dough.

Pâton A piece of butter dough that is about to be rolled out.

Pincer To make an edge with a knife or by pinching with your fingers around a pie or *tarte*.

Pointage The time after the kneading of a dough and the first fermentation.

Pousse Fermentation time between the kneading and baking.

Puncher To drown babas and *savarins* in rum.

Rognures Butter dough leftovers.

Sabler To crumble butter and flour between your fingertips before adding baking fluids.

Tamiser To sift.

Travailler To knead a dough until it is smooth.

Flour

Cereal is a common term for a variety of grains and grain products. It most likely originates from the Near East and was already used in Sweden in the Stone Ages.

Fresh stone-ground flour, preferably from small mills and without additives, is the best if you ask me. Flour should be stored in a cool, dry, and dark place. When stored for too long, the moisture and fat levels tend to change, sometimes also affecting the weight of the flour. The fat oxidizes and may acquire a rancid taste. You may notice after a while that the flour tastes a bit bitter. Untreated flour requires old-fashioned baking methods for sourdoughs and pre-doughs as well as more time to ferment than ordinary flour from larger mills. The dough needs to be kneaded more carefully and the results tend to vary from mill to mill. The ability of the flour to absorb water always varies.

In Sweden and Scandinavia, bread-baking recipes are usually based on 1 liter (1,000 grams/4½ cups) of water, whereas the continental recipes usually are based on 1 kilogram of flour. For every kilogram (7¼ cups) of wheat flour, add 600–650 grams (2½–2¾ cups) of water, and for 1 liter (4½ cups) of water add 1,600–1,900 grams (11¾–14 cups) of wheat flour. Coarse flour, such as rye, requires a little more water since it swells more slowly; about 700 grams (3 cups) per kilogram (7¾ cups) of rye flour, or about 1,500–1,600 grams (11¾–12½ cups) of rye flour per liter (4½ cups) of water. In France, Switzerland, and Italy, the consistency of the dough is often looser than how we traditionally make it, which makes for airy and light loaves. Aged flour absorbs more water than fresh flour, since flour dries out over time. Therefore, you should always have fresh flour at home; it tastes better, too. Only add more water if the dough feels dry. It could be due to the recipe or the fact that flours from different mills vary in their ability to absorb water. Use your common sense. Stone-ground flour is preferable, as it tends to become more aromatic and doesn't heat up as much during milling as flour from some of the quicker mills. The temperatue during the milling process should ideally not rise above 35°C (95°F).

In the early days, flour quality was not as good or consistent as it is now. Harvesting took a long time and the drying process was entirely dependent on the weather. Consequently, the enzyme activity in the flour was often high. In old recipe books, you might come across the term "baking with sweet flour," referring to when enzymes would have already broken down some of the starch and turned it into sugar. Baking with such flour was not easy, and making good rye bread was the most difficult of all. The idea to scald bread spread across the country from the southeast of Sweden, where rye was often grown. Whether it was a Swedish idea or came with one of the merchant ships that visited our southeastern coast is hard to tell. Boats came from Germany, Denmark, and Russia, among other places. In any case, someone discovered that it was easier to bake with rye if you started by pouring boiling water over it (in other words, scalding the rye, or *skållade*). The scalded mixture, *skållningen*, was left to rest until the following day. At this point, more flour was kneaded into the dough and the loaves were finished.

In Sweden, we mostly use the four traditional seeds—wheat, rye, barley, and oats—but in recent years, as the general public has taken a greater interest in baking, many other kinds of flour have become popular as well. Spelt meal is more popular than ever because of its strong aroma, whereas Kamut, Emmer, single grain, and Durum wheat are now used by professionals as well as amateurs. There is also Dwarf wheat, Miracle wheat (aka English wheat), whole Durum, Winter Emmer, yellow wheat; the list is endless. All of these different kinds of flour also come in different grinds, such as whole, cross, and sifted.

Wheat

Wheat *(Triticum)* is a grass species of which there are more than 20 varieties. It originates from across Transcaucasia and is one of the oldest cultivated plants. The cultivated kinds of wheat were developed from wild grass. Today we use wild Emmer and wild single grain hybrids.

The cultural history of wheat is debated and complicated. In ancient Egypt they primarily grew Kamut wheat. Today, ordinary wheat, or bread wheat, dominates crops and is the most common seed in the world. The harvest follows the sun from the Northern to the Southern Hemisphere. Hard wheat is separated from soft. Hard, or strong, wheat is generally higher in gluten and more conducive to baking than soft wheat. In other words, soft wheat is lower in gluten and less capable of containing gas. Hard wheat is grown in Canada, the USA, Russia, and Argentina. Öland wheat is a delicious flour grown quite a bit in Denmark, but not in Sweden. Single grain also has a special and lovely flavor and dates back to the oldest seeds.

Wheat contains gluten and is therefore the most conducive flour for baking. The gluten binds the gas from the yeast and enables the dough to rise. Wheat is the most popular seed due to the gluten-producing substances gliadin and glutenin. The egg white substances in the wheat also have the special ability to absorb water during the kneading process and make the dough tough and elastic.

Spring wheat (sown in the spring) is considered the finest quality wheat. Most of the crop consists of autumn wheat, but the protein quality and content is typically not as high as in spring wheat.

There are many kinds of wheat for different purposes.

Emmer wheat *(Triticum dicoccum)* is one of the original types of wheat. Its gluten structure is quite weak, but it is high in protein and minerals. For good baking results, use old methods such as baking with sourdough and levain and letting the dough rise for a long time. Remember not to work the dough at the highest speed. You can stretch the dough a little toward the end, but be careful not to collapse the gluten web.

Kamut wheat *(Triticum turanicum)* Kamut, or whole Durum, is a hard wheat that originates from the Nile delta. It was the most popular wheat in ancient Egypt, and Kamut is the Egyptian name for wheat flour. It was forgotten for many years, and it is thanks to the American farmer Bob Quinn that it was brought back in the 1990s.

Kamut has a round, yellowish core about 20–40% higher in protein than soft wheats and 2–3 times larger than ordinary wheat cores. Because of its high protein content, Kamut is excellent for baking. From a nutritional perspective, Kamut is fantastic for its richness in amino acids, fatty acids, vitamins, and selen. Much like Emmer wheat, Kamut is best when used with sourdough and pre-dough and given a long rising time.

Spelt meal *(Triticum spelta/polonicum)*, a.k.a. Dinkel wheat. During the Middle Ages, spelt meal was the most common wheat in Europe. The seed itself is encased by a spelt, and special peeling machines are required to roll off the shell. Spelt meal is high in gluten moisture, which enables the gluten to stretch well. Its use is a bit limited, but you can achieve nice results using old-fashioned methods such as sourdoughs, pre-doughs, and long rising times. Nutritionally, spelt meal is quite advantageous, as it contains many more nutrients than regular wheat. It has a strong seed flavor that makes for delicious bread.

Yellow wheat (dates back to the *Triticum aestivum* family; *Luteus*, *Safrania*, *Citrus*, and *Caroti* are typically the kinds that are grown) The pigment that gives this wheat its yellow color comes from carotene. This flour, grown in Italy and Switzerland, can be used the same way as white wheat flour. It is high in protein with a powerful gluten structure that creates large air bubbles in the bread and a tough consistency as well as a crispy crust, tasty aroma, and beautiful color. When I was working in Switzerland, we often used yellow wheat flour, especially for Italian breads and panettone.

Durum wheat *(Triticum durum)* is a hard, yellow, and glasslike wheat high in protein (14%). Swedish Durum wheat is grown on the island Ven, but otherwise it is mainly imported. Durum wheat flour is primarily used for pasta dough but works well for all kinds of baking. The swollen whole seeds also make for an excellent risotto. You will find both fine and coarse Durum wheat in the market.

Rye

Rye *(Secale cereale)* is a gray-green, thin, and relatively young seed that most likely originates from Asia Minor. Rye tolerates the cold better than wheat and is of great importance in countries with colder climates. Finnish and Russian rye is considered the best by many, since the cold creates smaller seeds. This creates more shell parts, which in turn yield a darker and more flavorful flour. It is used mostly for rye bread and bread in which wheat and rye are sifted together. Rye flour has a lower baking ability than wheat flour. Baking can be made possible by adding sourdough, which enables the pentosans in the rye to swell. Rye bread keeps well.

Barley

Barley *(Hordeum sativum)* originates from the northeast of Africa. Barley is the most commonly grown seed in Sweden. A small part is ground into flour (which is used for flat bread from Norrland), but most of it goes to the brewery business.

Oats

Oats *(Avena sativa)* are originally from Southeastern Europe and the Near East. They contain important vitamins and minerals, but no gluten. When baking with oats, first scald the grains, or the bread will become crumbly.

Corn

Corn *(Hordeum distichum)* is an annual grass that can grow to be 6 meters (19 feet 8 inches) high and originates in Africa. All types of corn are dependent on a warm climate. The different species of corn vary in shape, color, and quality. Corn flour and starch are used for breads and pastries, and for preparations such as vanilla cream.

Rice

Rice *(Oryza sativa)* plants grow to be about 1 meter (3 feet 3 inches) tall with single flowered mini-ears in panicles. Rice is higher in starch and lower in protein than other seeds. It is usually consumed as a seed but can also be ground into flour and powder. It is rarely used for baking, but it can be used for tiger–glazing bread (see page 40).

Buckwheat

Buckwheat *(Fagopyrum exculentum)* is not a grass but a willow herb. It is currently grown to a small extent in the USA, East Asia, Germany, and Austria. Buckwheat has no gluten, which makes it poor for baking, but I have used it in this book for making delicious *blinier* (blintzes) (see page 229).

Quinoa

Quinoa *(Chenopodium quinoa)* is a seed from the goosefoot family. Quinoa is an Inca-Indian name for "mother seed." It grows at altitudes up to 4,000 meters (13,000 feet) in dry climates in the Andes such as Peru and Bolivia. Quinoa is extremely nutritious and works well for both cooking and baking. It is gluten free, but still makes for tasty and moist bread. Whole-cooked quinoa can be mixed into the dough, which creates a nice structure. Use no more than 50% quinoa flour for baking, otherwise the dough will be difficult to work with. It is important that the dough is loose, since quinoa flour tends to swell a bit toward the end of the process. Let the dough rise slowly, by using a pre-dough or sourdough, and the bread will turn out great.

Flour for baking

Developing flour is a complicated process. The seed is ground and sifted into various pieces, called fractions. The whole seed is ground together for wholemeal, whereas the outer parts of the shell and germ rich in protein, vitamins, and oil are removed when making other flours. The remaining white part of the seed, which also contains the starch, comprises 85% of the seed altogether. The white of the seed is the part used when grinding white flour. Besides wheat flour, it is also common in Sweden to grind rye, oats, and barley into flour.

Wheat Flour

When baking white, airy, and light bread, one should preferably use stone-ground flour high in protein. Swedish bakeries often use protein-enriched wheat flour (10.5% protein) and *bagarns bästa* (a Swedish brand, 11% protein).

In the case of rustic wheat flour, only the shell and a small part of the germ is sifted off. It is darker, more flavorful, and contains more fibers and proteins than regular wheat flour.

Saltå Kvarn uses no additives in their flour, unlike some of the major mills that treat theirs with amylase, ascorbic acid, iron, and vitamin B. When working with this fine flour, one should keep in mind not to knead the dough too hard, and to use old methods such as sourdough and long rising times to bring the best out of the flour.

Regular wheat flour, or extra fine, is lower in gluten than rustic wheat flour and does not bake as well. I use it for cookies, pie dough, and sponge and Madeira cakes, as well as for cake plates.

For professional bakers and chefs there is extra-strong wheat flour with 13.5% protein, such as Manitoba Cream from AbdonMills and Nord Mills Blue Mountain. Until recently these only existed as wholesale brands, but they are now becoming more accessible. These types of wheat flour should be used for table bread.

For sweet doughs and pastries you could use flour with 10% protein, but I prefer using a stronger flour for these as well, as it tends to make the bread softer and more airy.

Graham flour is a flavorful and tasty whole wheat flour. It comes in fine and coarse grinds and contains about 10% protein. Scalding the flour when baking bread makes it moist. It was the American Sylvester Graham who first discovered the high nutrition in co-ground wheat flour, hence the name.

There are also wheat bran, rye bran, wheat germ, cut and crushed wheat, and wheat flakes, all of which are great for making coarse bread.

Rye flour

Rye flour comes in fine and coarse grinds and contains about 8% protein. It is a very flavorful flour with a strong aroma, unlike wheat, which has a more neutral flavor. Cut or crushed rye, rye flakes, etc., work well for several kinds of whole wheat bread, and flakes are great for decorating bread surfaces. Pure sifted rye contains about 7% protein.

Mixed flour

Sifted rye flour contains about 51% sifted rye and 49% wheat flour. The brand *4 sädesslag* (4 seeds) is simply a mixture of the four seeds. Personally, I almost never use mixed flours, as I prefer mixing them myself.

Miscellaneous

Other kinds of flour that are good for baking and do not contain any gluten are white, yellow, and blue corn flour; polenta and semolina grains; chestnut flour; rice flour; Jerusalem artichoke flour; pea flour; buckwheat flour; and so on.

A brief flour glossary

Aleurone layer
The aleurone layer of flour is closest to the shell in wheat and rye seeds.

Amylase
Amylase is the enzyme that breaks down the starch of the flour to fermentable maltose. This is a process in two steps: first with alfa-amylase from starch to dextrine, and next with beta-amylase from dextrine to maltose.

Ash content
Ash content, or mineral content, indicates the yield that can be expected during milling and is determined by incinerating a sample (at about 700–800°C/1300°F) and then weighing the residue. The higher the ash content of the flour, the higher the milling degree.

Enriched flour
Flour enriched with ascorbic acid additives (vitamin C) as a ripening agent to improve its baking ability.

Soaking
Soaking is used for cut and crushed wheat and rye when making whole wheat bread. Leave the seed to soak overnight. The water's temperature should not rise above 50°C (122°F). At higher temperatures, the starch starts to pre-gelatinize and the seeds do not absorb the water; instead, the starch pre-gelatinizes on the surface of the seed.

Enzymes
Enzymes can be defined as proteins with the ability to catalyze reactions in living cells despite the fact that they appear in small amounts. From a baking perspective, the carbohydrate-active, amylase, invertase, and maltase; the protein active, protease; and the fatty active, lipase, are the most important enzymes.

Falling number
This is a method to measure the alfa-amylase activity in flour and seeds. Its name refers to its execution—you let a rod fall through a certain amount of pre-gelatinized flour starch and time the number of seconds this takes.

Pre-gelatinizing
This quality of starch makes it absorb water and swell at higher temperatures. The pre-gelatinizing temperature varies for different types of starch. For wheat starch it is at 60–65°C (140–150°F) and for rye starch at 58–62°C (136–143°F). Starch can absorb water several times its own weight.

Containability of carbonic acid
This refers to the ability of the flour to contain carbonic acid formed during the fermentation process and depends on the quality of the gluten. A flour high in gluten is capable of containing more carbonic acid than a flour low in gluten. The amount of protease, which breaks down proteins, affects the containability of carbonic acid through the destructive effect of the enzymes on the gluten. Kneading with too much or too little force, as well as low protein quality or content, has a lowering effect on the flour.

Gluten

Gluten is a common name for the two protein fractions in flour, glutenin and gliadin. Their quantity and quality determine the baking capability of the flour. A strong wheat flour is higher in good quality gluten than a weak flour. Together, glutenin and gliadin account for about 80% of the protein in the flour. A strong wheat absorbs about 2.5 times its weight in water during the kneading process. Rye flour contains glutenin and gliadin but still cannot produce gluten.

Oxidation

Oxidation is the process in which a substance reacts with oxygen.

Pentosans

Sometimes referred to as rye slime, as rye has plenty of it. Pentosans swell in water and therefore greatly influence the viscosity and ability of the rye to absorb water. These qualities make rye suitable for baking. Pentosans cannot be pre-fermented. Although wheat also contains pentosans, it is less important than in the case of rye.

Proteins

Egg white substances, the particles of highest nitrogen content in plants and animals. Proteins are a large family in which all substances are comprised of amino acids. These amino acids are linked together into peptide chains with tens or hundreds in each chain. Each protein molecule consists of a varying number of peptide chains.

Starch

Flour contains starch in the shape of tiny seeds with a core and an outer layer. The outer layer absorbs water and swells. At 30°C (86°F) the starch seeds crack and pre-gelatinize.

Milling degree

Milling degree indicates the extent to which the whole core is included in a flour, counting from the center. The milling degree of whole wheat flour is 100%, whereas the milling degree of wheat kernel, which has a lighter color, is about 72%.

Water content

The extent of existing water in flour can vary a great deal, depending on the type of flour as well as harvest and storage conditions. Over 14% is usually considered unfit, to avoid mold. While the flour is in storage it is important to keep its moisture level low, at around 15% at most, until it is time to use it.

Water absorption

Dough liquid gets absorbed by the various components in flour. A large amount is taken care of by starch. It does not swell, but the water is absorbed by starch seeds.

Dough liquids

The most common dough liquid is water. You can also use wort, beer, vegetable puree, milk, yogurt, cream cheese, buttermilk, light beer, and more. All such additives come with different advantages and disadvantages, but, more importantly, these doughs do not require the same amount of flour as water-based dough, as these liquids are more viscous. Regarding dough liquid temperatures, see pages 23 and 35.

Water

After flour, water is bread's most important ingredient. Kneading flour and water activates the enzymatic process. The water soaks the gluten inside the flour, which is a condition for the dough to develop gluten and for the starch to pre-gelatinize. The more water the dough contains, the more efficiently the nutrients will dissolve, which increases the kneading tolerance.

Flour, yogurt, cream cheese

When using milk in the dough, the bread gets a soft inside with closed pores and browns faster while baking. Milk requires less flour than water does for baking. Milk is used for making sweet doughs, tea biscuits, hot dog and hamburger bread, rolls, sandwich bread, crispies (biscuits), and certain crispbreads. I always use whole milk, with 3% fat, for baking. For some doughs, I use yogurt, as it tends to bake well and gives great volume to the bread. Cream cheese makes the bread moist and tasty. Ricotta cheese, mascarpone cheese, and other soft cheeses can also bring good results in breads and pastries.

Flavors

Salt

The purest salt is regular table salt, with 99.9% sodium chloride (NaCl). It is called stone salt and is taken out of gigantic underground salt deposits. Another great source of salt is the ocean, where salt is extracted by evaporation. *Fleur de sel*, the finest and most delicious salt, is sea salt from salt beds in France. Gourmet salt is produced by boiling seawater in large pans until only the fragile crystals remain. I prefer sea salt and normally use 20 grams (3½ teaspoons) per kilogram of flour. For coarse breads, you can reduce the amount of salt by a few grams, since there is already salt in the shells of the seeds.

Salt serves several functions in a dough. It improves the flavor, helps the elasticity of the dough and keeps it moist, and soothes the fermentation process. Adding salt late in the preparation of a dough makes the dough more elastic and the inside of the bread and the crust whiter. Using too little salt makes the dough runny, sticky, and less elastic, and reduces its capability to bind carbonic acid/gas. Also, the bread will be smaller and paler, and will taste bland. Too much salt causes the dough to be runny and moist, and to ferment more slowly. The bread will also brown too quickly in the oven and taste too salty.

Sugar

Granulated sugar consists of fructose and glycose molecules that dissolve easily in water. The yeast uses the glycose as a nutrient while the fructose stays in the dough and affects the color of the bread. Small amounts of sugar in the dough accelerate the fermentation, whereas larger amounts slow it down. Sugar gives the bread a sweet flavor and surface color. Farin (a brown, syrup-infused Swedish granulated sugar), Muscovado sugar, and cane sugar all have different flavors.

Honey

Honey also adds a different flavor and improves fermentation ability. It can be used as a substitute for malt at home.

Malt

Malt, light and dark, is one of the oldest baking agents. Produced from malted seeds, malt brings flavor and can improve the baking abilities of weak flours.

Wort

Wort is an intermediate product from malting while brewing beer. It gives the bread a special flavor, darker color, and better moisture.

Syrup

Syrup consists of 80% dry substances and 20% water. A deciliter (1/3 cup + 1 1/2 tablespoons) of syrup weighs 140 grams (4.9 ounces). There are 6 kinds of syrup: white, yellow, brown, dark brown, black, and malt. Syrup is a natural ingredient in many Swedish doughs, and it is preferred in scalded table breads from Skåne (a region in the south of Sweden) and in *kavring*, with its moist and sweet flavor, as well as in various types of rye cakes.

Egg

An egg yolk weighs about 20 grams (0.7 ounces), an egg white about 30 grams (1 ounce), a whole egg about 50 grams (1.6 ounces) and including the shell about 60 grams (2.1 ounces). Make it a rule to always weigh eggs, as they tend to vary in size.

The lecithin in the egg yolk distributes the fat, makes the dough elastic, and increases its containability of carbonic acid. Airy Berliner doughnuts and Karlsbader dough should only contain yolk. Doughs for Danishes (Wiener/Viennese), croissants, and brioche bread contain whole eggs that help distribute the fat in the dough. Eggs also make the dough dry out faster, so these breads and pastries should always be enjoyed fresh.

Butter

Butter added to sweet dough should always be at room temperature. The firm fat binds more air into the dough, which makes it ferment better and helps the dough get soft and more elastic. During the leavening and baking processes, the air bubbles in the dough grow bigger, which increases the volume of the bread. Never use melted butter, although many books will tell you to do so. It absorbs more flour than soft butter and gives the bread a heavier consistency. Melted butter also cannot increase in volume like soft butter does. Add the butter a little at a time, when the dough has been worked for a few minutes. This way the dough will be more elastic and increase nicely in volume. Butter also increases moisture and freshness and makes the bread keep longer.

Never replace butter with margarine; it neither sounds nor tastes good.

Oil

Olive oil is added to give the dough a Mediterranean flavor. The oil creates a shorter inside and a tougher consistency. Liquid fat makes the bread more tender but creates less volume. Its lack of fat crystals reduces the containability of carbonic acid. Rapeseed oil and sunflower oil are also excellent for many of the doughs in which no particular oil flavor is desired.

Classic bread spices

Anise spices

Anise, also known as sweet cumin, is mostly sold in the shape of tiny oval seeds (anise seeds) and appears in both breads and pastries. The leaves are thin, bushy, and very aromatic, and can be used as dill. Star anise can also be ground and used as a bread spice, but in moderation—it can easily become too

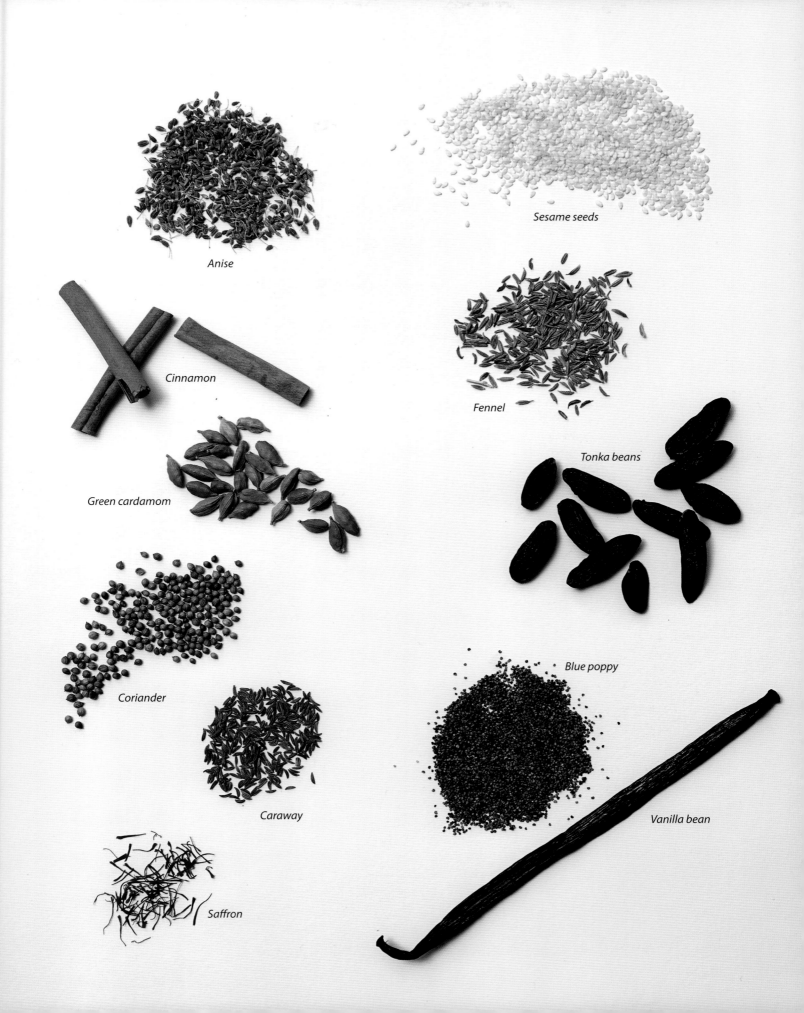

Anise

Sesame seeds

Cinnamon

Fennel

Green cardamom

Tonka beans

Coriander

Blue poppy

Caraway

Vanilla bean

Saffron

much of a good thing. Fennel seeds, the source of grown fennel, are used in the same way as anise, whole or ground.

Cinnamon

The bark of the cinnamon tree is harvested and used as a spice. Real cinnamon, or Ceylon cinnamon, is the most expensive kind. It is grown in Sri Lanka, Kenya, and Tanzania, among other places.

Household cinnamon, or Cassia cinnamon, which we see much of in Sweden, comes from China, Vietnam, and Indonesia in significantly longer and coarser bark sticks. Real cinnamon is characterized by a lighter brown color and significantly thinner and longer sticks.

Cardamom

Cardamom is a tall, perennial tropical herb related to ginger. Try to get ahold of green cardamom; it tastes fresher. It also comes in white and black.

The seed pod, which is tough and strong, provides protection for the tiny dark brown seeds used as spices. Roast the pods in a pan or in a warm oven until the skins loosen. Remove the pods and pound the cardamom directly when you are ready to use it. The flavor quickly fades when ground, just like cinnamon.

Coriander

Ground coriander is often used to season bread dough, but since I do not like the taste of dried coriander, I do not use it. However, I really like fresh coriander.

Caraway

Caraway is an important ingredient in many breads and cakes in which the seeds create a contrast both in taste and texture. Keep in mind that they go rancid if storage conditions are too warm. Keep it in a cool, dry place. Caraway stays fresh for about a year.

Saffron

The autumn-blooming saffron crocus yields the most expensive of all spices. More than 250,000 flowers are required to produce less than half a kilogram (about 1 pound) from the dried strings that give it its characteristic yellow color. Fortunately, saffron is so powerful that you only need a pinch; too much of it will completely dominate the flavor.

Sesame

Sesame, appreciated for its oil, has a more prominent nut flavor than any other spice seed. We sprinkle whole white sesame seeds over buns, breads, and cookies and let them brown while baking. Raw sesame seeds are ground into tahini (sesame paste used in Middle Eastern cuisine), often used in hummus. Black sesame seeds are also decorative.

Cumin

Cumin is often confused with caraway, but it has a different, earthy smell. Black cumin tastes more like pepper than the light and white. White cumin resembles caraway. All kinds of cumin can make for nice seasoning in bread.

Tonka beans

The tonka bean is originally from Venezuela. It comes from the Fabaceae family, like peas and other beans. The fruit is about 7–10 centimeters ($2^3/_4$–$3^{15}/_{16}$ inches) in length and meaty. The fruit contains seeds (beans) that are dried. They are then soaked in rum or other alcohol and dried again. The aroma is strong. When grating a tonka bean, it releases a scent a little like spicy vanilla. Tonka beans can be used in the same ways as vanilla, as spicy seasoning for desserts. In Germany, the tonka bean is always used for *Dresdner Weihnachtsstollen*.

Poppy

The only poppy with edible seeds is the opium poppy. The seeds do not contain any opium, however; it is extracted from the seed capsule. The most common seed is grayish blue, but there is a pale yellow version (couscous) that grows in India. The black poppy seeds are also often used for sweet dough fillings and cakes.

Vanilla

Vanilla is one of the most important spices to bakers and pastry chefs. I prefer using Tahiti or Bourbon vanilla from Madagascar. Bourbon is the classic vanilla, but Tahiti vanilla is somewhat bigger and sweeter with a rounder taste.

Yeast

Fermentation is a complicated yet simple phenomenon. It is basically a question of the formation of gas bubbles inside the dough, which causes it to rise. Gas develops after adding yeast. There are two types of yeast: natural and chemical. These must be discussed separately, as they work differently in the dough.

Six thousand years ago there already were airy and light breads, and the discovery of leavened bread most likely originated with the Egyptians. Someone probably left a mixture of flour and water sitting for too long, allowing microscopic fungus to develop in the dough, and to the great delight of the baker, it started to rise. In all likelihood, the baker mixed the dough leftovers with new flour and water, and the new dough became just as good, light, and flavorful. The baker in question should be eternally blessed by the patron saint of the bakers, Saint Honoré!

Fresh yeast

Yeast fungus (*Saccharomyces*) exists everywhere in nature, and natural yeast consists of microorganisms reproducing and eliminating residue. It was not until the year 1680 that yeast microorganisms were discovered under a microscope. Afterward, it was primarily the breweries who delivered brewery yeast to the bakeries. Louis Pasteur extracted the kind of yeast we use most often today, press yeast. It is the most common yeast in our stores, containing about 10 billion yeast cells per gram. Nowadays there are two kinds of yeast, one of which is especially suitable for sweet dough.

Once the yeast is added, the dough comes alive from the sugar, proteins, and nitrogen products and develops the gas required to swell. The yeast needs liquid and heat to activate. The most conducive fermentation temperature is 38°C (100.4°F). Under 20°C (68°F) and over 40°C (104°F) leavening is slower, and at 45°C (113°F) the yeast dies.

Yeast is a single-celled organism that, with the right nutrition, multiplies and forms new, independent cells. The cells can multiply through new substances. Yeast cells need energy and receive it through sugar-burning enzymes. The combustion also requires oxygen, which is taken from the air. Carbon dioxide (lifting the dough), water, and heat are released when the yeast is burned. During kneading, the yeast multiplies.

The ideal dough temperature is 24–28°C (75–82°F). Many cookbooks say you should heat the dough liquid to 37°c (98.6°F) for baking. This is entirely correct if kneading the dough by hand. It takes 20 to 30 minutes to work a dough by hand to be very elastic, and it is very difficult to achieve good friction with water that is cold or at room temperature. However, working the dough in a machine increases the friction and the temperature 24–26°C (75–79°F) during kneading. In this case, heating the liquid would cause the temperature to get too high, the dough to rise too fast, and the aromatic substances to suffer. Never let the dough get warmer than 28°C (82.4°F).

Always keep fresh yeast in a tightly sealed container in the refrigerator, preferably at 4°C (39.2°F).

Dry yeast

Keep dry yeast dry—do not let it become moist. Dry yeast contains about 4–6% water. It is practical and easy to store, but I prefer fresh yeast, because I think it yields better results. The dough liquid needs to be heated to 45–50°C (113–122°F) to activate dry yeast.

Chemical yeast or propellant

Chemical yeast can be baking powder, bicarbonate of soda, cloudberry salt, pot-ash, or soda. Chemical yeast reacts quickly with water and releases carbon dioxide. Chemical leaveners can be used for certain doughs, such as soda bread in Great Britain. Natural yeast multiplies and increases in volume during the entire leavening process, whereas chemical leaveners are quickly consumed when reacting with water. Adding too little yeast, not mixing the dough properly, and not giving the dough enough time to react like it should are all factors that will have a negative effect on the end result.

There is a difference between bread and soft products that rise with biological yeast and sponge cakes, Swiss rolls, cake plates, meringues, etc., that rise by mechanical force, in which case air bubbles are whisked into the batter. For sponge cakes, soft gingerbread cakes, and cookies, chemical leaveners are added to make the cakes rise in the oven and become airy. Regular yeast cannot handle the large amount of fat and sugar in these items.

Leavening and fermentation

When the dough is mixed and put to rest, it should not be covered with a baking cloth, although that is what most books will tell you. A cloth always lets in air and dries the surface of the dough. Let the dough rise for the first time in a plastic container that holds up to 10 liters (2.6 gallons) covered with a lid instead. Oil the container lightly with a neutral food oil, unless the recipe tells you otherwise. The oil keeps the dough from sticking and makes it easier to work with.

In practice, the amount of yeast and time allowed for leavening determine the flavor and aroma when the bread is finished. A dough with 10–25 grams (2½–6¼ teaspoons) of yeast per liter (¼ gallon) of water needs about 3 hours to become ready for baking. Dough with 50–60 grams (4–5 tablespoons) of yeast per liter (¼ gallon) of water requires 60–90 minutes, whereas 80–100 grams (6¾–8⅓ tablespoons) require about 30–45 minutes.

dough
preparation

By mastering a variety of kneading methods, you can create special and specific breads and pastries and learn how to make your own favorites.

Sourdough

The original fermentation method involves wild yeast. Simply put, sourdough is a mixture of flour and water that has been left to rest long enough to rise on its own; wild yeast starts to multiply. The sourdough stays active through frequent additions of flour and water. It forms bacteria, lactic acid, acetic acid, aromas and, in some cases, yeast. Bacteria are single-celled microorganisms that exist wherever there is life. When lactic acid bacteria is heterofermentative, it can form both lactic acid and and acetic acid. Homofermentative bacteria produces only lactic acid. Wholemeal flour is always more acidic than sifted flour.

Sourdough was originally used only as a leavener. In Swedish bakeries, sourdough is added primarily for the sake of flavor and aroma. The bakeries do not take the time to let the dough rise, but add press yeast to speed up the acid process.

Although sourdough can be used both as a starter and for flavor, both are simply referred to as "sourdough" in Swedish. The context of the usage of "sourdough" in this book should clarify its meaning.

Two frequently occurring bacteria in sourdough are *Lactobacillus plantarum*, which produces mostly lactic acid and makes the dough aromatic and elastic, and *Lactobacillus brevis*, which mostly produces acetic acid, carbon dioxide, and alcohol and gives the bread a good taste. *Lactobacillus fermentum* is heterofermentative and can form both lactic acid and acetic acid in the dough.

The final result of a sourdough is greatly determined by its pH value. It affects the absorbability of rye flour and the enzyme activity in dough, which affects its consistency, ability to bake, flavor, and aroma. Coarse breads made from sourdough and rye flour are very healthy compared to white and airy breads, which quickly raise your blood sugar levels.

The sugar, or saccharose, is broken down during the fermentation process, and the carbohydrates in sourdough and whole wheat bread are absorbed slowly into the bloodstream. The acids formed when making sourdough tend to make absorption in the stomach slower. Sourdough keeps better because of its low pH value, which suppresses unwanted microorganisms. In whole wheat breads, the starch is encapsulated, which prevents the enzymes from reaching the starch. This slow process gives the body a stable and even blood sugar level.

Nutritionally, sourdough bread is beneficial because of its high enzyme activity. Lactic acid activates the phytase, which

in turn breaks down the fatty acids in the flour. This makes it easier for the body to absorb iron from the bread.

Acetic acid is important to the flavor of the bread. The acetic acid level in sourdough should be at about 15–25% in order to taste good. At higher levels, it gets too acidic, and at lower levels, it becomes flavorless. Acetic acid has a preservative effect and protects the bread against mold.

Lactic acid is an organic acid formed by fermenting sugars with lactic acid bacteria. The acid gives the bread a sour taste and protects against infection from foreign microorganisms.

When the sourdough is ready, the pH value should be under 4.0. Higher levels create a bad taste and texture. The acid production eventually subsides, but the lactic acid bacteria continue their activity if you just keep adding water and flour. Bakers refer to this as reviving the sourdough.

Put the sourdough in the refrigerator between bakings and always take the bowl out the day before baking to freshen it with equal amounts of water and flour. Use the amount you will be using in the recipe—this way you always have a back-up ready. Let the sourdough rise at room temperature until the next day. It should be bubbly and look alive. If it doesn't, put it in a lukewarm bath to awaken it. If this is not successful, try adding a small grated apple or onion. If this should also fail, the dough is dead. Then you just start over again.

Advantages of baking with sourdough

Sourdough gives bread its own character full of flavor and aroma; a beautiful, tight texture; and a moist inside. The bread cuts well. Sourdough bread is also very healthy and improves cholesterol levels, among other things. It has also been proven that diabetics can lower their insulin levels by eating rye sourdough bread.

Acidic and even tart bread has not currently been popular in Sweden for very long. However, prior to 1939, sourdough was common in Swedish bakeries. In our eastern and southern neighboring countries, one could hardly even picture a bakery without sourdough rye. Our interest in sourdough, however, appears to be back.

Originally, when there was no access to refined yeast, the intention of sourdough was for use as a leavening agent (levain baking with natural sourdough). These days sourdough is primarily used for its texture. In the right amount, the bread does not taste acidic, but has a rich flavor and aroma.

What happens in a sourdough?

In rye sourdough, the pentosans of the flour expand and prevent the proteins from swelling. The absorption capabilities of the pentosans are important when baking rye bread, as rye lacks the gluten-forming qualities of wheat. In a sourdough,

there are about a billion yeast cells per 100 grams (3.5 ounces) of dough.

A loose dough that requires a long time to rise (overnight in the refrigerator) creates large pores, like in French and Italian breads. In Germany and Eastern Europe, bread is often more acidic than in the rest of Europe. You let the dough rise at lower temperatures and keep it in the refrigerator. This way the acetic acid bacteria take over and make the dough stiffer. French and Italian sourdough breads are mild in flavor, and sometimes you can sense merely from the fine quality that there must be sourdough in it. Swiss breads are somewhere in between.

A sourdough tastes acidic and has a pH value under 4.0. When mixed with flour and water, the value rises to about 5.5. As the bacteria obtain nutrition they start to multiply with renewed force; meanwhile, they keep producing acid. After 16 hours, there will be so much acid that the value drops back down to 3.8–4.0 again.

Wheat sourdough (white sourdough) and rye sourdough

Start by making a wheat sourdough and a rye sourdough, and you will soon be able to make fantastic breads at home in your own oven. Sourdough is easy to make—it practically takes care of itself. It feels amazing to have a sourdough to take care of at home—it is almost like having a new addition to the family!

I have tried making sourdough in hundreds of different ways and concluded that the following recipe suits me most. Use preferably unbleached organic rye or wheat flour. Naturally, you can use other flours as well, such as Emmer or Kamut; the bread comes out great, and it is fun to vary.

The flour contains about 100 lactic acid bacteria per gram. A raw grated apple will get the fermentation process started more quickly than the traditional water and flour. Some use honey, raw grated potato, organic grapes, or raisins to speed up and improve the leavening.

This is how I make it:

DAY 1–3

Mix 100 grams (1/3 cup + 3 1/2 tablespoons) of water with 200 grams rye (1 1/2 cups + 1 1/2 tablespoons) or wheat (1 1/2 cups) flour and 100 grams (3/4 cup) raw grated apple in a stainless steel bucket. The dough should be thick, but loose enough to pour. Add water if it is too thick until it has the right consistency. Pour into a 2-liter (1/2-gallon) glass jar with a lid. Put the jar in a warm place, ideally at 26–30°C (78.8–86°F), for 3 days. If you cannot achieve this temperature at home, keep the jar in a turned-off oven or on top of the refrigerator. Speed up the fermentation by stirring with a ladle once a day.

DAY 4

Scrape the dough down into a big bucket. Add 200 grams (1 1/2 cups + 1 1/2 tablespoons for rye, or 1 1/2 cups for wheat) of flour and 200 grams (3/4 cup + 1 1/2 tablespoons) of preheated water at 35°C (95°F). Stir thoroughly with a ladle and let it sit for another 24 hours at the same temperature as before.

DAY 5

Now we have a sourdough ready. Keep it in the refrigerator until it is time to use it.

Back-up sourdough

Add more of the same flour you used before, mixing it into the dough until it is dry and crumbly. Pour it out on a table and let it dry for 2 days at room temperature. Then pulverize it into flour in a food processor. Store it in a jar to keep it dry.

The next time you bake with sourdough, take some of the dry sourdough and whisk with lukewarm water into a thick porridge. Put the jar with the sourdough in lukewarm water so that the fermentation process gets going—it takes about 3–4 hours. Then pour in a little more water and some flour to activate the sourdough. Cover with plastic and let it rise until the next day at room temperature. The sourdough is now fully sour

and can be used for baking without going through all the other steps in the process.

Always have a dry sourdough back-up. This way you will not have to start all over again in case the sourdough should die. Never freeze sourdough, as some people suggest. Many of the bacteria die when freezing, which makes it difficult to reactivate the dough.

Spelt sourdough

I do not use grated apple for this, but add honey instead to quicken the process.

Heat up 150 grams (1/2 cup + 5 tablespoons) of water to 35°C (95°F), pour it over 100 grams (1/2 cup) of spelt wholemeal (or Kamut or Emmer) and 15 grams (5 tablespoons) of honey, and stir into a slightly tough paste. This is the same method as for traditional sourdough, by the way.

Levain/natural starters

Baking bread with a natural starter demands a lot of attention from the baker.

Then again, it does become a bread of the highest quality in accordance with old French baking tradition.

A natural starter is usually made with wheat flour and fruit juice that has been left to rise for a week in a hermetically sealed glass jar. The yeast in the fruit juice is usually from raisins or apples, and sugar or honey is often added to speed up the fermentation process. Fruit yeast is the mother, if you will, of the fermentation, and some refer to it as "mother" (*la mere*, in French).

Once flour has been added to the mother and it has been refreshed once with flour and water, it becomes a "chef," which is the second stage in baking with natural starters. It is freshened once more and then turns into levain, or a natural starter.

According to French rules, you may add about 3% yeast per kilogram of flour and still call it levain bread. This is to ensure the leavening process in the bakery.

A properly made starter can be stored for many years. It is very important to pay attention to this leavening process, so that it does not go rancid or die.

A natural starter contains neither yeast nor salt. It is kneaded with white wheat flour high in gluten, preferably stone ground, which rises better.

The natural starter improves the consistency of the dough as well as its elasticity, which makes it smooth and easy to work with. It also keeps the bread together and creates a nice structure in the oven. It improves the taste and helps the bread keep longer. Bread made with natural starters gets a lovely natural acid and strong flavor with a heavy, crisp, and tough crust. It is important to bake the bread well to bring out the roasted flavor and toughness as well as a nice elastic inside that lasts. Always keep it wrapped in cloth: the crust will not get soft the way it does when kept in a plastic bag.

Raisin yeast for levain

If you do not wish to use sugar or honey, you can start the process with only raisins. In that case, exclude sugar and honey, as it would take another day for the raisins to rise.

1,000 grams (4¹/₄ cups) water
500 grams (3¹/₂ cups) California raisins
250 grams (1¹/₄ cups) granulated sugar
100 grams (5 tablespoons) Swedish honey

1. Heat the water to 30–35°C (90–95°F). Measure the ingredients into a large glass jar with a lid. Mix everything together and shake the jar until the sugar is melted.
2. Put the jar in a warm place, at about 26–30°C (78.8–86°F), to speed up the leavening. If you do not have a good place for it, you could also put it in a turned-off oven, though it might take another day for it to rise. Let it rise for 4–6 days. Shake the jar once a day. When you lift the lid and it almost pops, bubbles on the surface, and smells like alcohol, then it is done.
3. Pour the liquid over the raisins into a strainer, catching the liquid, and press the raisins out with the back of a ladle. Throw away the pressed raisins—it is the liquid that is going to be used.

4. Keep the raisin yeast in a jar with the lid tightly shut in the refrigerator, where it will keep for months.

La mère—"mother"

125 grams (¹/₄ cup) raisin yeast
175 grams (1¹/₄ cups) wheat flour high in protein, preferably stone ground

Mix the raisin yeast and wheat flour and work the dough at low speed for 5 minutes. Then put the dough in a 2 liter (¹/₂ gallon) plastic container covered with a lid and let it rise in a warm place or in a turned-off oven for 4 hours. The dough should double in size.

If you wish to use white sourdough instead, which works just as well as with raisin yeast or apple yeast, you can take 200–250 grams (1–1¹/₈ cups) of fertile white sourdough (see page 27) and use the same method.

Raisin yeast

Chef

In order to use a dough as a starter in the fermentation process, the chef has to be activated or refreshed by adding water and flour. This natural sourdough usually keeps for a week in the refrigerator if kept in a plastic container covered with a lid. If you bake often, you can simply multiply the recipe; this way you have a natural starter, levain, ready for the whole week.

Scrape the leavened mother back into the baking bowl and freshen with:

125 grams (1½ cups) water
175 grams (1¼ cups) wheat flour high in protein, preferably stone ground

Work the dough for another 5 minutes and put it back into a plastic container covered with a lid. Let it sit for 4 hours, or until it has doubled in size. Now you have a chef, which should be homogenous and dry on the surface.

Be careful how you handle your chef. Remember, for instance, to save 200 grams (7 ounces) for the next day when you will be starting a levain. French bakers often keep the chef in the refrigerator for 2–3 days before making the levain to make it stronger when it rises. In Italy, where this technique is used, they usually put the chef on a clean and floured cloth, fold in the edges like a package (not too tight) and keep it in the refrigerator at a low temperature, 2–4°C (35.6–39.2°F). The chef

will sour more slowly this way than if kept in a jar. It lasts for about 14 days, depending on the refrigerator's temperature.

When baking a bread calling for, for instance, "400 grams levain," you have to make the following preparations the day before. Bread that is made this way has a unique taste and consistency that is well worth all the work. What is left over can be kept under a lid in the refrigerator. The levain is dead when it starts to collapse and smells sour.

200 grams (7 ounces) chef
600 grams (2½ cups) water
1,080 grams (8 cups) wheat flour high in protein, preferably stone ground, or 900 grams (7 cups) fine rye flour if you want to make a rye levain

Flour from different mills can absorb water a little differently. The dough should be stiff but not hard. If it should seem too hard, just add some more water.

1. Cut 200 grams (7 ounces) of the chef and put it in a baking bowl with water and flour. Knead the dough for 5 minutes at low speed.
2. Put the dough in a plastic container with a lid greased in a bit of neutral oil (see photograph below).
3. Let rise in a warm place or in a turned-off oven for 5–6 hours, or until the dough has doubled in size. Now the levain is ready to use.

Mother

Chef

Freshening the chef

1,000 grams (7⅓ cups) wheat flour high in protein, preferably
  stone ground
500 grams (1 pound 1.6 ounces) chef
500 grams (2 cups) water

1. Make an elastic dough by kneading for 15 minutes at the
   lowest speed. The ideal temperature for the dough is 24.5°C
   (76.1°F), and it should preferably not be over 25°C (77°F).
2. Let the dough sit and ripen for 10 minutes, covered to
   keep it from drying.
3. Check the dough temperature. Shape the dough into a ball
   and put it in a plastic container covered with a lid in the
   refrigerator for 16 hours at 4°C (39.2°F).

*TIP: If you want to bring the chef somewhere else for baking,
mix the dough with flour until it becomes crumbly. Put it in a
bucket and bring a cooler bag; this way, you can awaken it later
with water and knead a new chef when you arrive.*

Apple yeast for levain

1,000 grams (4 cups) water
500 grams (4½ cups) diced green apples

Let it sit and rise the same way as raisin yeast. Strain the fruit
juice from the apples and press the juice out by using a strainer
and the back of a spoon.

Émile Cauvière's levain with apple yeast

Mother
375 grams (2¾ cups) wheat flour high in protein, preferably
  stone ground
250 grams (1 cup) apple yeast

The same method as with raisin yeast, except the dough
should double in volume and sit for 6 hours instead of 4.

Chef
625 grams (4½ cups) wheat flour high in protein, preferably
  stone ground
250 grams (1 cup) water

The same method as with raisin yeast, except the dough
should double in volume. This normally takes 4 hours.

Levain

500 grams (1 pound 1.6 ounces) chef
1,000 grams (7⅓ cups) wheat flour high in protein, preferably
  stone ground
500 grams (2 cups) water

The same method as for levain with raisin yeast.

Apple levain from Pasticceria Motta in Milan

4 green apples
1,200 grams (5 cups) water

1. Wash the apples in lukewarm water and dice them to the
   size of sugar cubes.
2. Put the apple cubes in a large glass jar, pour warm water at
   35°C (95°F) into the jar, and close the lid. Let it sit for 4–5
   days to rise. Shake the jar every day. If it hisses when you
   open it, then it is ready.
3. Put the mix in a juicer to extract the juice. If you do not have
   a juicer, you can also use a food processor and a strainer.

all the apple juice
1,750 grams (12¾ cups) wheat flour high in protein, preferably
  stone ground
300 grams (10.6 ounces) white sourdough
2 grams (½ teaspoon) yeast

1. Knead an elastic dough at the lowest speed for about 10–
   15 minutes.
2. Put the dough in a lightly oiled plastic container covered
   with a lid and let it sit in a warm place to double in size.
3. Put the natural starter in the refrigerator until it is time to
   use it.

Natural starter as they make it in Italy:
the Milanese method

2 x 100 grams (⅓ cup) apple puree from fresh green apples
2 x 200 grams (1½ cups) wheat flour
2 x 100 grams (½ cup) still mineral water, Italian

1. Wash and puree two freshly cut green apples and strain
   the puree using a sieve.
2. Mix 100 grams (⅓ cup) of apple puree, 200 grams (1½ cups)
   of flour, and 100 grams (½ cup) of mineral water with a ladle
   into a tough dough. Let it rise at 26–28°C (78.8–92.4°F) for

about 48 hours covered with plastic wrap. If no such place exists, put it in a turned-off oven instead. It might need another 24 hours before it is properly fermented. In any case, it should triple in size.

3. Add another 100 grams (1/3 cup) of apple puree, 200 grams (1 1/2 cups) of wheat flour, and 100 grams (1/2 cup) of mineral water. Knead a dough, put it in an oiled plastic container covered with a lid, and let it triple in volume. Now you have a Milanese chef. With this you can make natural starters, levain, in the same way as with raisin yeast.

Natural starter with white sourdough

Make it the same way as levain with raisin yeast (see page 28), but replace the raisin yeast with a white, highly fertile, bubbly and foamy sourdough.

STEP 1
Start a white sourdough (see page 27).

STEP 2
Mother
about 200–300 grams (7–10.6 ounces) white sourdough, depending on consistency, for 175 grams (1 1/3 cups) wheat flour high in protein, preferably stone ground

Mix the flour with the dough until you have a soft yet firm dough. Knead it at low speed for 5 minutes. Then put it in a 2-liter (1/2-gallon) plastic container covered with a lid and let it rise in a warm place or in a turned-off oven for 4 hours (it should double in volume; otherwise, it gets to sit for a little longer, but 4 hours is usually enough).

STEP 3
Chef
Scoop the mother back into the baking bowl and freshen with 125 grams (1/2 cup) of water and 175 grams (1 1/4 cups) of wheat flour high in protein, preferably stone ground. Knead the dough for another 5 minutes and put it back in the jar. Let it sit for another 4 hours until it has doubled in volume. Now you have a chef that should be homogenous and dry on the surface.

This is the same process as for baking with raisin yeast.

Pre-dough

Starting with a pre-dough when baking bread is always to your advantage. It increases the fermentation capabilities and volume and improves the consistency and aroma in the bread

when it is ready.

If you bake a lot of bread you can make a *pâte à fermeté* (white leavening dough) and keep it in the refrigerator at 4°C (39.2°F). This kind of dough keeps for about a week if tightly wrapped in a cloth and for about 4 days in a plastic container covered with a lid. In this book there are several examples of pre-doughs without yeast, as they rise quickly anyway.

Bakers usually refer to a dough started by using a pre-dough as an indirect dough, as it is kneaded in two steps, and to dough made without first using a pre-dough as a direct dough, as all ingredients are mixed together at once. I almost always use a pre-dough in different ways when I bake bread because the results are significantly better. The major bakeries have stopped using this method, which has resulted in lots of flavorless bread of great volume and crumbly crumb. A real baker makes many kinds of pre-dough, scalded breads, and sourdough and creates aromatic bread with small amounts of yeast. The less yeast you use when baking, the more aromatic the bread. The texture will be better, too, since the flour gets plenty of time to absorb the water in the dough.

Quick pre-dough

Should you be in a hurry or forget to make the dough a day ahead, you can use a shortcut. Put the dough in a big bucket of lukewarm water (about 35°C /95°F), not over 40°C (104°F). Take the dough out when it has risen to the surface. If this is a Brioche dough, add in the butter and let it rest for 2 hours in a lightly oiled plastic container covered with a lid until the dough has doubled in volume. Push the dough together (see page 36) and let it rest in the refrigerator for 3 hours, then it is ready to work with. For croissants, you can speed up the fermentation the same way and then push the dough together with some flour. Let it cool for 1 hour and roll in the butter as usual.

Quick pre-dough for *savarins* is a classic method of getting the dough to rise more efficiently and become porous. Naturally, the aroma will not be quite as good as when doing it properly, but the dough will still develop enough to strengthen the gluten structures, and the difference is insignificant.

Quick pre-dough has saved us many times in the restaurant and cruise business when there are suddenly more guests than expected or someone has forgotten to place an order with the bakery.

White leavening dough

This is known in France as *pâte à fermeté* and usually consists of 500 grams (2 cups) of water, 750 grams (5 1/2 cups) of wheat flour high in protein, between 1 and 5 grams (1/4–1 1/4 tablespoons) of yeast, and 20 grams (1 tablespoon) of sea salt. Knead the flour and water into an elastic dough and add the salt to suppress the fermentation. The dough should rise in a plastic container or covered with plastic for 6 hours at room temperature between 20 and 25°C (68–77°F) or for at least 11 hours in the refrigerator to develop enough acid to strengthen the gluten and improve the baking abilities and aroma of the final main dough. At bakeries like Olof Viktor's, there is always a substantial reserve of this dough to prevent having to make pre-dough from scratch for every single loaf.

Poolish

This method was invented in 1840 by Polish bakers. The famous baker Poilâne called the dough *pâte à crêpes*, which is pancake batter. The consistency is about as thick as pancake batter.

Baking bread with poolish means extra work, but it yields a better and more airy bread. It increases the elasticity of the dough and requires less kneading, since it quickly becomes elastic and you do not have to add any leavening agents. It has a nice porous consistency with beehive-like pores. Poolish also

gives the bread a slightly acidic aroma, a certain toughness in the crust, and a creamy color. Cuts into the dough made with a knife also open beautifully this way, and the bread stays fresh longer. However, remember not to store the poolish for too long, or it will turn into sourdough instead. Use it as soon as it starts to collapse in the middle—that is when it is ready for baking. The quantity of poolish required for the main dough depends on the recipe. It can be anything between ½ to ¼ of the total weight of the dough.

Measure 500 grams (2 cups) of water, 500 grams of flour of any kind, and 5 grams (1¼ teaspoons) of yeast. Heat the water to 35°C (95°F) and dissolve the yeast with a whisk.

First add half of the flour and whisk the mix into a pancake-like batter, then add the rest of the flour and whisk until the batter is smooth and a little tough. Cover with plastic wrap and let it rise for 3–6 hours at room temperature or for 12–15 hours in the refrigerator until the mix has swelled and formed lots of aroma and light acid.

Scalding

Prior to kneading the dough, you sometimes scald it. You usually pour 500 grams (2 cups) of boiling water over, for example, rye flour. You never use wheat flour for this, but you could use Graham flour, in which the seed shell is kept. Scalding enables the dough to bind more water and gives the bread a moist and slightly sweet crumb. This method is used for classic Skåne breads such as rustic, various rye breads, *laputa*, and bitter-sweet bread, and is typical for breads from the Skåne region.

You usually use 250 grams of flour for 500 grams (2 cups) of water. Work the dough until it is smooth with a ladle. Cover with plastic wrap and let it sit overnight. The temperature of the scalded dough will be around 70°C (158°F).

Sometimes the dough is mildly scalded. In this case, the water should be just below boiling, which pre-gelatinizes the starch somewhat less than boiling water would. The bread pores become coarser and it tastes nice. Let it sit covered with plastic overnight. The final temperature of the scalded bread will be around 50°C (122°F).

Scalding with smaller amounts of flour (*anrörning*) is mostly used for making *kavring* (dark rye bread from Skåne) or breads with a dense crumb. Boil 500 grams (2 cups) of water and pour it over 175 grams (1¾ cups) of rye flour, stir heavily with a ladle into an even porridge. Cover with plastic wrap and let it sit overnight. The temperature of the scalded bread will be around 85–90°C (185–194°F).

Quick-dough

For certain recipes (such as *vörtbröd* and *kavring*; see recipes) I use a quick-dough to start and speed up the fermentation.

These types of dough are heavy and need the quick-dough to help make the bread moist and tasty.

Kneading

I use a machine for kneading and have based the estimated kneading times in this book on that. The number of machines on the market rises all the time, from the good old-fashioned Electrolux to the fabulous-looking KitchenAid machines. The prices vary, and you can find an excellent one at a cheap price. A large bucket is an advantage, whereas the power of the motor effect is less important. Ask around and test a few different ones to find your own preference. You can, naturally, knead by hand, but it takes a long time to bring out the gluten in the dough and the bread will not achieve the same quality or volume. A poorly worked dough is less capable of containing acid/gas.

The salt is always added toward the end of the kneading. It strengthens the gluten, and makes the dough more plastic and elastic and can keep the acids in place.

Keep in mind that all flour in a dough should be kept at room temperature and that everything should be included from the start, otherwise the flour will not be worked evenly and will not achieve the desired volume.

Always make a gluten test (see below) before you finish kneading.

Wheat flour dough

Mix the liquid and yeast with a whisk until the yeast is dissolved. Pour in the flour and pre-dough (if there was one). Mix at low speed to start with, for about 13 minutes (depending on the recipe), without salt. The liquid should wet the wheat in order for the gliadin and glutenin to make it swell and form gluten. Add the salt and knead for another 7 minutes for a total of 20 minutes. Increase the speed toward the end to stretch out the gluten properly. To improve the gluten, the dough should be kneaded for a few minutes before adding any fat.

Rye flour dough

Knead slowly for about 15 minutes. Add the salt after 5 minutes. Rye flour tends to swell slowly and needs time to absorb the water. Rye has completely different abilities than wheat and cannot form gluten. It is relatively high in pentosans that bind water and it swells when adding sourdough. That is why I always add sourdough when baking with rye.

When making dough from a mixture of rye and wheat, you have to keep in mind that the dough cannot tolerate the same intensive kneading as a wheat flour dough, since rye flour is weaker than wheat flour. When dough gets shiny on the surface it has been kneaded for too long. It can no longer contain the gas and the dough gets runny.

Combining

Bortgörning (combining the many separate parts) is an old term for finishing kneading the dough. The ingredients are kneaded into the dough to become evenly distributed and to develop gluten. Air is mixed in as small bubbles, enabling a light and airy result. During the kneading process, the gluten gets stretched out, but if the kneading gets too intense, it rips the gluten apart and the dough collapses.

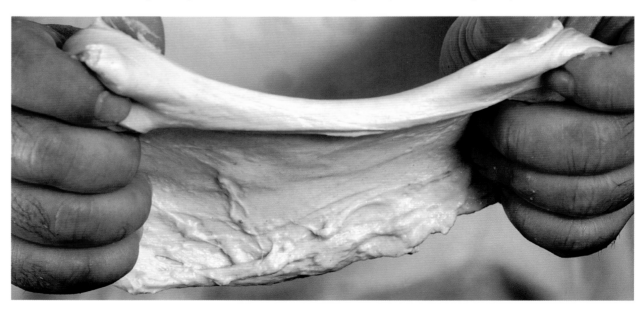

Gluten test

It is important to check the consistency of the dough while kneading. Take a piece of the dough and stretch it between your thumb and forefinger. It should create a thin elastic film. If the dough comes apart too easily, it needs to be worked more. However, if it bursts too easily, it has been worked too much.

It is hard to know when rye dough is kneaded enough, as it still feels sticky when it is stiff. Keep in mind that rye dough should never be as stiff as wheat dough, since it stiffens while rising.

Temperature and kneading

Many recipes suggest an ideal dough temperature. It is important to bake bread at the right temperatures. Always use cold water straight from the faucet: This way the leavening will not speed up, but proceed slowly. The hardness of the water indicates the amounts of calcium, magnesium, and other salts present, which is of a certain importance when baking. Hard water tastes better and gives the gluten a certain firmness, but at the same time it also obstructs the swelling abilities of the

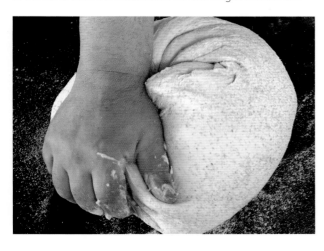

flour. For wheat dough with milk, I take the milk straight from the refrigerator when it is time to knead the dough. The friction from kneading in a machine causes the temperature to rise.

Most kinds of wheat dough should be kneaded for 20 minutes. Strong flour requires heavier kneading than weak flour to develop gluten. I usually knead rye dough for 15 minutes since it does not form gluten, but the temperature rises quite significantly anyway. It is always more difficult to determine when a rye dough is finished kneading.

The dough usually reaches a temperature of 24–26°C (75.2–78.8°F) when kneaded finished in a machine—the more efficient your machine is, the more quickly the temperature rises. This is often an ideal temperature, unless the recipe tells

you otherwise. With more experience using your machine, you can learn to control the dough temperature.

When making nice baguettes, the dough cannot be too warm or rise too quickly. Use cold water, which should bring the temperature to 24–25°C (75–77°F), the ideal temperature. For Ciabatta dough, it is important to maintain a higher temperature; 28°C (82.4°F) is ideal for optimal rising effect. The Italians often set aside 7% of the dough liquid to add when the dough is finished kneading, to make the bread tougher and more airy with a strong crackle.

Check with a thermometer and learn how to control the dough temperature; you will achieve much better results this way. You could also approach it from a scientific point of view like the professional bakers. It only takes a minute; this is how you do it:

How to calculate the dough temperature (in Celcius) for "direct dough," in which all ingredients are mixed at the same time without using a pre-dough.
The most common practice is to multiply the desired dough temperature by 2. Subtract the flour temperature from this amount and then add the baking factor of 2, and you have the liquid temperature.

Example: The recipe suggests a desired dough temperature at 26°C. Multiply 26 by 2, which is 52°C. Measure the temperature of the flour. If it is 20°C, subtract 20°C from the calculated temperature, which comes out to 32°C. Add the baking factor, 2°C, for a cold baking bowl. Hence, the water should be 34°C.

How to calculate the dough temperature (in Celcius) for quick-dough, scalding, pre-dough, or poolish.
Multiply the desired dough temperature by 3. Subtract the total of the flour temperature and the quick-dough/pre-dough/scalding/poolish temperature from this amount. Add 2 for the baking factor, and you have the liquid temperature.

Example: The desired dough temperature is 27°C. Multiply 27 x 3 = 81. The flour temperature is 18°C and the quick-dough/pre-dough/scalding/poolish temperature is 25°C, so the total is 43°C; 81 – 43 = 38 + baking factor of 2 = 40. In other words, the liquid temperature should be 40°C.

In order to calculate the temperature of an indirect dough (a dough including a pre-dough), you must also measure the temperature of the pre-dough to determine the liquid temperature.

Rising time—the first fermentation
Fold the dough like a pillow and put it in a lightly oiled plastic container covered with a lid. While rising, the gluten absorbs

water and the dough gets a dry surface that indicates that it is ready for baking.

The time required for dough to be ripe for baking varies from 1 to 3 hours. The less yeast, the more time the dough needs. While fermenting, the dough is forming acids and alcohol, which react together and give the bread its flavor and aroma. The flour swells and forms an elastic gluten web that creates structure in the dough. Without time to rise, the dough cannot become elastic. On the other hand, gluten is sensitive to acid and can lose its elasticity if left to rise for too long. It then collapses instead and becomes impossible to bake with. Cold temperatures suppress acidic activity in the dough and can enable the dough to rise for a lot longer without going rancid. In other words, you can let dough rise overnight in the refrigerator and start shaping it into loaves right away the next morning. The only downside to leaving dough to rise overnight is that the bread and buns become a little smaller. Try not to leave the dough sitting for more than 12–15 hours.

Rye dough rarely needs more than 1 hour to rise; too much time makes it runny. In the case of rye dough, you let the aroma and flavor develop in the pre-dough, sourdough, quick-dough, and scalded bread.

Pushing out the air

This method primarily applies to wheat flour dough. At 20–25°C (68–77°F) acetic acid is formed, which slows the fermentation process. When the air is pushed out of the dough, most of the acetic acid disappears. Some of it remains in the dough, however—the acetic acid and the milder lactic acid form the aroma.

Put the dough on a floured baking table and push out the air by hand. Fold the edges of the dough toward the middle into the shape of a pillow and put it back into the plastic container with the seam of the dough downward (see photograph to the right). When the dough is shaped this way, it becomes extra stretchy. The temperature gives new nutrition to the yeast cells. When you remove the carbonic acid from the dough, the fermentation becomes more powerful. The yeast multiplies, creating more air bubbles, and the dough rises faster. Pushing out the air this way gives the bread more volume, better bak-

ing abilities, and a finer, more elastic crumb. Some dough is pushed together twice, and, in the case of looser dough, even 3 times to make it more stable.

Shaping the loaves

When the dough is ready, it gets divided into pieces with a dough scraper and a scale to make all the pieces equal in size and weight. In most cases, the dough pieces are rolled into tight buns. Swedish bakers refer to this as "riva bröd," and you usually use both of your hands for this to make it faster.

Cover the dough with plastic or a baking cloth and let it relax for about 10 minutes. Shape a regular loaf by flattening the dough with your right hand and folding it together 3 times (see photograph, page 38). Position the seam across from you and use your right palm to hit the dough to make the seam stick to the table.

Round loaves are usually placed directly onto a tray, cloth, or basket to rise. Traditional bread rises on trays, floured wooden boards, or floured cloth, in which case the cloth is pulled up between the loaves so that they rise upward rather than sideways (see photograph, page 54). They can also rise in special leavening baskets, heavily floured to keep the dough from sticking. The baskets also make the bread rise upward, which allows you to bake with dough of loose consistency and large pores inside. Put the seam downward in the basket if you want the bread to be broken from the top, and put it upward if you want the bread to have a smooth upper surface.

If you want to make bread with air bubbles in the crumb, you have to treat the dough tenderly, like when making baguettes. Fold the dough together 3 times and do not press out the air. Cover with plastic or cloth and let the dough relax. Roll out the dough without pressing, or the precious air bubbles will disappear.

Other breads I just fold carefully and place in baskets with the seam facing downward. This yields beautiful breads that crackle in the oven.

The first fermentation. The doughs (rye and wheat) are resting.

When rolling (tearing) buns, it is not so important to use both hands at once like the professionals do. The important thing is that there is tension in the dough and that the buns are rolled evenly. When I was a boy, we received proper training in tearing buns during the "Fat Tuesday" (a Swedish pastry also known as *semla*) season. Thankfully, most bakeries and pastry shops could not afford to buy automatic bun-cutting machines.

Leavening—the second fermentation

Bakers refer to this as quickening (*raska*) the bread, and the space in which this process takes place is often referred to as *raskrum* (quick-room). Bakeries usually keep a temperature of 37°C (98.6°F) and 70–80% air humidity to keep the dough from drying out on the surface and rising too quickly. I use this method only for wheat dough. It is quite heavy but gets light and airy if you let it rise the right way.

Brioche and Karlsbader dough, which are heavy, rise well in a turned-off oven.

Most breads take about 1–3 hours to rise a second time at room temperature. It all depends on the temperature in the room, and that is why I always specify that the breads should rise to twice their size. At home you can let the bread rise in a turned-off oven and spray a little water in now and then to improve the fermentation and prevent the dough from drying out. I almost always let dough rise overnight in the refrigerator, as it gives the dough a fantastic aroma and structure. The bread can also rise on floured cloth with fabric on top (to keep the

Tearing buns

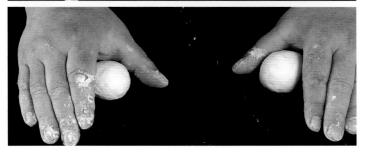

Tearing round loaves

Shaping the bread:

Flatten the dough.

Fold in the seam.

Fold and lock the bread.

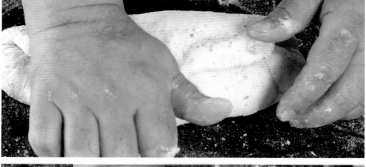

Push together the seam.

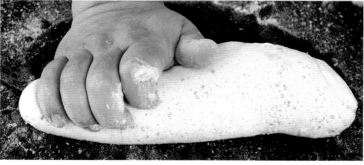

Roll out the bread.

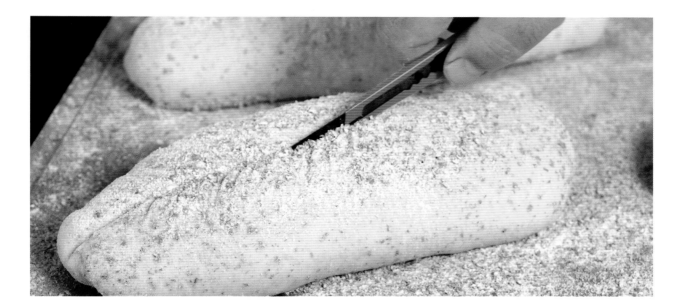

dough from drying on the surface). The traditional leavening method on cloth is ideal. It yields great volume and makes it rise easily.

The same is true of fermenting bread in baskets. Never raise the temperature during fermentation, or you will have bread of industrial character instead of nice quality.

When is the bread finished rising?

Determining when a loaf of bread is finished rising becomes a habit when you bake often. When bread is left to rise for too long, it risks collapse, loses its shape, and gets runny and flat at the bottom. When it gets too little time to rise, it usually cracks on the sides. Check if the bread is done rising by pressing it with your forefinger; it should be elastic and a little springy.

Cutting

Cut the bread with a special knife just before putting it in the oven. Cutting too early will cause any patterns to fade. You can use a sharp razorblade, and the bread will open differently depending on how you angle the cut. For baguettes, you make deep and quite long cuts to achieve their characteristic look.

Cutting little incisions in the bread before putting it in the oven primarily serves a technical purpose, namely to distribute the gluten tension for the sake of volume. Certain cuts are, however, more for the sake of decoration.

Baking

I want to teach you how to bake delicious bread at home, even if you do not have a firewood oven.

This book uses the same methods as we do at Olof Viktor's Bakery. You can copy this style of baking at home by getting a granite baking plate, which you oil generously to keep the breads from sticking to the stone. Heat the stone to 250°C (480°F). If you do not have a baking stone, you can use a tray and heat it the same way.

Put the leavened bread directly onto the hot stone or tray with a spatula. The professionals use long baker's peels, called rods. In old baker's Swedish, we say to *skuvar* the bread (squeeze the bread tightly together) when putting loaves in the oven. Spray a little water in with a squirt bottle, mimicking the heat of an old-fashioned steamy firewood upright oven. At the bakeries, we spray in steam.

I use a high starting temperature in most of my recipes, 250°C (480°F). I preheat the stone or tray in the oven. When the bread is in the oven, I spray in some water to soften the surface of the dough and help the bread expand. The dough temperature rises and the gases grow and widen the pores; the bread rises and some of the gas disappears into the oven.

The egg white in the gluten eventually hardens (coagulates), and the bread forms a skeleton that gives off water to the starch cells, which in turn swell and pre-gelatinize. The bread gets a firm crumb. When the bread is ready, the internal temperature for white bread should be 95–96°C (203–205°F) at the lowest and for heavier bread 96–98°C (205–208°F).

After 5 minutes, I lower the heat to 200°C (390°F) to keep from browning the crust too much. I open the door briefly after 10–20 minutes to bring drier air into the oven and make the crust crispier. I usually repeat the venting a couple of times during baking, since much of the flavor and aroma is in the crust.

GOOD TO KNOW: The expansion of air pockets during the baking process is in accordance with the law of physics stating that a gas expands $1/273$ times its own volume per 1°C of increased temperature.

Baking times

I usually weigh the dough for each kind of bread to calculate the amount of baking time to get a good crust.

French bread or white bread
400 grams (14 ounces): about 35–40 minutes
500 grams (1 pound 1.6 ounces): about 45–55 minutes
750 grams (1 pound 9.6 ounces): about 55–60 minutes
1000 grams (2 pounds 3.2 ounces): about 75 minutes

Baguettes that weigh 350–400 grams (12–14 ounces) require less time in the oven than larger breads, so I usually bake them for about 25–30 minutes, depending on the type.

When baking bread in a pan, such as *kavring* and whole wheat bread, you should always check the internal temperature with a thermometer.

Flat breads, such as "hole-cakes" and tea biscuits, should bake at high temperatures the entire time to keep from becoming dry.

I put most breads on an oven rack as soon as they are out of the oven. If I want the surface to crackle, which I think is important for light breads, I use a squirt bottle to spray them with water.

Making sure that the bread is ready

Follow my times if you want crispy breads and use a thermometer when in doubt, especially for whole wheat bread. Some people turn the bread over and knock on it; the idea being that it should sound hollow, but this method is not guaranteed to work. The bread could be ready on the inside but maybe not have developed a flavorful crust.

Crusts

The bread temperature is around 30°C (86°F) when it is put in the oven. Adding steam also speeds up the heating. The steam condenses on the cooler dough and transfers heat. The top of the dough heats up much faster this way. The water content of the crust of freshly baked bread is around 5%.

The crust of bread baked without steam has entirely different qualities. In this case, there is no pre-gelatinized starch on top. Instead, the starch remains unchanged, since the surface dries when the dough is put in the oven. Without water, the starch cannot pre-gelatinize.

Maillard reaction

This process causes certain sugars (the reducing ones) such as glucose, maltose, and fructose, when heated with proteins and amino acids, to turn brown. This contributes, among other things, to the appetizing color of the crust. Maillard products are also formed in the crust of a steak.

Brushing

Bread glaze

The bread is brushed with a glaze to make it glossy. Mix 10 grams (3 teaspoons) of potato flour and 50 grams (1/4 cup) of water. Boil 200 grams (3/4 cup + 1 1/2 tablespoons) of water, whisk the flour, and let it cook. In this book, I use bread glaze for wort bread, coarse Skåne bread, and syrup loaves.

Stroking the bread with an egg

Whisk an egg and a bit of salt. For a high gloss, use an egg, an egg yolk, and a pinch of salt. Always brush wheat dough, Karlsbader dough, Danish (Viennese) bread, croissants, and brioche with egg before rising and one more time just prior to baking in the oven for a beautiful gloss. A badger brush is traditional.

Water and milk

Brush dough with water for seeds and grains to stick to it: for example, poppy on a French roll. You can also use milk, though it browns a lot more. I usually brush gingerbread with milk.

Butter

Brush bread with butter after baking it in the oven to enhance its flavor. Cream buns get brushed with butter for the sugar to stick to the bun. Clarify the butter by heating it and letting the sediment sink. Use the clarified butter and throw away the sediment, which comprises about 20% of the butter.

Tiger glaze

This glaze looks like tiger fur—very decorative. Brush buns or bread with it and let them rise until it crackles properly. The dough rises more slowly when glazed. Bake in the oven as usual, except do not spray in any water.

125 grams (1/2 cup) water
6 grams (1 1/2 teaspoons) yeast
125 grams (1 cup) rice flour
8 grams (2 teaspoons) granulated sugar
8 grams (1 3/4 teaspoons) cooking oil
3 grams (1/2 teaspoon) sea salt

Dissolve the yeast in the water and whisk in the rest of the ingredients. Cover with plastic wrap and let it rise for 30 minutes.

Aging of bread

I always keep freshly baked bread wrapped in a cloth at room temperature. This way, the crust can breathe and the bread still tastes good the next day. White bread ages the quickest. Heavier and scalded breads keep better and can be eaten all week without the quality changing much. Levain bread without commercial yeast keeps the longest, along with panettone made from apple yeast.

Freezing and thawing bread

Freeze the bread in a plastic bag as soon as it has cooled and then thaw it in the plastic bag. Soft breads and breads with a crispy crust become just like freshly baked bread when you put them in the oven at 100°C (212°F) for about 5 minutes for buns and 8–10 minutes for loaves. Check that they feel warm inside before taking them out. If you want the bread to have a crispy crust, simply take it out of the plastic bag before thawing.

Toasting

Toasting bread is a simple way to freshen it, and it is important for the flavor that it gets properly toasted. Most breads taste better when toasted.

Americans, much like the English, love having toast for breakfast. The Italians fill their bread and roast it with a beautifully checkered pattern on the outside and soft fillings.

Mold on bread

Mold is caused by various fungi, which all multiply by sporulation.

The spores grow in a variety of ways, each specific to its kind of mold, and only on open surfaces, like a crust or a slice of bread. Moisture is the ideal condition for growing mold; 14% water content is the limit for bread. This is why it is important not to package bread until it has cooled properly; otherwise, the moisture will condensate inside the bag.

bread

The finest and most aromatic bread you can bake is levain bread, which has in recent years seen new popularity across the world. French bakers normally begin the leavening process with either raisin or apple yeast, but you can also use sourdough, which has the same rising capacity.

Pain au levain

This flavorful bread of neutral taste and mild acidity never fails to please. I tend to vary between equal amounts of spelt wholemeal, whole Kamut, or Emmer wheat.

Dough temperature 26°C (79°F)
Sits 2 hours and 50 minutes

For 4 loaves
65 grams (½ cup) graham flour, preferably stone ground
65 grams (½ cup) coarse rye flour, preferably stone ground
1,125 grams (8¼ cups) wheat flour high in protein
875 grams (3½ cups + 2 tablespoons) water
800 grams (1 pound 12 ounces) levain (see page 27–29)
25 grams (4 teaspoons) sea salt

1. Place the flour in a baking bowl and pour the water over it. Add the levain and knead the dough at low speed for approximately 13 minutes. Add the salt, increase the speed, and knead the dough for roughly 7 more minutes, until it's completely elastic and fully developed.
2. Put the dough in a lightly oiled plastic container covered with a lid and let it rest for 90 minutes.
3. Place the dough on a floured table, push out the air inside the dough (see page 36) and fold it like an envelope. Let rest in the container for another 80 minutes.
4. Push the dough back together and let it relax for 10 more minutes.
5. Divide the dough into 4 equal pieces, roll them carefully into round balls, and place them on a floured baking cloth. Dust some flour over them as well. Put them in a warm place for 60-90 minutes to rise (ideally 28–30°C / 82–86°F) until they have increased ¾ in volume.
6. Preheat the oven to 250°C (482°F) and place a baking stone or oven tray inside. Put 2 of the loaves in the refrigerator to halt the leavening until baking.
7. Make a deep cut on top of the loaves with a sharp knife (see page 39). Put 2 of the loaves in the oven with a baker's peel. Spray a generous amount of water using a squirt bottle and lower the heat to 200°C (392°F) after 5 minutes.
8. After 20 minutes, vent the oven by briefly opening the door. Repeat venting once more during baking to achieve a crispy crust.
9. Bake the bread for a total of 1 hour, checking with a thermometer that their inner temperature is 98°C (209°F). Place them on a metal rack to cool. Repeat the process with the loaves in the refrigerator.

Pain au levain with graham flour

Pain au levain med grahamsmjöl

A very tasty and aromatic bread with a strong taste.

Dough temperature 26°C (79°F)
Sits 2 hours and 50 minutes

For 4 loaves
1,000 grams (8⅓ cups) graham flour, preferably stone ground
650 grams (2¾ cups) water
800 grams (1 pound 12 ounces) levain (see pages 27–29)
20 grams (3½ teaspoons) sea salt

1. Follow the first 4 steps of *Pain au levain* on page 43, only knead the dough at low speed the entire time.
2. Gently shape the dough into round loaves with both hands, without pushing out the air.
3. Dip the loaves in graham flour and and use a cookie cutter or glass to make the round indentation on top (shown). Let them rise on a floured cloth, lifting up the cloth between the loaves (see photograph on page 54).
4. Let the loaves rise for 75–90 minutes. Follow the baking directions for *Pain au levain blanc* (opposite page).

Pain au levain with spelt wholemeal

Pain au levain med fullkornsdinkel

This is a fantastic and lasting bread. Take care not to knead the dough too quickly.

Dough temperature 26°C (79°F)
Sits 2 hours and 50 minutes

For 4 loaves
1,000 grams (5¾ cups) spelt wholemeal, preferably stone ground
650 grams (2¾ cups) water
800 grams (1 pound 12 ounces) levain (see pages 27–29)
20 grams (3½ teaspoons) sea salt

1. Follow the first 4 steps of *Pain au levain* on page 43, only knead the dough at low speed the entire time.
2. Turn out the dough on a breadboard floured with spelt wholemeal and sprinkle a little on top.
3. Divide the dough into 4 equal pieces using a dough scraper.
4. Shape each into a bow, as shown, and let them rise for 75–90 minutes.
5. Follow the baking directions for *Pain au levain blanc* (opposite page).

Pain au levain blanc

Keep in mind that wheat dough must be fully kneaded to develop gluten!

Dough temperature 26°C (79°F)
Sits 2 hours and 50 minutes

For 4 loaves
1,000 grams (7¼ cups) wheat flour high in
    protein, preferably stone ground
630 grams (2⅔ cups) water
800 grams (1 pound 12 ounces) levain (see
    pages 27–29)
20 grams (3½ teaspoons) sea salt

1. Follow the first 4 steps of *Pain au levain* on page 43.
2. Divide the dough gently into 4 equal pieces. Sift a generous amount of
   white flour on a baking cloth, fold the dough over with the seam in the
   bottom, and put 2 and 2 next to each other. Lift up the cloth between the
   loaves (see photograph on page 54) and let them rise for 75–90 minutes.
3. Preheat the oven to 250°C (482°F) and place a baking stone or tray inside.
   Place 2 of the loaves inside the refrigerator to halt the leavening.
4. Put 2 loaves into the oven with a baker's peel. Spray generously with cold
   water using a squirt bottle and lower heat to 200 °C (392°F) after 5 minutes.
   Vent the oven now and then to let in air in order to achieve a crispy crust.
5. Bake loaves for a total of 50 minutes, checking with a thermometer that
   their inner temperature is 98°C (209°F).
6. Place the loaves on a metal rack to cool and spray some water to make
   them crackle beautifully. Repeat the process with loaves in the refrigerator.

Using this dough, I made the 400-gram (1-pound) large baguettes that are
visible in the background of the photograph above.

Pain au levain with bran and vinegar

Pain au levain med havrekli och vinäger

While bran does not contain any gluten proteins, it has many other nutrients such as lipids, lysine, and vitamins. You can divide the dough into 8 parts instead of 4, then shape the pieces into small oblong loaves, brush them with water, and roll them in bran and other grains.

Dough temperature 26°C (79°F)
Sits 2 hours and 50 minutes

For 4 loaves
500 grams (3²/₃ cups) wheat flour high in protein, preferably stone ground
650 grams (2¾ cups) water
800 grams (1 pound 12 ounces) levain (see pages 27–29)
500 grams (8²/₃ cups) bran
10 grams (2 teaspoons) vineger
20 grams (3½ teaspoons) sea salt

1. Follow the first 4 steps of *Pain au levain* on page 43, also adding the bran and vinegar and kneading the dough only at a low speed the entire time.
2. Divide the dough into 4 equal pieces and cut 50 grams (1.6 ounces) of dough off of each piece for the leaf. Shape gently into round loaves with a little wheat flour.
3. Roll out the small pieces of dough to a thickness of 5 millimeters (about ³/₁₆ inch) and cut out leaves as shown in the photograph.
4. Brush the loaves with a little water, add the leaves, and mark the leaf veins with the back of a knife. Dust with a little flour and place them on a floured cloth to rise for 75–90 minutes.
5. Follow the baking directions for *Pain au levain blanc* on page 45.

You can also make loaves if you feel that the leaves are difficult. Sprinkle grains or seeds and cut as shown.

Pain au siegle–Levain bread with rye flour

Pain au siegle–Levainbröd med rågmjöl

This is one of my favorite kinds of bread; it's great with oysters, meat, and aged cheeses. Remember that rye dough must be kneaded for at least 15 minutes to develop its baking abilities. This bread is suitable for freezing in plastic bags. Let it thaw in the bag at room temperature.

Dough temperature 28°C (82°F)
Sits 1 hour

For 3 loaves
1,000 grams (9¾ cups) fine rye flour, preferably stone ground
700 grams (3 cups) water
1,000 grams (2 pounds 3 ounces) levain (see pages 28–29)
20 grams (3½ teaspoons) sea salt

1. Pour all of the ingredients except the salt into a bowl. Knead the dough for 10 minutes at low speed. Add the salt and continue to knead at low speed for 5 minutes (rye dough becomes a bit fuzzy on the surface when it is ready). Transfer the dough to a lightly oiled plastic container covered with a lid and let it rest for 1 hour.

2. Take 3 round baskets and sprinkle them with fine rye flour plentifully, so that the loaves do not stick to the basket.

3. Place the dough on a floured work table and divide it into 3 equal pieces. Roll the pieces into round buns and place them with the seams facing downward into the baskets. Sift over a little bit of rye flour and cover the buns with a cloth. Let them rise for about 60–75 minutes at room temperature.

4. Preheat the oven to 250°C (482°F) and place a baking stone or tray inside.

5. Place all of the loaves in the oven at once using a baker's peel and spray generously with water using a squirt bottle. Lower the temperature to 190°C (375°F) after 5 minutes. After another 20 minutes, vent the oven by briefly opening the door in order to achieve a crispy crust.

6. Bake the loaves for a total of 50 minutes, checking with a thermometer to see that they are finished. The inner temperature should be at least 98°C (209°F) when baking rye bread.

7. Remove the loaves from the oven and let them cool on a rack. Let them rest until the next day.

Hazelnut and raisin bread

Hasselnöts- och russinbröd

Pairs wonderfully with cheese.

For 4 loaves
When using *Pain au siegle* dough for making hazelnut and raisin bread, add 350 grams (2½ cups) of soaked and drained raisins and 400 grams (1¾ cups) of peeled and roasted hazelnuts to the dough. Shape oblong loaves and put them in oblong baskets floured with rye flour to rise in the same way as the bread to the left. Place 2 loaves in the refrigerator to stop the leavening.

Preheat the oven to 250°C (482°F), and carefully put them in the oven with a baker's peel. Spray a generous amount of water into the oven using a squirt bottle.

Vent the oven after 20 minutes by briefly opening the door. Repeat this once more during baking. Bake for a total of 50 minutes, checking the bread's internal temperature by using a thermometer. It should be at least 98°C (209°F).

Let them cool on a rack and repeat the process with the other 2 loaves.

Rye bread with figs and walnuts

Rågbröd med fikon och valnötter

Also a wonderful bread with cheese. Try to get ahold of French walnuts from Grenoble and fine dried figs.

350 grams (1½ cups) soaked figs chopped into small pieces
400 grams (3½ cups) walnuts

Follow the steps for the Hazelnut and raisin bread.

Pain au levain with whole Emmer wheat

Pain au levain med fullkornsemmermjöl

This bread has a lovely color, great aroma, and a delicious crust with a truly original taste.

Dough temperature 26°C (79°F)
Sits 2 hours and 50 minutes

For 4 loaves
1,000 grams (5¼ cups) whole
  Emmer wheat
650 grams (2¾ cups) water
800 grams (1 pound 12 ounces)
  levain (see pages 27–29)
20 grams (3½ teaspoons) sea salt

Topping
100 grams (½ cup) Emmer flakes

1. Follow the first 4 steps of *Pain au levain* on page 43, only knead the dough at low speed the entire time.
2. Divide the dough into 4 equal pieces and gently shape them into round loaves.
3. Roll out ⅓ of each loaf with a rolling pin and then fold it back over the loaf.
4. Brush the loaves with water and sprinkle with Emmer flakes. Let them rise on a floured cloth for 70–90 minutes.
5. Follow the baking directions for *Pain au levain blanc* on page 45.

Pain au levain with whole Kamut wheat

Pain au levain med fullkornskamutmjöl

A bread with a yellowish tone and a delightful seed taste. Egypt does not feel so far away.

Dough temperature 26°C (79°F)
Sits 2 hours and 50 minutes

For 4 loaves
1,000 grams (5⅓ cups) whole
  Kamut wheat
650 grams (2¾ cups) water
800 grams (1 pound 12 ounces)
  levain (see pages 27–29)
20 grams (3½ teaspoons) sea salt

Topping
100 grams (1⅓ cups) oatmeal,
  sunflower seeds, and pumpkin
  seeds

1. Follow the first 4 steps of *Pain au levain* on page 43, only knead at low speed the entire time.
2. Divide the dough into 4 parts, cut off ⅓ of each part, and gently shape 4 large and 4 small round buns.
3. Roll out the small buns to the size of saucers using a rolling pin and some flour. Brush them with water and sprinkle with oatmeal, pumpkin seeds, and sunflower seeds.
4. Brush the larger loaves with water and place the smaller pieces on top of them. Dust with a bit of flour and press the rolling pin lightly on the middle of the loaves.
5. Place the loaves on a floured cloth to rise for 70–90 minutes, then follow the baking directions for *Pain au levain blanc* on page 45.

Pain de Campagne with apple yeast

Pain de Campagne med äppeljäst

Dough temperature 26°C (79°F)
Sits 2 hours

For 2 loaves

1,000 grams (7¼ cups) wheat flour high in protein, preferably stone ground

300 grams (1¾ cups) spelt wholemeal

700 grams (3 cups) water (32°C/90°F)

425 grams (15 ounces) apple levain (see page 31)

20 grams (1 tablespoon) honey

3 grams (¾ teaspoon) yeast

25 grams (4⅛ teaspoon) sea salt

1. Mix all the flour with water and knead the dough for about 4–5 minutes. Transfer the dough to a lightly oiled plastic container covered with a lid and let it rest for 1 hour in a warm place.

2. Put the dough back in the machine, and add the levain dough, honey, and yeast. Knead at lowest speed for 10 minutes. Add salt and knead more quickly for about another 7 minutes until the dough is elastic. Make a gluten test (see photograph on page 34). Do not knead for too long, as spelt meal makes the dough more sensitive to heavy kneading.

3. Transfer the dough back to the container and let it rest for 1 hour.

4. Put the dough on a baking surface and push the air out of it (see photograph on page 36). Fold it over and put it back in the container with the seam facing downward. Let it rest for an additional hour.

5. Remove the dough from the container and push the air out one more time. Cut the dough in half and gently shape 2 round loaves using both hands. Place them on a floured cloth to rise 70–90 minutes, until the volume has increased by 75%.

6. Preheat the oven to 250°C (482°F) and place a baking stone or tray inside. Cut incisions around and across the middle of the loaves with a sharp knife. Place one loaf inside the refrigerator to stop leavening.

7. Put one loaf into the oven using a baker's peel. Spray generously with water using a squirt bottle. Lower the heat to 200°C (392°F) after 5 minutes. Vent the oven after 20 minutes by briefly opening the door. Repeat this once more during baking to make the crust crispier.

8. Bake the bread for about 50 minutes, checking with a thermometer that its internal temperature is 98°C (209°F).

9. Place the baked bread on a rack to cool and repeat the process with the second loaf in the refrigerator.

Rustic apple yeast bread

Äppeljäst lantbröd

Dough temperature 26°C (79°F)
Sits 2 hours and 50 minutes

For 4 loaves

900 grams (3¾ cups) water

12 grams (3 teaspoons) yeast

1,000 grams (7¼ cups) wheat flour high in protein, preferably stone ground

100 grams (¾ cup) coarse rye flour, preferably stone ground

200 grams (1 cup) spelt whole-meal, preferably stone ground

250 grams (1⅓ cups) whole Kamut wheat, preferably stone ground

400 grams (14 ounces) apple levain (see page 31)

25 grams (3½ teaspoons) honey

30 grams (5 teaspoons) sea salt

1. Dissolve the yeast in water using a whisk and pour it over all of the flour in a bowl. Add the apple levain and honey and knead the dough at low speed for 10 minutes.

2. Add salt and knead for about another 5 minutes until the dough is elastic. Do not knead for too long, as there is plenty of coarse flour in the dough.

3. Transfer the dough to a lightly oiled plastic container covered with a lid and let it rest for 1 hour.

4. Place the dough on a lightly floured surface and push the air out of it (see page 36). Put it back in the container with the seam facing downward and let it rest another hour.

5. Push the air out again and then let the dough rise for another 50 minutes.

6. Carefully shape 4 round loaves and fold them like crescents (see *Pain au levain* with whole Emmer wheat on page 50). Let them rise for 60–90 minutes on a floured cloth with a little bit of spelt wholemeal on top.

7. Preheat the oven to 250°C (482°F) and place a stone plate or baking sheet inside. Place 2 of the loaves inside the refrigerator to halt leavening.

8. Put 2 loaves into the oven with a baker's peel and spray generously with water using a squirt bottle. After 20 minutes, vent the oven by briefly opening the door. Repeat this once more during baking to achieve a crispy crust.

9. Bake the loaves for 45–50 minutes, checking with a thermometer that their internal temperature is 98°C (209°F).

10. Place the loaves on a rack to cool and repeat the process with the remaining loaves in the refrigerator.

Baguette de Tradition Française—French sourdough baguettes

Baguette de Tradition Française—Franska surdegsbaguetter

For this recipe, you will have to have started both levain, a natural starter, and a white sourdough. But I promise you it is worth the effort. The dough can also be used for all regional French bread.

This baguette has a very mild flavor and a nice crispy crust. The texture is full of bubbles, and this bread is a perfect table bread or for making a sandwich with ripe Brie de Meaux, cured ham, or salami.

French bakers have wild discussions about the temperature of baguette dough. The question is whether the finished dough should be at 24, 25, or 25.5°C (75, 77, or 78°F). In any case, it should not be more than 26°C (79°F) after kneading. Check with a thermometer that the dough is at the right temperature: It affects the leavening, and dough that gets too hot rises too quickly and will not taste as you would like. On the other hand, if it gets too cold, it rises too slowly and will not develop enough air pockets. The proportions of 1 part levain to 1 part white sourdough gives this bread a distinct flavor. You can also use a *pâte à fermeté* instead of white sourdough, but then you have to reduce the flour by 40 grams (⅓ cup) to get the same texture.

TIP: Remember that French baguettes should not rise for too long, because then they lose their strength and do not crackle as they should in the oven. Also, do not spray too much water or steam into the oven, or the cuts will not split open like they should.

Dough temperature 25.5°C (78°F)
Sits 1 hour

For 4 baguettes
500 grams (2 cups) water
9 grams (2¼ teaspoons) yeast
100 grams (3.5 ounces) white sourdough (see page 27)
100 grams (3.5 ounces) levain (see pages 27–29)
800 grams (5¾ cups) wheat flour, or preferably French
    wheat flour (*Farine de Tradition*)
18 grams (3 teaspoons) sea salt

In the photograph on the right I have formed the baguette dough into various classic French shapes and styles.

1. Dissolve the yeast in water, add the white sourdough, levain, and wheat flour, and knead the dough at low speed for 13 minutes. Add the salt, increase the speed, and knead for 7 more minutes. Make a gluten test (see page 35).

2. Transfer the dough to a lightly oiled plastic container covered with a lid and let it rest for 1 hour.

3. Cut and weigh 4 equal pieces of 400 grams each. Fold the pieces together 3 times (see page 36). Let rest for 30 minutes under a cloth.

4. Shape oblong baguettes by rolling the dough out from the middle and making the ends a bit pointy. Put them with the seam facing upward on a floured cloth and pull the fabric up a little between the baguettes to maintain their shape and make them expand upward rather than sideways. Let them rise for 75 minutes at room temperature (ideally 25°C/77°F) or until they have doubled in size.

5. Preheat the oven to 240°C (464°F) and place a baking stone or tray at the bottom.

6. Place the baguettes on a small board or a ruler longer and wider than a baguette. Cut as shown above and put the loaves on the stone or tray. Bake 2 at a time or, if you're using a tray, all at once.

7. Spray generously with water using a squirt bottle. Lower the temperature after 5 minutes. After another 10 minutes, open the oven door to let in air. Repeat this twice.

8. Bake for a total of 30 minutes. Baguettes are better over-baked than the other way around, or they will soon become too soft and chewy.

9. Take the baguettes out of the oven and set them on a rack. Spray them with water to improve the crackle.

TIP: If you want to bake them the next day, put them in the refrigerator to rise overnight.

Pain Dijonnaise

The first time I visited the mustard city of Dijon, I had this bread with dry-cured ham and Dijon honey mustard and a glass of nice wine. It was practically a religious experience for me and my classmates from the Coba school in Basel. For our entree, I remember that we had roast saddle of rabbit with mustard sauce, baked apples, and prunes.

Dough temperature 26°C (79°F)
Sits 1 hour and 30 minutes

For 4 loaves
150 grams (1 cup) sunflower seeds
100 grams (3.5 ounces) white sourdough (see page 27)
600 grams (4⅓ cups) wheat flour high in protein, preferably stone ground
125 grams (¾ cup) rye flakes
100 grams (1 cup) graham flour, preferably stone ground
100 grams (6½ tablespoons) Dijon mustard, classic Maille
450 grams (2 cups) water
20 grams (5 teaspoons) yeast
15 grams (2½ teaspoons) sea salt
100 grams (1 cup) Gruyère cheese, grated

Topping
75 grams (½ cup) yellow mustard seeds
150 grams (1 cup) sunflower seeds
20 grams (7 teaspoons) wheat flour

1. Preheat the oven to 200°C (392°F). Pour the sunflower seeds into a small pan and roast them until golden brown for about 8–10 minutes. Let cool.
2. Combine the sourdough, wheat flour, rye flakes, graham flour, and mustard in a bowl. Dissolve the yeast in the water with a whisk and pour it in. Knead at low speed for about 13 minutes. Add the salt, increase the speed, and knead for about 5 minutes. Make a gluten test (see page 35).
3. Knead the sunflower seeds and cheese into the dough. Transfer to a lightly oiled plastic container covered with a lid and let it rest for 45 minutes. ➤

4. Place the dough on a floured table, push the air out (see page 36), and fold the dough like a pillow. Put it back into the container with the seam facing downward and let it rest another 45 minutes.

5. Push the air out of the dough again and let it relax for another 10 minutes.

6. Divide the dough into 4 pieces and shape them into round buns. Place them on a cloth and wait 5 minutes.

7. Shape the buns into short, oblong loaves. Brush them with water and then roll them, first in the mustard seeds, then in the sunflower seeds, and finally in a little wheat flour. Place them on the floured cloth, pull up the cloth between the loaves (see page 54) to keep their shape and let them expand upward rather than sideways, and let them rise 45–50 minutes until they have almost doubled in size.

8. Preheat the oven to 250°C (482°F) and place a baking stone or tray inside. Place 2 of the loaves inside the refrigerator to stop leavening.

9. Put two loaves into the oven with a baker's peel. Spray generously with water using a squirt bottle and lower the heat to 200°C (392°F) after 5 minutes. After 20 minutes, vent the oven by briefly opening the door. Repeat this once more.

10. Bake for a total of 40 minutes, checking with a thermometer that the loaves' internal temperature is 98°C (209°F). Set them on a rack to cool, and spray a little water with a squirt bottle to help the crackle. Repeat the process with the loaves in the refrigerator.

Pain Brie

This butter-flavored bread comes from the province of Normandy, which is known for its dairy products, fine cheeses, and cider and calvados. Make this bread when you are already baking baguettes—you will not regret it. This bread comes into its own with a good butter, a ripe Brie de Meaux, and a nice glass of wine.

Dough temperature 26°C (79°F)
Sits 30 minutes

For 3 loaves

750 grams (1 pound 9 ounces) baguette dough (see page 52), which has been resting in a lightly oiled plastic container covered with a lid for 4 hours
200 grams (1 cup + 1½ tablespoons) water
500 grams (3¾ cups) wheat flour high in protein, preferably stone ground
15 grams (2½ teaspoons) sea salt
100 grams (7 tablespoons) butter, room temperature

1. Knead the water, flour, and salt into the baguette dough at low speed for 15 minutes.
2. Add the butter and work the dough for another 5 minutes until it is smooth and elastic. Make a gluten test (see page 35). Place the dough into a lightly oiled plastic container covered with a lid to rest 30 minutes.
3. Divide the dough into 3 equal pieces, tear the dough into round buns, cover them with a cloth, and wait 10 minutes.
4. Place the loaves on a floured cloth to rise for about 2 hours until they have doubled in size.
5. Preheat the oven to 240°C (464°F) and place a baking stone or tray inside.
6. Cut the loaves as shown in the photograph with a sharp knife. Place them into the oven with a baker's peel. Spray generously with water using a squirt bottle and lower the heat to 210°C (410°F). After 5 minutes, vent the oven. Repeat this once more while the bread is in the oven to achieve a crispy crust.
7. Bake the loaves for 45 minutes, checking with a thermometer that the loaves' internal temperature is 98°C (209°F). Set them on a rack to cool.

Baguette de Tradition Française with poolish

Baguette de Tradition Française med poolish

The method of baking baguettes with poolish was introduced in Paris in the 1920s when the baguette first became popular. I got this recipe from the world champion of bread baking, who honored the French flag at the World Cup of baking held every other year in Paris. Cauvière Emile is a fantastic baker and believes that he makes the best baguettes in all of France. Try the recipe and see what you think. Emile could talk about poolish baking for hours, and this is how to make a proper poolish for baguette dough, according to him. Use the poolish as soon as it begins to collapse in the middle. The baguettes may taste best if you let them ferment overnight in the refrigerator, though it can be difficult to make room in the refrigerator at home.

Dough temperature 25°C (77°F)
Sits 1 hour and 30 minutes

For about 5 baguettes
Poolish
250 grams (1 cup) water
1 gram (¼ teaspoon) yeast
250 grams (2 cups) wheat flour, or
    preferably French *Farine de Tradition*

1. Dissolve the yeast in the water with a whisk, and whisk half of the flour into a pancake-like batter. Whisk in the rest of the flour until the dough is a bit tough, and then let it rise at room temperature for 1 hour covered with plastic wrap. The ideal temperature is 25°C (77°F).
2. Set the dough inside the refrigerator for the next day (12–15 hours).

Combining (Bortgörning)
225 grams (1 cup) water
3 grams (¾ teaspoon) yeast
600 grams (4½ cups) wheat flour high in
    protein, preferably stone ground, or
    the French *Farine de Tradition*
500 grams (1 pound 1.6 ounces)
    fermented poolish
18 grams (3 teaspoons) sea salt

1. Dissolve the yeast in the water with a whisk and pour it over the flour and the poolish in a bowl. Knead at low speed for 15 minutes. Add the salt, increase the speed, and knead the dough until it is elastic for 5 minutes. Make a gluten test (see page 35).
2. Transfer the dough to a lightly oiled plastic container covered with a lid and let it rest for 90 minutes.
3. Cut the dough into 350-gram (12-ounce) pieces, fold them together gently 3 times (see page 36), cover them with a cloth, and let rest for 30 minutes.
4. Shape the dough into oblong baguettes by rolling them out from the middle and make the ends a bit pointy. Put them with the seam facing upward on a floured cloth and pull up the fabric between the baguettes (see page 54) to help maintain their shape and let them expand upward rather than sideways. Let them rise for 75 minutes at room temperature or until they have doubled in size.
5. Preheat the oven to 240°C (464°F) and place a baking stone or tray inside.
6. Place the baguettes on a board that is longer and wider than a baguette. Make cuts as shown on page 54 and then put the baguettes on the baking stone or tray. Bake in 2 batches.
7. Spray generously with water using a squirt bottle. Lower the temperature to 200°C (392°F) after 5 minutes. After another 10 minutes, vent the oven to let in air. Repeat this twice more during baking to achieve a crispy crust. Bake for a total of 30 minutes.
8. Remove the baguettes from the oven and set them on the rack. Spray them with water to crackle more. Bake the remaining baguettes the same way. Let them cool and eat them fresh.

Fig baguettes

Fikonbaguetter

Add 350 grams (2½ cups) of chopped figs to the base dough and separate the dough into equal 400-gram (14-ounce) pieces instead of 350 grams (12 ounces). Follow the baking directions above.

Fig Baguettes

Pain de metiel

The classic French bread for oysters. Serve it with good butter and a bit of flake salt on top. Cut the bread into thin slices to serve with oysters or cold cuts. In the case of oysters, Brasserie Gare du Nord is clearly a favorite in Paris.

Dough temperature 26°C (79°F)
Sits 1 hour

For 2 loaves

DAY 1
Poolish
500 grams (2 cups) water
3 grams (¾ teaspoon) yeast
165 grams (1½ cups + 5 teaspoons) fine
    rye flour
165 grams (1¼ cups) wheat flour high in
    protein, or preferably the French *Farine
    de Tradition*

Dissolve the yeast in the water. Add half of the flour and whisk into a thick batter using a heavy whisk. Whisk in the remaining flour until the dough is smooth and a bit tough. Let it sit at room temperature for 12–15 hours covered with plastic wrap.

DAY 2
Combining (Bortgörning)
833 grams (1 pound 13.4 ounces) poolish
20 grams (5 teaspoons) yeast

500 grams (3¾ cups) wheat flour high in protein, preferably stone ground
500 grams (5 cups) fine rye flour, preferably stone ground
33 grams (5½ teaspoons) sea salt

1. Pour the poolish into a bowl, add the yeast, and keep going until it has dissolved. Add the flour and knead the dough at low speed for 10 minutes. Add the salt and knead for another 5 minutes, until the dough begins to feel elastic (do not work the dough for too long, as it contains rye flour).
2. Transfer the dough to a lightly oiled plastic container covered with a lid and let it rest for 1 hour.
3. Put the dough on a board floured with fine rye flour. Divide it into 2 equal pieces and shape them into round buns. Cover them with a cloth and let them rest for 5 minutes.
4. Shape the buns into oblong loaves and place them into heavily floured baskets to rise for 1 hour. If you do not have leavening baskets, place them on a cloth and pull up the fabric between the loaves to help maintain their shape and let them expand upward rather than sideways (see page 54).
5. Preheat the oven to 250°C (482°F) and place a baking stone or tray inside.
6. Put the loaves into the oven with a baker's peel. Spray a little water and lower the temperature to 200°C (392°F). After 20 minutes, vent the oven by opening it briefly. Repeat this once more during baking to achieve a crispy crust.
7. Bake about 50 minutes, checking with a thermometer that the internal temperature is 98°C (209°F). Place the loaves on a rack to cool.

Rye buns

Rågbullar

Using the *Pain de metiel* dough, I have also made various rye buns that go well with breakfast and lunch, dinner, or sandwiches. Don't forget plenty of salted butter and good cheese, or jam and marmalade. The buns weigh about 60 grams (2 ounces) each. You can freeze them in plastic bags.

(See the photograph to the right) Upper right: I rolled these buns into the shape of hot dog bread bread (see page 6), then brushed them with water and rolled them in a mixture of sunflower seeds, pumpkin seeds, and oats.

Middle right: I rolled these into buns and let them rise halfway, and then marked them in the center with a rolling pin.

Bottom right: I rolled these into the shape of hot dog bread, then brushed them with water and dipped them in fine rye

flour. When they had risen, I made an incision across the long side with a sharp knife.

Bottom left: I mixed 350 grams (2½ cups) of soaked raisins into the dough and shaped the buns, brushed them with water, and dipped them in fine rye flour. I let them rise and made an incision just before baking them.

Middle left: I greased the baking table with a little olive oil and tore the buns so that they were not completely sealed on

the bottom. I let them rise on a rye-floured cloth with the ends facing down. Turn the buns over to the right side facing up before baking, and they will come out beautifully.

Top left: I shaped the buns and then rolled out ⅓ of the dough like a tongue with a rolling pin. Then I made an incision in the tongue and put it over the buns. After that I powdered them with fine rye flour.

The buns need to rise until doubled in volume; about 1 hour. Preheat the oven to 250°C (482°F) and bake them until golden brown, approximately 12–15 minutes. Spray a little water with a squirt bottle at the beginning of the baking process. Let them cool on an oven rack.

German rustic bread from Bavaria

Tyskt lantbröd från Bayern

I sometimes call this Silvia Bread after our lovely Queen, who is from Bavaria. However, since I did not ask the Queen for permission, I will officially call it German rustic bread instead.

Serve this rustic, tangy bread with prosciutto (*Rohschinken*), pickles and caraway cheese, and a thinly sliced black radish with flake salt. After that, a generous portion of cured pork (*Eisbein*) with Sauerkraut as the main course, with potato and green pea puree with crispy bacon on top, hot mustard, and foamy beer. Perhaps an apple brandy (*Apfelkorn*) to go with it.

Dough temperature 27°C (81°F)
Sits 2 hours

For 2 loaves
500 grams (2 cups) water
10 grams (2½ teaspoons) yeast
500 grams (3¾ cups) wheat flour high
    in protein, preferably stone ground
500 grams (3 cups) spelt wholemeal,
    preferably stone ground
500 grams (1 pound 1.6 ounces) rye
    sourdough (see page 27)
20 grams (9½ teaspoons) whole cumin
30 grams (5 teaspoons) sea salt

1. Dissolve the yeast in the water with a whisk and pour it into the bowl with all of the flour, sourdough, and carway. Knead the dough at low speed for about 12 minutes. Add the salt and knead more quickly for another 8 minutes until the dough is tough and elastic. Make a gluten test (see page 35). Do not knead the dough for too long, or it will burst.
2. Transfer the dough to a lightly oiled plastic container covered with a lid and let it rest for 1 hour.
3. Put the dough on a floured table and push the air out of it (see page 36). Put it back in the container with the seam facing downwards to rest for another hour.
4. Push the air out again and let it rest for 10 minutes.
5. Divide the dough in half and roll it gently into 2 round loaves. Put them into 2 large, round, heavily floured baskets to rise to double their volume, which will take about 45–60 minutes. If you do not have baskets, let them rise on a floured cloth.
6. Preheat the oven to 250°C (482°F) and place a baking stone or tray inside.
7. Turn out loaves on a baker's peel, and place them in the oven. Spray with water using a squirt bottle and lower the heat after 20 minutes by opening the oven door to let in air. Repeat this once more during baking to achieve a crispy crust.
8. Bake for a total of 1 hour, checking with a thermometer that the loaves' internal temperature is 98°C (209°F). Set them on a rack to cool.

Lucerne Bread

Luzernbröd

Also known in Switzerland as *Luzernerweggen*. I have a special relationship with Lucerne because I got part of my education there, at the Richemont school and at the Montana school.
This crispy bread should have the rustic taste of sourdough and seeds and a rich color.

Dough temperature 27°C (81°F)
Sits 1 hour and 10 minutes

For 3 loaves
DAY 1
Quick-dough (Raskdeg)
250 grams (2½ cup) fine rye flour, preferably
    stone ground
190 grams (¾ cup) water
10 grams (0.35 ounces) rye sourdough
    (see page 27)

Knead the ingredients into a dough for 5
minutes. Put it in a bowl, cover it with plastic
wrap, and let it sit at room temperature for
10–12 hours.

DAY 2
Combining (Bortgörning)
450 grams (1 pound) quick-dough
750 grams (5½ cups) wheat flour high in
    protein, preferably stone ground
520 grams (2 cups) water
25 grams (6¼ teaspoons) yeast
20 grams (3⅓ teaspoons) sea salt

1. Place the quick-dough in a bowl with the
   flour. Dissolve the yeast with a whisk in
   the water and pour it in. Knead the dough
   at low speed for 12 minutes. Add the salt
   and knead more quickly for another 7–8
   minutes to a tough, elastic dough. Make a
   gluten test (see page 35).
2. Transfer the dough to a lightly oiled
   plastic container covered with a lid and
   let it rest for 35 minutes. Put it on a lightly
   floured table and push the air out of it
   (see page 36). Put it back in the container
   with the seam facing downwards to rest
   for 35 minutes.
3. Push the air out again. Put the dough
   back in the container for 10 minutes.

4. Divide the dough into 3 equal pieces, tear them into round buns, cover
   them with a cloth, and let them rest for 5 minutes.
5. Shape the loaves into ovals, put them with the seam facing up on a floured
   cloth and pull up the fabric between the loaves to help maintain their shape

and let them expand upward rather than sideways (see page 54). Let it rise about 30 minutes.

6. Place the loaves on a floured table and press deeply into the middle using a rolling pin. Let them rise for about another 20–30 minutes.

7. Preheat the oven to 250°C (482°F) and place a baking stone or tray inside. Place one of the loaves inside the refrigerator to halt leavening.

8. Put 2 loaves into the oven with a baker's peel. Spray generously with water using a squirt bottle and lower the heat to 200°C (392°F) after 5 minutes. After 20 minutes, vent the oven by briefly opening the door. Repeat this once more during baking to achieve a crispy crust.

9. Bake the loaves for 50–60 minutes, checking with a thermometer that their internal temperature is 98°C (209°F). Place them on a rack and spray lightly with water to make them crackle beautifully. Repeat the process with the loaf in the refrigerator.

Wallis rye bread

Wallis rågbröd

I bake this Swiss bread often, because it is difficult to live without once you have become used to it. Besides, it is healthy. With its strong flavor, it is excellent for cold cuts and aged cheese. Cut the bread into thin slices and spread butter on with a little bit of flake salt. It is important that the dough is fairly warm so that it rises well and crackles on the surface. If you want to speed up the leavening process, you can add 5 grams (1¼ teaspoons) of yeast, but the bread tastes better without it.

Dough temperature 28°C (82°F)
Sits 1 hour

For 2 loaves
DAY 1
Quick-dough (Raskdeg)
250 grams (1 cup) water
375 grams (3½ cups + 8 teaspoons) fine rye
    flour, preferably stone ground
25 grams (0.9 ounces) rye sourdough
    (see page 27)

Mix everything together into a dough and leave it covered with plastic wrap at room temperature for 12–15 hours.

DAY 2
650 grams (1 pound 7 ounces) quick-dough
700 grams (6¾ cups + 5 teaspoons) fine rye
    flour, preferably stone ground
500 grams (2 cups) water
25 grams (4¼ teaspoons) sea salt

1. Knead all of the ingredients at low speed until the dough creases on the surface. This is how you know that a rye dough is finished, which usually takes about 15 minutes. Place the dough in a lightly oiled plastic container to rise for 1 hour.
2. Place the dough onto a floured table and divide it in half. Shape into 2 round loaves and place them on a floured cloth. Dust generously with rye flour and press a little into the loaves. Let them rise at room temperature until the bread has crackled on the surface, which can take between 45 and 90 minutes depending on the temperature in the room.
3. Preheat the oven to 250°C (482°F) and place a baking stone or tray inside.
4. Put the loaves in the oven using a baker's peel and lower the temperature to 180°C (456°F) after 5 minutes. After 20 minutes, vent the oven by briefly opening the door.
5. Bake the loaves well for about 60–70 minutes. Check with a thermometer that their internal temperature is at least 98°C (209°F). Set on a rack to cool.

Rye herb bread

Rågkryddbröd

This bread has a rustic flavor of typical Austrian character. It tastes like real bread should, with a strong crust and wonderfully tasty crumb. After wheat, rye is the grain mainly used for bread production.

When in Innsbruck, you must visit Gotthard and Marco Valier on Maximilianstrasse 27. Do not miss their *Topfenstrudel*, and also try *Indianerkrapfen* and *Kaisersemmel*, which was created for Emperor Franz Josef's birthday.

Dough temperature 27°C (81°F)
Sits 1 hour and 15 minutes

For 4 loaves or rings
DAY 1
Rye pre-dough (Rågfördeg)
480 grams (4¾ cups) fine rye flour
370 grams (1½ cups) water
50 grams (1.8 ounces) rye sourdough
   (see page 27)

Knead the ingredients into a dough, then put it in a lightly oiled plastic container covered with a lid and let it rest at room temperature for 7–10 hours. Then place it inside the refrigerator for 12–15 hours. Remove the dough 2 hours before baking so that it is not too cold.

DAY 2
Combining (Bortgörning)
900 grams (2 pounds) rye pre-dough
670 grams (5¼ cups) coarse rye flour,
   preferably stone ground
330 grams (2½ cups) wheat flour with a
   high protein content, preferably stone
   ground
50 grams (¼ cup + 3 teaspoons)
   graham flour, preferably stone ground
5 grams (2½ teaspoons) ground cumin
5 grams (2¾ teaspoons) ground coriander
5 grams (2½ teaspoons) anise seeds,
   ground
5 grams (2½ teaspoons) fennel seeds,
   ground
735 grams (3 cups) water
28 grams (7 teaspoons) yeast
40 grams (2 tablespoons) sea salt

1. Put the rye pre-dough in a bowl with all of the flour and spices. Dissolve the yeast in the water with a whisk and pour it into the bowl. Knead the dough at low speed for 10 minutes, add the salt, and knead for another 7 minutes.
2. Transfer the dough to a lightly oiled plastic container covered with a lid and let it rest for 45 minutes.
3. Push the air out of the dough on a floured baking table (see page 36). Let it rest for 10 minutes.
4. Fold the dough together and put it with the seam facing downwards. Divide it into 4 equal pieces, cut each piece into 8 parts, and tear them into round, tight buns. Place 8 buns together in each of the 4 heavily floured round baskets. If you do not have any baskets, connect them in circles on the floured cloth, as shown. Sift over a little rye flour and set them to rise for 45–60 minutes until they have doubled in volume.
5. Preheat the oven to 250°C (482°F) and place a baking stone or tray inside.
6. Turn the loaves on a baker's peel, and place the 2 loaves in the oven. Spray generously with water using a squirt bottle. Place 2 of the loaves inside the refrigerator to halt leavening until they are baked.
7. Lower the heat to 200°C (392°F) after 5 minutes. After 20 minutes, vent the oven by briefly opening the door. Repeat this once more during baking to achieve a crispy crust.
8. Bake the loaves for 45 minutes, checking with a thermometer that their internal temperature is 98°C (209°F). Place them on a rack to cool. Repeat the process with the loaves in the refrigerator.
(If you have chosen to make the bread circles instead, cut them with a sharp knife before baking for 30 minutes.) They should be golden brown when finished.

Italian creased bread with white sourdough

Italienskt bigabröd med vit surdeg

The beautiful crumb of this bread is created by adding water at the end, which makes the dough stringy. The bread is slightly acidic with a lovely aroma and a lasting crumb. It keeps well and goes with almost every food.

Dough temperature 28°C (82°F)
Sits 3 hours

For 4 loaves
Combining (Bortgörning)
675 grams (2¾ cups + 5 teaspoons) + 75 grams (⅓ cup) water
5 grams (1¼ teaspoons) yeast
500 grams (1 pound 1.6 ounces) white sourdough (see page 27)
1,250 grams (9⅛ cups) wheat flour high in protein, preferably stone ground or, ideally, Italian wheat flour
35 grams (2 tablespoons) sea salt

1. Dissolve the yeast in 675 grams (2¾ cups + 5 teaspoons) of water with a whisk and pour it onto the flour and white sourdough in a bowl. Knead the dough at low speed for 13 minutes. Add the salt, increase the speed, and knead for another 7 minutes until the dough is completely elastic. Add 75 grams (⅓ cup) of water and knead until elastic again. Make a gluten test (see page 35).
2. Let the dough rest for 90 minutes in a lightly oiled plastic container covered with a lid.
3. Push the air out of the dough (see page 36) on a floured baking table and put it back in the container with the seam facing downwards. Let it rest another 90 minutes and then push the air our again.
4. Divide the dough into 4 equal pieces. Fold them gently without damaging the air pockets and dust with a bit of flour. Place the loaves to rise on a floured cloth for about 90 minutes at room temperature, or place them inside the refrigerator overnight, take them out in the morning, and let them stand for 1 hour at room temperature before baking.
5. Preheat the oven to 250°C (482°F) and place a baking stone or tray inside. Place 2 of the loaves inside the refrigerator for later.
6. Put 2 loaves into the oven with a baker's peel, and spray in a bit of water with a squirt bottle. Lower the heat to 200°C (392°F) after 5 minutes. After 20 minutes, vent the oven by briefly opening the door. Repeat this once more during baking to achieve a crispy crust.
7. Bake the loaves for about 45–50 minutes. Check with a thermometer that their internal temperature is 98°C (209°F). Place them on a rack to cool. Repeat the process with the other 2 loaves.

Italian creased bread with rye sourdough

Italienskt bigabröd med rågsurdeg

Luca Mannori in Prato, Italy is a pastry chef and a baker. You must not miss visiting his bakery when you are there; it is located on Via Lazzerini 2. This bread is not as airy as the recipe with wheat sourdough, but is just as delicious.

Dough temperature 28°C (82°F)
Sits 3 hours

800 grams (3⅓ cups) water
6 grams (1½ teaspoons) yeast

600 grams (1 pound 5 ounces) rye sourdough (see page 27)
1,250 grams (9⅛ cups) special wheat flour or, ideally, Italian wheat flour
40 grams (2 tablespoons) sea salt

Follow the steps of the recipe for Italian creased bread with white sourdough on page 70.

French sourdough *batarde*

Fransk surdegsbatarde

The best bread of this kind that I have ever had was in the French countryside, especially in Provence. It should be lightly acidic but not too much, because that is simply not how it is done in France.

Dough temperature 25°C (77°F)
Sits 1 hour and 30 minutes

For about 6 loaves
DAY 1
Poolish
500 grams (2 cups) water
5 grams (1¼ teaspoons) yeast
500 grams (3½ cups + 2½ teaspoons) wheat flour high in protein, preferably stone ground

Dissolve the yeast in the water with a whisk. Whisk half of the flour into the water until a smooth batter forms. Add the remaining flour and whisk the batter smooth again. Let it rise at room temperature for 1 hour in a bowl covered with plastic wrap. Then, let it sit in the refrigerator (4°C/39°F) for 12–15 hours.

DAY 2
Combining (Bortgörning)
300 grams (1¼ cups) water
10 grams (2½ teaspoons) yeast
1,000 grams (7⅓ cups) wheat flour high in protein, preferably stone ground
300 grams (10.6 ounces) white sourdough (see page 27)

1,005 grams (2 pounds 3.5 ounces) poolish
30 grams (5 teaspoons) sea salt

1. Dissolve the yeast in the water with a whisk, pour it over the flour in a bowl, and add the white sourdough and poolish.
2. Knead the dough at low speed for about 15 minutes. Add the salt, increase the speed, and knead for about another 5 minutes until it is elastic.
3. Transfer the dough to a lightly oiled plastic container covered with a lid and let it rest for 90 minutes.
4. Break off 400-gram (14-ounce) pieces of dough, fold them together gently, place them on a floured cloth, and let them rest for 30 minutes.
5. Roll the dough into short *batarde* shapes or round loaves. Put them on the floured cloth with the seam facing upward and pull up the fabric between them (see page 54) to help maintain their shape and let them expand upward rather than sideways. Let them rise for about 90 minutes until doubled in volume.
6. Preheat the oven to 240°C (464°F) and place a baking stone or tray inside.
7. Turn the *batarde* loaves upside down on a baker's peel and cut incisions with a sharp cut knife as shown on page 39. Put 3 loaves in the oven using a baker's peel and spray generously with water using a squirt bottle. Place the other 3 loaves in the refrigerator to stop halt leavening.
8. Bake the loaves until they are golden brown, about 25 minutes. After 10 minutes, vent the oven by briefly opening the door and lower the temperature to 200°C (392°F). Vent the oven once more during baking to achieve a crispy crust.
9. Place the loaves on a rack, spray them lightly with water, and let them cool. Repeat the process with the loaves in the refrigerator. See the photograph on page 116.

Restaurant Academy bread

Restaurangakademiens bröd

This bread was invented by chef legends Björn Halling and Örjan Klein, and is managed every day by chef Mark Löfgren and his disciples at the Academy. It is the ideal table bread.

Try to get ahold of Manitoba Cream flour, which is high in protein, to make light and airy bread with large air pockets, a tough crumb, and a crispy crust. You also need a high-speed kneading machine for this recipe, otherwise the dough may not loosen from the bowl.

Dough temperature 25–26°C (77–79°F)
Sits 1 hour

For 2 loaves
500 grams (2 cups) water
12 grams (3 teaspoons) yeast
500 grams (3½ cups + 2½ teaspoons)
   Manitoba Cream wheat flour
15 grams (2½ teaspoons) sea salt

1. Dissolve the yeast in the water with a whisk and pour it over the flour. Add the salt. Knead the dough at the highest possible speed in the machine until the dough loosens from the bowl, which can take 15–20 minutes.
2. Transfer the dough to a lightly oiled plastic container covered with a lid and let it rest for 1 hour.
3. Place the dough gently on a floured baking table without destroying the air pockets. Divide it in half and very gently shape the 2 loaves by rolling them on a baking tray. Let them rise at room temperature for 1 hour.
4. Preheat the oven to 250°C (482°F).
5. Put the loaves into the oven and inject water using a squirt bottle.
6. Bake the bread for 10 minutes, then lower the heat to 200°C (392°F) and bake for another 30 minutes. Let the loaves cool on a rack.

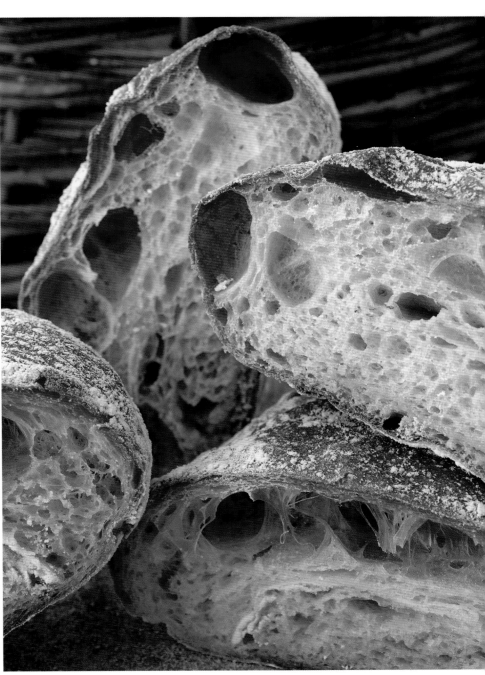

Miche bread with sourdough

Michebröd med surdeg

You could never tire of this light French bread. It goes with everything. The best Miche bread I've ever tried was at the Troisgros brothers' fantastic restaurant in Rouen. They had not, however, made it themselves, they said, but it came from a bakery in town. In Rouen you also have the wonderful pastry shop Pilati et fils on Avenue de Paris 42300 and the French baking academy École supérieure de la boulangerie.

Dough temperature 26°C (79°F)
Sits 1 hour and 15 minutes

For 4 loaves

DAY 1

Pre-dough (Fördeg)

130 grams (1 cup + 4½ tablespoons) fine rye
    flour, preferably stone ground
50 grams (⅓ cup) wheat flour high in protein,
    preferably stone ground
130 grams (½ cup) water
10 grams (0.35 ounces) rye sourdough
    (see page 27)

Mix everything into a dough and let it rise at room temperature for 1 hour. Put it in the refrigerator for 12–15 hours.

DAY 2

Combining (Bortgörning)

320 grams (11.3 ounces) pre-dough
820 grams (6 cups) wheat flour high in
    protein, preferably stone ground
5 grams (1 teaspoon) honey
500 grams + 30 grams (2 cups +
    3 tablespoons) water
16 grams (4 teaspoons) yeast
23 grams (1 tablespoon) sea salt

1. Put the pre-dough and flour in a bowl with the honey. Dissolve the yeast in 500 grams (2 cups) of water with a whisk and pour it into the bowl.
2. Knead the dough at low speed for 15 minutes. Add the salt, increase the speed, and knead until the dough is very elastic. Make a gluten test (see page 35). Knead in the rest of the water (30 grams) until the dough is stringy.
3. Put the dough in a lightly oiled plastic container covered with a lid and let it rest for 35 minutes.
4. Push the air out of the dough on a floured baking table (see page 36). Put it back into the container and let rest for another 40 minutes.
5. Push the air out of the dough again and let the dough relax for 10 minutes.
6. Divide the dough into 4 equal pieces and shape them carefully into round loaves without crushing the dough. Dust a little wheat flour using a sieve. Put the bread on a floured cloth to rise and double in volume for about 90 minutes.
7. Preheat the oven to 250°C (482°F) and place a baking stone or tray inside. Put 2 of the loaves in the refrigerator to keep them from leavening further before baking in the oven.
8. Put 2 loaves in the oven using a baker's peel and spray in water with a squirt bottle. Lower the heat to 200°C (392°F) after 5 minutes. Vent the oven after 20 minutes by opening the door briefly. Repeat venting one more time while the bread is in the oven.
9. Bake the loaves until crispy for about 45 minutes. Check with a thermometer that their internal temperature is 98°C (208°F). Put them on a rack to cool. Repeat the process with the 2 loaves in the refrigerator.

Pane Valle Maggia

This flavorful bread comes from Lugano in the Italian part of Switzerland. It is cut in thick slices and goes well with, for example, Italian and Spanish cold cuts and olives. This is a very loose dough, but it gets firm in the end anyway from pushing so much air out when preparing the dough. At the restaurants in Lugano they often served coppa, bresaola, and mortadella sausage with the delicious bread. This beautiful town is always great to visit. Do not forget to buy a panettone and a box of the wonderful and tough almond biscuits, Amaretti, that are everywhere in the bakeries and pastry shops of this town.

Dough temperature 26°C (79°F)
Sits 3 hours

For 2 loaves
1,000 grams (4 cups + 3 tablespoons) water
30 grams (2½ tablespoons) yeast
240 grams (2½ cups) fine rye flour,
    preferably stone ground
1,000 grams (7⅓ cups) wheat flour high in
    protein, preferably stone ground, or
    ideally yellow Italian wheat flour
150 grams (5.3 ounces) white sourdough
    (see page 27)
24 grams (1 tablespoon) sea salt

1. Dissolve the yeast in the water with a whisk and pour it over all the flour and the sourdough in the bowl. Knead the dough at lowest speed for about 10 minutes.
2. Add the salt, increase the speed, and knead for about 5 minutes into a tough and elastic dough. Make a gluten test (see page 35). Do not knead the dough for too long, or it could burst and lose its rising abilities since there is rye flour in the dough.
3. Put the dough in a lightly oiled plastic container covered with a lid and let rest for 90 minutes.

4. Put the dough on a floured table. Push the air out of the dough (see page 36) and fold it like a pillow. Put it back in the container with the seam facing downward and let it rest for 90 more minutes.
5. Push the air out again, put the dough back in the container, and let it relax for 10 minutes.
6. Divide the dough in half and fold it carefully into 2 round buns. Roll it out with a little bit of fine rye flour into round cakes, about 30 centimeters (about 11 inches) in diameter. Put them on a floured cloth and let rise until they have increased by ¾ in volume. Cut 5 incisions across the long side with a sharp knife.
7. Preheat the oven to 250°C (482°F) and place a baking stone or tray inside. Put one of the loaves in the refrigerator to keep it from rising for too long.
8. Put the other loaf in the oven using a baker's peel. Spray in a generous amount of water with a squirt bottle. Lower the temperature to 200°C (392°F) after 5 minutes. After another 20 minutes, vent the oven by opening the door briefly. Repeat this once while the bread is in the oven to get a crispy crust.
9. Bake for a total of about 50–60 minutes. Check with a thermometer that the bread's internal temperature is 98°C (208°F). Take the bread out of the oven and put it on a rack to cool. Repeat the procedure with the bread in the refrigerator.

Ciabatta according to Peck in Milan

Ciabatta som hos Peck i Milano

You will find the best ciabatta in Milan at Peck's. Do not miss a visit to their fantastic gourmet store close to the cathedral and the Vittorio Emanuele mall. This Italian bread with a taste of the Mediterranean is popular all over the world.

One of the conditions for bread to become as airy as I like it is a loose dough, good olive oil, and wheat flour high in protein—preferably yellow Italian wheat flour with good stretching abilities.

With this basic dough you can make many different breads in a variety of flavors. This bread goes well with sandwiches, prosciutto, mortadella, salami, bresaola, and Italian cheese. It is also ideal for panini.

The olive oil in the dough gives the bread a lovely texture and makes it last longer. At the end of the kneading process it is important to check that the temperature is quite high (28°C/82°F) so that it can rise and stretch well.

Sits 120 + 20 minutes
Dough temperature 28°C (82°F)

DAY 1
Poolish
500 grams (2 cups + 2 tablespoons) water
5 grams (1¼ teaspoons) yeast
500 grams (2⅗ cups) fine Durum wheat,
    preferably stone ground

Dissolve the yeast in the water with a whisk. Add half of the flour and whisk into a pancake-like batter. Whisk in the rest of the flour until the dough gets a little tough. Cover with plastic wrap and let it rest for 12 hours at room temperature.

DAY 2
Combining (Bortgörning)
625 grams (2½ cups) water
10 grams (2½ teaspoons) yeast
1,005 grams (2 pounds 3.5 ounces) poolish
250 grams (8.8 ounces) white sourdough
    (see page 27)
1,200 grams (8¾ cups) wheat flour high in
    protein, preferably stone ground or
    ideally Italian wheat flour
½ deciliter (6 tablespoons + 2½ teaspoons)
    olive oil
60 grams (3 tablespoons) sea salt

1. Dissolve the yeast in the water with a whisk and pour it over the poolish and the sourdough in the bowl. Add the flour and knead the dough for 13 minutes at lowest speed.
2. Add olive oil and salt, increase the speed, and knead for another 7 minutes until the dough is very elastic. Make a gluten test (see page 35). Make sure that the temperature is 28°C (82°F) for the dough to rise properly—it is important in order to get nice air pockets in the crumb.
3. Put the dough in a lightly oiled plastic container covered with a lid. Let rest at room temperature for 1 hour.
4. Put the dough onto the baking table and push out all the air (see page 36). Put it back in the container and let it rest for another hour.

5. Push together the dough like before. Let it relax for another 20 minutes.
6. Press the dough out onto a floured cloth with your fingertips with a little wheat flour, being careful not to lose too much air, until it is about 5 centimeters (about 2 inches) thick. Let it rise on the cloth for 1 hour.
7. Preheat the oven to 250°C (482°F) and place 2 trays or a baking stone at the bottom for about 10 minutes before baking.
8. Cut up the dough into ciabatta bread by using a metal scraper right before baking. Put 3 loaves on each tray using a spatula. Spray in water with a squirt bottle and bake the bread for about 18 minutes until golden brown. Vent the oven now and then to make them really crispy. Put the baked bread on a rack to cool.

TIP: The bread will turn out best if you let it sit on a cloth in the refrigerator for 16–18 hours. This makes the aroma even stronger and the crust more flavorful.

When you feel like varying with different flavors:

Olive ciabatta
Take 1,000 grams (2 pounds 3 ounces) of ciabatta dough and knead in 150 grams (1 cup) of chopped green or black olives. Shape the bread as usual.

Provencal ciabatta
Knead in 15 grams (3 tablespoons) of *herbes de Provence* and 12 grams (1½ tablespoons) of crushed garlic into 1,000 grams (2 pounds 3 ounces) of ciabatta dough.

Lemon ciabatta
Knead the zest from a washed lemon into 1,000 grams (2 pounds 3 ounces) of ciabatta dough and shape it as usual.

Garlic ciabatta
Knead 15 grams (2 tablespoons) of crushed garlic into 1,000 grams (2 pounds 3 ounces) of ciabatta dough.

Bacon ciabatta with turmeric
Knead 220 grams (1½ cups) of crispy fried and drained bacon and 10 grams (1½ tablespoons) of turmeric into 1,000 grams (2 pounds 3 ounces) of ciabatta dough.

Basil ciabatta with sundried tomatoes
Knead 125 grams (2⅓ cups) of sundried tomatoes and 25 grams (5½ tablespoons) of chopped fresh Basil Genovese into 1,000 grams (2 pounds 3 ounces) of ciabatta dough.

Cheese ciabatta
Knead 150 grams (1½ cups) of grated 4-year-old Parmesan cheese into 1,000 grams (2 pounds 3 ounces) of ciabatta dough. Garnish with 25 grams (¼ cup) of *Emmenthaler* (Swiss) cheese on top.

Spelt wheat ciabatta

Dinkelciabatta

Spelt wheat flour, with its strong aroma and flavor, makes this bread delicious. At St Gotthard Hotel in Zürich I recently had a fantastic spelt wheat ciabatta. When I asked who had made it, they answered Bäckerei Kleiner, one of the classic bakeries in Zürich famous for their Zürcher Langbrot.

Dough temperature 28°C (82°F)
Sits 2 hours

For 2 large or 4 regular ciabatta loaves

DAY 1

Quick-dough (Raskdeg)
100 grams (6 tablespoons) water
2 grams (½ teaspoon) yeast
160 grams (1 cup + 3 tablespoons) white
  spelt wheat flour, preferably stone
  ground
4 grams (½ teaspoon) sea salt

Dissolve the yeast in the water and pour it over the flour and salt. Knead into a dough, put it in a bucket, cover with plastic wrap, and let it sit at room temperature for 1 hour. Then put it in the refrigerator for 12–18 hours.

DAY 2

Combining (Bortgörning)
266 grams (9.4 ounces) quick-dough
840 grams (6 cups) white spelt wheat flour,
  preferably stone ground
450 grams (2¾ cups) water
280 grams (1 cup + 2 tablespoons) milk
10 grams (½ tablespoon) honey
35 grams (3 tablespoons) raw sugar
35 grams (8¾ teaspoons) yeast
28 grams (1½ tablespoons) sea salt
½ deciliter (2 cups) olive oil (for greasing)

1. Put the quick-dough in a bowl with all the other ingredients except for the salt and oil. Knead the dough at lowest speed for 3 minutes. Add the salt, increase the speed, and knead for about another 17 minutes. Make a gluten test (see page 35).
2. Put the dough to rest in a plastic container, lightly greased with olive oil, covered with a lid for 2 hours.
3. Put the dough onto a floured table and push it together (see page 36). Put it back in the container with the seam facing upward and push the air out 2 more times with 40 minutes in between.
4. Put the dough onto an oiled baking table. Fold it together carefully without damaging the air pockets. Cut the dough into 2 large or 4 small loaves and dust over a little bit of the flour. Put them to rise properly for about 45–60 minutes on floured cloth.
5. Preheat the oven at 250°C (482°F) and place a baking stone or tray inside.
6. Put the bread in the oven using a baker's peel. Spray generously with water using a squirt bottle. Lower the temperature to 200°C (392°F) after 10 minutes. After about 20 minutes, vent the oven by briefly opening the door.
7. Bake the bread until golden brown and crispy, for about 35–40 minutes for the small and 55–60 minutes for the large. Put them on a rack to cool.

Ciabatta with sundried tomatoes.

Focaccia

This Italian bread comes in many versions, and most of them unfortunately have nothing to do with real focaccia bread. However, at the food empire Peck in Milan, much like at Motta in the same city, they know how it is done. Italian flour, which some gourmet stores carry, yields the best results. The dough should be light and airy and somewhat stringy.

Dough temperature 28°C (82°F)
Sits 3 hours

DAY 1
Pre-dough (Fördeg)
3 grams (¾ teaspoon) yeast
125 grams (½ cup) water
175 grams (1¼ cups) organic wheat flour, or ideally Italian wheat flour
5 grams (1 teaspoon) sea salt

Dissolve the yeast in the water with a whisk and pour it over the flour. Knead at lowest speed for about 13 minutes into an elastic dough. Add the salt, increase the speed, and knead for another 3 minutes. Put the dough in an oiled plastic container covered with a lid to rest for 6 hours at room temperature or 12 hours in the refrigerator.

DAY 2
(if the dough has been rising overnight in the refrigerator)
Combining (Bortgörning)
8 grams (2 teaspoons) yeast
500 grams (2 cups) water
308 grams (10.9 ounces) pre-dough

850 grams (6 cups + 3 tablespoons) wheat flour high in protein, preferably stone ground, or ideally Italian wheat flour
125 grams (½ cup + 2½ tablespoons) fine Durum wheat, preferably stone ground
125 grams white sourdough (4.4 ounces) (see page 27)
25 grams (2 tablespoons) olive oil
20 grams (1 tablespoon) sea salt
60 grams (¼ cup) water

Garnish
olive oil
rosemary
Parmesan cheese
preferably also tomatoes, salami, coppa, olives, cheese, etc.

1. Dissolve the yeast with a whisk in the water and pour it over the pre-dough, all of the flour, and the sourdough in the machine. Knead the dough at lowest speed for 10 minutes.
2. Add the oil and knead for another 3 minutes. Add the salt, increase speed, and knead for another 7 minutes into a tough and elastic dough. Make a gluten test (see page 35). If the dough is not elastic enough, just keep kneading.
3. Add 60 grams (¼ cup) of water and knead it in toward the end.
4. Put the dough in a plastic container, greased with a little bit of olive oil, covered with a lid and let it rise for 1 hour.
5. Take the dough out and push out all of the air (see page 36). Fold the dough together and put it back in the container with the seam facing downward. Repeat the procedure twice (total rising time 3 hours).
6. Roll out the dough and put it in a pan greased with olive oil. Prick it with your fingertips, brush with olive oil, and sprinkle generously with rosemary. Decorate it in different ways (see photograph) with something that you like. Let it rise at room temperature for about 90 minutes until doubled in size.
7. Preheat the oven to 250°C (482°F).
8. Bake the focaccia for about 8–10 minutes. Put it on a rack to cool. Cut into square pieces.

Top: focaccia with sundried tomatoes, green olives, and prosciutto. Below: with pepperoni, olives, and tomatoes.

Rustic bread from Palermo

Lantbröd från Palermo

This bread makes me think about the friendly city of Palermo in Sicily—grilled swordfish, delicious ice cream, and lovely marzipan fruits in the pastry shops along the beach promenade.

Dough temperature 26°C (79°F)
Sits 2 hours

For 2 loaves
Poolish
5 grams (1¼ teaspoons) yeast
500 grams (2 cups) water
500 grams (2½ cups) Durum wheat, preferably stone ground

Dissolve the yeast in the water with a whisk, and whisk in half of the flour for a pancake-like batter. Add the rest of the flour and whisk until the dough is slightly tough. Cover with plastic wrap and let sit at room temperature for 3 hours.

Combining (Bortgörning)
50 grams egg (about 1 egg)
10 grams (2½ teaspoons) yeast
450 grams (3⅓ cups) organic wheat flour, or ideally Italian wheat flour
1,005 grams (2 pounds 3.5 ounces) poolish
25 grams (2 tablespoons) extra virgin olive oil
20 grams (1 tablespoon) sea salt
25 grams (1½ tablespoons) water

1. Dissolve the yeast in the egg with a whisk and pour it over the flour in a bowl. Put in the poolish and knead the dough at lowest speed for about 15 minutes.

2. Add the oil and salt, increase the speed, and knead the dough for about 5 minutes. Make a gluten test (see page 35) and make sure that the dough is elastic. Add 25 grams (1½ tablespoons) of water and knead it in properly.

3. Put the dough in a plastic container greased in oil, put on the lid, and let it rest 1 hour.

4. Put the dough onto the table and push out all the air (see page 36). Fold it together, then put it back in the container with the seam facing downward and let rest for 1 more hour.

5. Push the air out of the dough again. Let it relax for 10 minutes.

6. Divide the dough in half, roll it out carefully, twist it together like a shell, and dust over a little bit of Durum wheat. Let it rise for about 1 hour on a floured cloth.

7. Preheat the oven to 250°C (482°F) and place a baking stone or tray inside.

8. Carefully lift the bread onto the stone or tray using a baker's peel. Spray in a generous amount of water with a squirt bottle, and lower the heat to 200°C (392°F) after 5 minutes. Vent the oven after 20 minutes by briefly opening the door. Repeat the process once while the bread is in the oven to make the bread crispy.

9. Bake for about 1 hour. Make sure with a thermometer that the bread's internal temperature is 98°C (208°F). Put the bread on an oven rack to cool.

Toscana Bread

Bröd från Toscana

This airy and light bread goes with all good food, not only Italian. It should be crispy with a flavorful crust and an airy crumb. Great for making bruschetta, or grill with nice toppings in the middle.

Dough temperature 27°C (81°F)
Sits 2 hours

For 4 loaves
DAY 1
Pre-dough (Fördeg)
250 grams (1 cup) water
5 grams (1¼ teaspoons) yeast
400 grams (2 cups) Durum wheat, preferably
    stone ground
2 grams (½ teaspoon) sea salt

Dissolve the yeast in the water with a whisk and measure the flour into a baking bowl. Pour in the yeast mixture and knead at lowest speed for 10 minutes. Add the salt, increase the speed, and knead for another 5 minutes into a tough and elastic dough. Put the dough in a lightly oiled plastic container covered with a lid and let it rest for 90 minutes at room temperature. Then put it in the refrigerator for 15–18 hours.

DAY 2
Combining (Bortgörning)
350 grams + 50 grams (1½ cups + ¼ cup)
    water
25 grams (6¼ teaspoons) yeast
300 grams (1¾ cups) spelt wholemeal,
    preferably stone ground
450 grams (3¼ cups) wheat flour high in
    protein, preferably stone ground, or ideally
    yellow Italian wheat flour
200 grams (7 ounces) white sourdough (see
    page 27)
657 grams (1 pound 7 ounces) pre-dough
75 grams (5½ tablespoons) olive oil
25 grams (4 teaspoons) sea salt

1. Dissolve the yeast in 350 grams (1½ cups) of water with a whisk and pour it over all the flour in the bowl along with the

sourdough and the pre-dough. Knead for 5 minutes at lowest speed, add the olive oil, and knead for another 10 minutes.

2. Add the salt, increase the speed, and knead for another 5 minutes. Make a gluten test (see page 35) and make sure that the dough is elastic. Add 50 grams (¼ cup) of water and knead it in—it yields a stringy crumb.

3. Put the dough in a lightly oiled plastic container covered with a lid and let it rest at room temperature for 1 hour.

4. Put the dough on a floured board and push it together so that the air is pressed out (see page 36). Fold it together like a pillow, put it back in the container with the seam facing downward, and let it rest for 1 hour.

5. Push the air out of the dough again, put it back in the container, and let it relax for 10 minutes.

6. Divide the dough into 4 equal pieces without pressing it too much. Shape carefully into round buns. Brush with water and roll them in spelt wholemeal. Put them on a floured cloth to rise for 1 hour until they double in size. Pull up the cloth between the loaves (see photograph on page 54).

7. Put 2 of the loaves in the refrigerator to stop the leavening. Preheat the oven to 250°C (482°F) and place a baking stone or tray at the bottom.

8. Cut the loaves as in the photograph with a sharp knife. Put 2 of the loaves in the oven using a baker's peel. Spray generously with water using a squirt bottle. Lower the temperature to 200°C (392°F) after 5 minutes. After another 20 minutes, vent the oven by briefly opening the door. Repeat once while the bread is in the oven to get a crispy crust.

9. Bake for a total of 50 minutes. Make sure with a thermometer that the internal temperature of the bread is 98°C (208°F). Put them on a rack to cool. Bake the other 2 loaves in the same way.

Cosa nostra bread

Cosa nostra-bröd

This lovely crispy bread truly tastes like Italy. When I was in Turin I got to try it at a baker's who looked very suspicious, hence the name, but he was a devil at baking bread. Try to get hold of Italian or Spanish almonds. Ripe cheese and fig marmalade with bay leaves works too (see my book *Jam and marmalade*).

Dough temperature 27°C (81°F)
Sits 2 hours

For 3 loaves
DAY 1
Soaking (Blötläggning)
190 grams (1½ cups) polenta grains
375 grams (1½ cups) water

Whisk together the polenta grains with the water, cover the bowl with plastic wrap, and let sit at room temperature until the next day.

DAY 2
Combining (Bortgörning)
250 grams almonds with peels
zest of 2 ripe yellow lemons (about 10 grams)
565 grams (1 pound 4 ounces) *blötläggning*
300 grams (1¼ cups) water
50 grams (12½ teaspoons) yeast
575 grams (3 cups) whole Emmer wheat,
    preferably stone ground
150 grams (5.3 ounces) white sourdough (see
    page 27)
40 grams (3 tablespoons) olive oil
25 grams (1½ tablespoons) sea salt
polenta grains

1. Preheat the oven to 200°C (392°F), pour the almonds onto a tray, and roast them for about 10 minutes to a golden brown. Crush the almonds coarsely with a rolling pin.
2. Wash and grate the lemons with a grater. Use only the outer yellow peel, or it will turn bitter.
3. Pour the soaked polenta grains in a bowl and whisk with water and yeast until the yeast is dissolved.
4. Measure the flour, lemon zest, and sourdough and pour it into the bowl over the yeast mixture. Knead the dough at lowest speed for 5 minutes. Add the olive oil and knead for another 10 minutes.

Add the salt, increase the speed, and knead for another 5 minutes. Make a gluten test (see page 35); the dough should be very elastic. Knead in the almonds toward the end.
5. Put the dough in a lightly oiled plastic container covered with a lid and let rest for 1 hour.
6. Put the dough on a lightly floured table. Push out all the air (see page 36) and fold the dough together like an envelope. Put it back in the container with the seam facing downward to rest for 1 hour.
7. Push the air out of the dough once more, put it back in the container again, and let it rest for another 10 minutes.
8. Divide the dough into 3 equal pieces, fold them carefully together into round buns, and let them relax for 5 minutes.
9. Shape the buns into short, oblong loaves. Brush with water and roll them in a generous amount of polenta grains. Leave them to rise for 1 hour to double in size on a floured cloth. Pull up the cloth between the loaves (see photograph, page 54).
10. Preheat the oven to 250°C (482°F) and place a baking stone or tray inside.
11. Cut the loaves on top like in the photograph on page 86 with a sharp knife. Put in all of the loaves with a baker's peel and spray generously with water using a squirt bottle. Lower the temperature to 200°C (392°F) after 5 minutes. After another 20 minutes, vent the oven by briefly opening the door. Vent one more time while the bread is in the oven to get a crispy crust.
12. Bake for a total of 50 minutes, making sure with a thermometer that the bread's internal temperature is 98°C (208°F). Put the loaves on an oven rack to cool and spray them lightly with water to make them crackle beautifully.

Pane Piemonte

In Italy it is common to add chestnut honey to this bread, but in such small amounts that you would not sense any difference using regular Swedish honey. This bread goes well with Italian cheese or a good jam or marmalade.

Dough temperature 27°C (81°F)
Sits 1 hour and 30 minutes

For 3 loaves

400 grams (3 cups) wheat flour high in protein, ideally Italian
100 grams (¾ cup) coarse rye flour
150 grams (1¼ cups) graham flour
100 grams (3.5 ounces) rye sourdough (see page 27)
25 grams (1 tablespoon) honey
450 grams (2 cups) water
20 grams (5 teaspoons) yeast
75 grams (⅓ cup) butter, at room temperature
15 grams (2½ teaspoons) sea salt
225 grams (1 cup) roasted peeled hazelnuts, preferably Italian from Piemonte or Spanish

1. Pour all of the flour along with the rye sourdough and honey into the bowl. Dissolve the yeast in the water and pour it in. Knead the dough for 10 minutes at lowest speed. Add the butter and knead for another 5 minutes. Add the salt and knead the dough for another 5 minutes until it is elastic and tough. Make a gluten test (see page 35). Gently knead in the hazelnuts.

2. Put the dough in a lightly oiled plastic container covered with a lid and let it rest for 45 minutes.

3. Put the dough on a floured table and push it together (see page 36). Put it back in the container with the seam facing downward and let it rise for 45 minutes.

4. Push the air out of the dough again and let the dough relax for another 10 minutes.

5. Divide the dough into 4 equal pieces and make them round. Cover with a cloth and let them relax for 5 minutes.

6. Shape the pieces into oblong loaves. Dust them with graham flour, put them on a floured cloth, and pull the cloth up between the bread. Let them rise for about 45 minutes to double their size.

7. Preheat the oven to 250°C (482°F) and place a baking stone or tray inside.

8. Cut an incision across the long side of the loaves with a sharp knife. Put them in the oven with a baker's peel and spray in water with a squirt bottle. Lower the temperature to 200°C (392°F) after 5 minutes. After 20 minutes, vent the oven by briefly opening the door. Repeat once more while the loaves are in the oven.

9. Bake the loaves until golden brown for about 45–50 minutes, making sure with a thermometer that their internal temperature is 98°C (208°F). Put them on an oven rack to cool.

Risotto Milanese bread

Risotto milanese-bröd

This bread is extra moist and goes well with fish soup and seafood. You can also add a few drops of truffle oil to the dough, which makes it even more delicious, but make sure to use real truffle oil—there are many imitations. You can also make grissini with this tasty dough (see page 110) and serve with antipasto.

Dough temperature 27°C (81°F)
Sits 1 hour

For 2 loaves
Risotto Milanese
50 grams (4 tablespoons) shallots, finely
  chopped
2 grams (3 teaspoons) saffron
50 grams (3½ tablespoons) butter
75 grams (½ cup) Arborio rice
50 grams (⅓ cup) dry white wine
150 grams (½ cup + 2 tablespoons) chicken
  broth

Fry the shallots and saffron in the butter until they start to soften—they should not brown. Add the rice and let it simmer with the shallots until slightly yellow. Pour in the wine and reduce by half. Pour the broth in a little at a time and keep stirring for about 15–17 minutes until the rice has absorbed the broth completely. Take the pot off the stove, cover with a lid, and let it cool in a cold water bath.

Combining (Bortgörning)
250 grams (1¾ cups) risotto
250 grams (8.8 ounces) Durum wheat, preferably stone ground
375 grams (2¾ cups) wheat flour high in
  protein, preferably stone ground, or
  ideally Italian flour
250 grams (8.8 ounces) white sourdough
  (see page 27)
10 grams (2¼ teaspoons) *herbes de Provence*
250 grams (1 cup) water
15 grams (3¾ teaspoons) yeast
20 grams (1 tablespoon) sea salt
100 grams (1 cup) Parmesan cheese, grated

1. Put the cold risotto in the bowl with all the flour, sourdough, and *herbes de Provence*. Dissolve the yeast in the water with a whisk and pour it into the bowl. Knead the dough at lowest speed for about 12 minutes. Add the salt, increase speed, and knead for another 6–8 minutes. Make a gluten test (see page 35). Knead in the cheese and put the dough in a lightly oiled plastic container covered with a lid to rest for 30 minutes.

2. Put the dough on a floured table and push it together (see page 36). Put the dough back in the container and let it rest for another 30 minutes.

3. Divide the dough into 2 equal pieces, roll them out, each 15 centimeters (about 6 inches) in length, and then roll them back together from two sides as in the photograph. Dust with a little Durum wheat. Let them rise to double their size for 45–60 minutes on a floured cloth.

4. Preheat the oven to 250°C (482°F) and place a baking stone or tray inside.

5. Put both of the loaves in the oven with a baker's peel and spray a generous amount of cold water into the oven with a squirt bottle. Lower the temperature to 200°C (392°F) after 5 minutes. After 20 minutes, vent the oven by briefly opening the door. Repeat once more while the bread is in the oven.

6. Bake the loaves for 45–50 minutes. Check with a thermometer that their internal temperature is 98°C (208°F). Turn bread onto an oven rack to cool.

Pain au vin

The first time I tried this bread was at a tiny restaurant in Alsace on a recommendation from the master chef Marc Haeberlin. They made the best oxtail ragu in the world with red wine, glazed shallots, salted bacon, and meadow mushrooms that had simmered for 24 hours on low heat. This was served with buttery mashed potatoes. The meal began with *Presskopf*, a pig's head brawn served with cornichons. Wine bread was served with the entire meal, with freshly made salted butter. The bread was made by a baker in the village especially for this restaurant. The cheese afterward was a classic Münster dipped in caraway seeds. Dessert consisted of rhubarb *tarte* with meringue, typical for this region. All of this was served with excellent wines from the district.

The next morning I spoke with the baker and admired his wonderful bread and old firewood brick oven, which had burned for many generations in the family. He was a real *Artisan Boulanger* who took great pride in his work and his old family traditions.

Dough temperature 26°C (79°F)
Sits 1 hour and 10 minutes

For 4 loaves

DAY 1
Pre-dough (Fördeg)
75 grams (⅓ cup) water
2 grams (½ teaspoon) yeast
125 grams (1 cup) graham flour, preferably stone ground

Dissolve the yeast in the water with a whisk and pour it over the flour in the bowl. Knead for 5 minutes at lowest speed. Cover the dough with plastic wrap and let it sit at room temperature for 1 hour. Then put it in the refrigerator for at least 12 hours.

DAY 2
Combining (Bortgörning)
400 grams (1¾ cups) water
20 grams (5 teaspoons) yeast
1,000 grams (8 cups) white spelt wheat flour, preferably stone ground
15 grams (2 teaspoons) honey
200 grams (7 ounces) pre-dough
270 grams (1 cup + 3 tablespoons) dry white wine, preferably from Alsace
27 grams (1½ tablespoons) sea salt

1. Dissolve the yeast in the water and pour it over the flour and the honey in the bowl. Add the pre-dough and pour in the wine. Knead at low speed for about 9 minutes. Add the salt, increase the speed, and knead for about 5 more minutes. Make a gluten test (see page 35).

2. Put the dough in a lightly oiled plastic container covered with a lid and let it rest for 45 minutes.
3. Put the dough onto a lightly floured table and push it together (see page 36). Put it back in the container with the seam facing downward and let rest for another 25 minutes.
4. Push the dough once more and let relax for another 10 minutes.
5. Divide the dough into 4 equal pieces and shape them carefully into round loaves with a little bit of flour without working the dough too much. Press a cross on top of the bread with a rolling pin and put each loaf in a floured basket (if you do not have any baskets, you can also let the loaves rise on a floured cloth; they will not rise to be as high but will certainly taste the same). Let them rise for about 60–90 minutes until doubled in size with a floured cloth on top.
6. Put in 2 baskets in the refrigerator to halt the leavening. Preheat the oven to 250°C (482°F) and place a baking stone or tray inside.
7. Put the bread in the oven with a baker's peel. Spray in a little water with a squirt bottle and lower the heat to 200°C (392°F) after 5 minutes. After 20 minutes, vent the oven and repeat a couple of times while the bread is baking to get a crispy crust.
8. Bake for a total of 1 hour. Use a thermometer to check that the bread's internal temperature is 98°C (208°F). Put them on an oven rack to cool. Repeat the process with the 2 loaves in the refrigerator.
9. Try the freshly baked bread with a piece of ripe Münster cheese dipped in caraway seeds and a nice wine from Alsace.

Olive *fougasse*

Oliv-fougasse

Pit Oberweis bakes perfect *fougasse* in Luxemburg. His bakery, which he runs with his sons Jeff and Tom, is on Grand Rue 19–21 in the capital and is well worth a visit. But most good bakeries in France make good *fougasse*, too.

Dough temperature 26°C (79°F)
Sits 1 hour

For 4 loaves
Base dough (Grunddeg)
700 grams (5 cups) wheat flour high in protein, preferably stone ground
100 grams (1 cup) fine rye flour, preferably stone ground
100 grams (1 cup) Graham flour, preferably stone ground
650 grams (2¾ cups) water
20 grams (5 teaspoons) yeast
15 grams (3⅓ tablespoons) *herbes de Provence*
50 grams (4 tablespoons) olive oil
20 grams (3⅓ teaspoons) sea salt
75 grams (1¼ cups) Italian salami or air-dried ham, finely diced
400 grams (1¾ cups) black pitted olives of highest quality

Topping
75 grams (5½ tablespoons) olive oil and 2 garlic cloves, crushed together with a mortar

Garnish
fresh rosemary, oregano, thyme, and flake salt

1. Mix the dry ingredients. Dissolve the yeast in the water with a whisk and pour it over the flour. Add the herb mixture.
2. Knead the dough at low speed for 3 minutes. Add the oil and knead for another 10 minutes.
3. Add the salt, increase the speed, and knead the dough for about 8 minutes until it is very elastic. Check the consistency of the dough and make a gluten test (see page 35).
4. Knead the salami or air-dried ham into the dough. Sprinkle a little wheat flour over the olives (this way they will not just glide around but actually stick in the dough) and knead them in as well. Put the dough in a lightly oiled plastic container covered with a lid. Let the dough rest for 1 hour, and push it together after 30 minutes (see page 36).

5. Divide the dough into 4 equal pieces and cut (or tear) 4 even buns. Cover with a cloth and let the dough relax for 5 minutes.

6. Flour the buns lightly and roll them into circles about 22 centimeters (about 8½ inches) in diameter, then stretch them into ovals. Place one of them on a floured cloth. Press a couple of holes into the dough with a dough scraper and stretch the dough to widen the holes. Now press pits in with your fingertips. Brush with the olive oil and garlic. Sprinkle with herbs and a little flake salt. Let rise until doubled in size, for about 45–60 minutes.

7. Preheat the oven to 250°C (482°F) and place a baking stone or tray inside.

8. Put in 2 loaves at a time and bake them until golden brown, for about 12–15 minutes. Put them on an oven rack to cool and repeat the process with the 2 remaining loaves.

Filled *fougasse*

Fylld fougasse

This is very popular in the South of France and is delicious with a green salad and a glass of wine. Here are two suggestions for fillings, but you can naturally fill them with anything that you like.

1. Divide the dough into 4 equal pieces and tear them into round buns. Put them on a cloth and let relax for 5 minutes.

2. Roll out each bun to be about 22 centimeters (about 8½ inches) in diameter, stretch them into ovals, and brush the lower edges with an egg.

3. On one of them I have put 3 split fresh figs, 8 walnut halves, and 100 grams (½ cup) of crumbled Roquefort cheese. I filled the second one with 12 drained preserved Italian cherry tomatoes and 2 tablespoons of pesto sauce (see recipe on page 108). On top of this, add a few slices of air-dried spicy sausage, pitted black olives, and a little bit of crumbled feta cheese.

4. Fold over the dough and press it together with a fork. Brush the whole bread with garlic oil and cut it on top with a sharp knife like in the photograph. Sprinkle with herbs.

5. Leaven and bake the bread in the same way as olive *fougasse*.

Caraway bread from Västerbotten

Kummin-och västerbottensostbrod

This lasting bread is a real treat with a layer of good butter on top. Serve preferably with nice cold cuts, pickles, and radishes with flake salt. Werner Vögeli, who once managed the Swedish royal kitchen, was passionate about the delicious Västerbotten cheese. Sadly, Werner is no longer with us, but his mission continues through every student who studied at Operakällaren.

Dough temperature 28°C (82°F)
Sits 30 minutes

For 2 loaves

DAY 1
Scalding (Skållning)
250 grams (1 cup) water
125 grams (1¼ cups) fine rye flour, preferably
    stone ground
10 grams (1¾ teaspoons) sea salt
10 grams (4¾ teaspoons) whole caraway

Cook up and pour the boiling water over the flour, salt, and caraway. Stir into a smooth paste with a ladle. Let sit at room temperature until the next day.

DAY 2
Quick-dough (Raskdeg)
250 grams (1 cup) water
40 grams (3 tablespoons + 1 teaspoon) yeast
395 grams (14 ounces) *skållning* from the day
    before
400 grams (4 cups) fine rye flour, preferably stone
    ground

Dissolve the yeast with a whisk in the water and pour it over the *skållning* in the bowl. Add the flour and mix the dough well (it should stay at 28°C / 82°F). Cover it with a cloth and let it rise for 1 hour.

Combining (Bortgörning)
1,085 grams (2 pounds 6.3 ounces) quick-dough
115 grams (5½ tablespoons) dark heather honey
425 grams (3 cups) wheat flour high in protein,
    preferably stone ground
25 grams (2 tablespoons) butter
100 grams (3.5 ounces) rye sourdough (see page
    27)
300 grams (2¼ cups) Västerbotten cheese, in
    small cubes

1. Pour the honey over the quick-dough along with wheat flour, butter, and rye sourdough. Knead at lowest speed for about 15 minutes into an elastic dough. Make a gluten test (see page 35).
2. Knead the cheese cubes into the dough. Put it into a lightly oiled plastic container covered with a lid and let it rest for 30 minutes.
3. Put the dough on a floured table, cut it in half, and roll into round buns. Put the bread into 2 heavily floured baskets with the ends facing upward. Let them rise under a cloth until doubled in volume for about 45–60 minutes.
4. Preheat the oven to 250°C (482°F) and place a baking stone or tray inside.
5. Turn the loaves out of the baskets and put them in the oven with a baker's peel. Spray a generous amount of water into the oven with a squirt bottle and lower the temperature to 180°C (392°F) after 5 minutes. After 20 minutes, vent the oven by briefly opening the door. Repeat once more while the bread is baking.
6. Bake the loaves for 60–70 minutes, and check with a thermometer that their internal temperature is 98°C (208°F). Put them on a rack to cool.

Two versions of caraway bread from Västerbotten, one of them flavored with pieces of salami added together with the cheese.

Bacon and onion bread with cheese

Bacon- och lökbröd med ost

One day I had this fantastic bread as an appetizer with a glass of Riesling from my favorite French region, Alsace. This was at the restaurant Belgian Queen in Brussels, which you have to visit when you are there. Do not forget to buy some pralines at Pierre MarcoLine in Place du Sablon—they are the best in Belgium. This bread is also fantastic for lunch with a nice mixed salad and Swiss salad dressing.

Dough temperature 27°C (81°F)
Sits 75 minutes

For 4 loaves
300 grams (1¼ cups) bacon, shredded
300 grams (3½ cups) yellow onion, peeled and sliced
300 grams (2¼ cups) Västerbotten cheese, grated
10 grams (1½ tablespoons) whole caraway
1 bunch of chives, finely chopped

Fry the bacon until it starts to release its fat, then add the onion and let it simmer until it is soft and transparent. Let it cool and then add cheese, caraway, and chives. Mix thoroughly.

Dough (Deg)
450 grams (2 cups) water
20 grams (5 teaspoons) yeast
800 grams (4½ cups) spelt wholemeal, preferably stone ground
75 grams (2.6 ounces) rye sourdough (see page 27)
20 grams (1 tablespoon) honey
20 grams (1 tablespoon) sea salt

Topping
100 grams (¾ cup) Västerbotten cheese, grated

1. Dissolve the yeast in the water with a whisk and pour it over the flour, sourdough, and honey in a bowl. Knead for 10 minutes at lowest speed. Add the salt, increase speed, and knead for another 5 minutes until it is a tough and elastic dough. Make a gluten test (see page 35).
2. Knead in the bacon mixture. Put the dough into a lightly oiled plastic container covered with a lid and let rest for 45 minutes.
3. Put the dough onto a floured table and push the air out of it (see page 36). Fold it like an envelope, put it back into the container with the seam facing downward, and let it rest for another 30 minutes.
4. Push the air out of the dough again and let it relax for 10 minutes.
5. Divide the dough into 4 equal pieces and roll them into round buns. Let them relax for 5 minutes under a cloth.
6. Shape the pieces into oblong loaves, brush them with water, and sprinkle with the grated cheese. Let them rise for 50–60 minutes on a floured cloth, pull up the cloth between the loaves to keep them rising upward rather than sideways (see photograph on page 54).
7. Preheat the oven to 250°C (482°F) and place a baking stone or a tray inside. Put 2 of the loaves in the refrigerator to stop the leavening.
8. Put 2 of the loaves in the oven with a baker's peel and spray in a generous amount of water with a squirt bottle. Lower the heat to 200°C (392°F) after 5 minutes. After 20 minutes, vent the oven by briefly opening the door. Repeat once more while the bread is baking.
9. Bake the bread to a golden brown for 40–45 minutes. Check with a thermometer that the internal temperature is 98°C (208°F). Put them to cool on an oven rack immediately. Repeat the process with the 2 loaves in the refrigerator.

Swiss salad dressing

Schweizisk salladssås

This delicious dressing works with all mixed salads.

For about 12 portions
50 grams (5 tablespoons) shallots, finely chopped (important)
1 gram (⅓ teaspoon) garlic clove, crushed
40 grams egg yolk (approximately 2 yolks)
60 grams (¼ cup) white wine vinegar
60 grams (⅓ cup) *crème fraiche*
5 grams (1 teaspoon) *Maggi* aroma seasoning
10 grams (4 teaspoons) powdered sugar
180 grams (1 cup) grapeseed oil
salt and freshly ground white pepper

Pour all of the ingredients except for the oil into a food processor and mix into a smooth cream. Pour the oil in at an even pace while constantly whisking. Keep in a bottle in the refrigerator. Shake well before pouring over the salad.

Potato bread with Mülhouse beer topping

Potatisbröd med öltopping som i Mülhouse

The sleepy little town of Mülhouse in Alsace is home to one of my favorite pastry shops, Pâtissérie Jacques. A piece of Münster cheese dipped in a little bit of caraway with this moist bread is incredibly tasty with a glass of wine. They always sell it at the marketplace next to the cathedral.

Dough temperature 27°C (81°F)
Sits 1 hour

DAY 1

Pre-dough (Fördeg)
250 grams (1 cup) water
2 grams (½ teaspoon) yeast
350 grams (2 cups) spelt wholemeal, preferably stone ground

Dissolve the yeast in the water with a whisk and pour it over the flour in the bowl. Knead the dough for 5 minutes and put it in a lightly oiled plastic container covered with a lid to rise in the refrigerator for 12–14 hours.

DAY 2

Combining (Bortgörning)
602 grams (21.2 ounces) pre-dough
350 grams (1½ cups) cooked, mashed potatoes
725 grams (5⅓ cups) wheat flour high in protein, preferably stone ground
250 grams (1 cup) light beer, preferably Kronenbourg from Alsace
15 grams (3¾ teaspoons) yeast
30 grams (5 teaspoons) sea salt

Topping
200 grams (1 cup) light beer
115 grams (1 cup) fine rye flour, preferably stone ground
5 grams (1¼ teaspoons) yeast

1. Put the pre-dough in the bowl with the potatoes and flour. Dissolve the yeast with a whisk in the beer and pour it into the bowl. Knead the dough for 10 minutes. Add the salt, increase the speed a little, and knead gently for about 5 minutes. Do not knead for too long as the potatoes suppress the forming of gluten, which could easily affect the rising abilities of the dough.

2. Put the dough in a lightly oiled plastic container covered with a lid to rest for 30 minutes.
3. Put the dough on a floured table, push the air out of it (see page 36), and fold it into a pillow. Put the dough back in the container with the seam facing downward and let it rest for another 30 minutes.
4. For the topping: Whisk the ingredients into a pancake-like batter and let it rest covered with plastic wrap for 30 minutes. If it should get too thick to brush on the bread, simply thin it out with some more beer.
5. Divide the dough into 4 equal pieces. Tear them into round buns and let them relax for 5 minutes.
6. Dust flour lightly on top of the buns and roll them out to be about 20 centimeters (about 8½ inches) in diameter. Fold in the dough from the sides as in the photograph so that the bread looks like a bicycle seat. Brush with the beer topping and sprinkle with spelt wholemeal. Put the bread to rise at room temperature until the surface has crackled well, about 45 minutes.
7. Preheat the oven to 250°C (482°F) and place 2 trays inside.
8. Put 2 loaves on each tray and lower the temperature to 200°C (392°F) after 10 minutes. After 20 minutes, vent the oven by briefly opening the door. Repeat this once while the bread is in the oven to get a crispy crust.
9. Bake the bread for 40 minutes until golden brown. Check with a thermometer that their internal temperature is 98°C (208°F). Lift them onto an oven rack to cool. Enjoy the bread with a good wine, air-dried cold cuts, and cheese.

Olive bread with garlic and pine nuts

Olivbröd med vitlök och pinjekärnor

This bread is slightly addictive. It goes well with a little bit of olive oil with a meal or as an appetizer with pesto, hummus, or guacamole, or tomatoes with a little bit of oil, salt, pepper, and fresh basil. At Guy de Savoy's in Paris, we had a similar bread with cheese, and it went like hotcakes.

Dough temperature 26°C (79°F)
Sits 1 hour and 30 minutes

For 4 loaves
Dough (Deg)
580 grams (4¼ cups) wheat flour high in
    protein, preferably stone ground
100 grams (1 cup) fine rye flour, preferably
    stone ground
500 grams (2 cups) water
20 grams (5 teaspoons) yeast
100 grams (3.5 ounces) rye sourdough
    (see page 27)
50 grams (3¾ tablespoons) olive oil
18 grams (3 teaspoons) sea salt

Filling (Fyllning)
50 grams (6 tablespoons) roasted pine nuts
200 grams (1 cup) green pitted olives of
    highest quality (buy them in bulk)
2 grams (⅔ teaspoon) garlic cloves (for
    about 20 grams)
20 grams (4½ tablespoons) fine herbs

1. Roast the pine nuts in a frying pan and pit the olives. Crush the garlic cloves with a knife with a little bit of salt. Mix everything together.
2. Mix the wheat flour and rye flour in a bowl. Dissolve the yeast in the water with a whisk and pour it over the flour. Knead the dough at lowest speed for about 5 minutes. Add the oil, knead for another 5 minutes, and add the salt. Increase the speed and knead for another 8–10 minutes until the dough is completely elastic. Make a gluten test (see page 35).
3. Knead the filling into the dough. Put it in a lightly oiled plastic container covered with a lid and let it rest for 45 minutes.
4. Put the dough on a floured table, push it together (see page 36), and put it back in the container with the seam facing downward to rise for 45 minutes.
5. Push the air out of the dough again and let the dough relax for 10 minutes.
6. Divide the dough into 4 equal pieces, roll them, cover with a cloth, and let them relax for 10 minutes.
7. Shape into 4 oblong loaves. Powder them lightly on top with a little bit of rye flour. Put them on a floured cloth and pull up the cloth between the loaves (see photograph on page 54). Let them rise until doubled in volume.
8. Preheat the oven to 250°C (482°F) and place a baking stone or tray inside.
9. Put all of the loaves into the oven with a baker's peel and spray generously with water using a squirt bottle. Lower the heat to 200°C (392°F) after 5 minutes. After 20 minutes, vent the oven by briefly opening the door. Repeat once more while the bread is baking to make the bread crispy.
10. Bake the loaves for 45–50 minutes. Use a thermometer and make sure that their internal temperature is 98°C (208°F). Lift the bread onto an oven rack to cool.

Caraway and saffron buns

Kummin- och saffransbullar

We used to bake these dinner rolls on cruise ships, and they were always appreciated by our passengers.

Dough temperature 27°C (81°F)
Sits 40 minutes

For about 38 buns
Poolish
250 grams (1 cup) water
200 grams (1½ cups) wheat flour high in
    protein, preferably stone ground
20 grams (5 teaspoons) yeast
10 grams (1½ teaspoons) honey

Whisk everything into a tough batter,
almost like a pancake batter. Cover
with plastic wrap and let rise at room
temperature for 1 hour.

Combining (Bortgörning)
480 grams (1 pound 1 ounce) poolish
500 grams (3½ cups) wheat flour high in
    protein, preferably stone ground
50 grams (¼ cup) water
25 grams (2 tablespoons) raw sugar
2 grams (3 teaspoons) saffron
12 grams (2 teaspoons) sea salt
100 grams (½ cup) extra virgin olive oil
caraway

1. Pour the poolish into a bowl with all the
   ingredients except for the salt, oil, and
   caraway. Knead at low speed for 2
   minutes, add the oil, and knead for
   another 5 minutes. Add the salt,
   increase the speed, and knead the
   dough for about 10 more minutes
   until elastic. Make a gluten test
   (see page 35).
2. Put the dough in a lightly oiled plastic
   container covered with a lid and let it
   rest for 40 minutes.
3. Divide the dough into 300-gram (10.6-ounce) pieces and divide each piece
   into 10 parts. Tear them into round buns and put them on a tray with baking
   paper. Brush them carefully with egg and let them rise until doubled in volume.
4. Brush one more time with egg and sprinkle with caraway. Preheat the oven to
   220°C (428°F).
5. Bake the buns for about 10 minutes until golden brown, and let them cool on a
   rack.

Dinner rolls with orange and rosemary

Dinner rolls med apelsin och rosmarin

These buns originate from my years in the cruise business, when we had time to create new recipes. They go with most foods but are also great for sandwiches.

Dough temperature 27°C (81°F)
Sits 90 minutes

For about 30 buns
25 grams (2 tablespoons) fresh rosemary
25 grams (2 tablespoons) olive oil

Brown the rosemary in the oil at low heat and let it sit and cool.

2 large oranges, washed
30 grams (2½ tablespoons) granulated sugar

Grate the orange peel with a grater without getting any of the white inner part. Rub it with the sugar using a cooking palette.

Dough (Deg)
225 grams (1 cup) water
25 grams (6¼ teaspoons) yeast
500 grams (3½ cups) wheat flour high in
    protein, preferably stone ground

100 grams (½ cup) extra virgin olive oil
10 grams (1½ teaspoons) sea salt

1. Dissolve the yeast in the water with a whisk and pour it over the flour. Add the orange zest, sugar, and the browned rosemary and knead for 2 minutes. Add the olive oil and knead for another 8 minutes. Add the salt, increase the speed, and knead for another 8 minutes into a tough and elastic dough. Make a gluten test (see page 35).
2. Put the dough in a lightly oiled plastic container covered with a lid. Let it rest for 30 minutes.
3. Put the dough on a floured table and push it together (see page 36). Let it rest for 30 minutes.
4. Push the air out of the dough again. Let it rest for 30 minutes.
5. Divide the dough into 300-gram (10.6-ounce) pieces, roll them out, and divide each piece into 10 parts. Roll them into hot-dog-shaped buns, a little more pointier at one end than the other. Twist together as in the photograph, slightly angled, and put them on a tray covered with baking parchment. Brush them with water, sprinkle a little bit with rosemary, and dust on some Durum wheat. Leave them to rise for about 45–60 minutes until doubled in size.
6. Preheat the oven to 230°C (446°F).
7. Bake the buns until golden brown for about 10–12 minutes. Put them on a rack to cool.

Barolo and onion buns

Barolo- och lökbullar

These dinner rolls are great for an exciting dinner with good food. The wine gives the bread a special character. The inspiration came from a visit to a vineyard in Italy and a fantastic roasted *poularde* (pullet) with cep risotto, glazed chestnuts, and a sauce made with Barolo wine.

Dough temperature 27°C (81°F)
Sits 1 hour

For about 40 buns
25 grams (2 tablespoons) butter
150 grams (1⅓ cups) red onion, sliced
150 grams (9½ tablespoons) red wine,
    preferably Barolo

Brown the onion until golden brown in the butter, pour in the wine, and cook together until all liquid is absorbed. Let cool.

Combining (Bortgörning)
250 grams (1 cup) milk
25 grams (6¼ teaspoons) yeast
500 grams (3½ cups) wheat flour high in
    protein, preferably stone ground
50 grams (¼ cup) red wine, preferably
    Barolo
100 grams (½ cup) ricotta cheese
50 grams (3½ tablespoons) butter, soft
12 grams (2 teaspoons) sea salt

Decoration
sliced red onion
oregano

1. Dissolve the yeast in the milk with a whisk, pour it over the flour, and pour in the wine and ricotta cheese.
2. Knead the dough 3 minutes at lowest speed, add the butter, and keep kneading for 7 minutes. Add the salt and knead at a higher speed for about 8 minutes until the dough is elastic. Make a gluten test (see page 35).
3. Knead in the onion and wine paste and put the dough in a lightly oiled plastic container covered with a lid. Let rest for 30 minutes.
4. Put the dough on a floured table and push it together (see page 36). Put the dough back into the container with the seam facing downward and let it rest for another 30 minutes.
5. Divide the dough into 300-gram (10.6-ounce) pieces and then divide each piece into 10 parts. Roll them into round buns, put them on baking parchment on a tray, brush them with water, put a tiny slice of red onion on top, and sprinkle with oregano. Let them rise until doubled in size, for about 45–60 minutes.
6. Preheat the oven to 230°C (446°F).
7. Bake the bread until golden brown, for about 10–12 minutes. Let them cool on a rack.

Tomato buns with toasted pine nuts

Tomatbullar med rostade pinjekärnor

These light and flavorful rolls go well with good food without dominating the taste too much. The crispiness of the roasted pine nuts has a piquant quality. I had a similar roll for the first time at Grand Hôtel in Monte Carlo. This is where the chef Alain Ducasse resides. His restaurants are characterized by bakers baking fresh bread all the time. He has 2 3-star restaurants in France.

   The buns can be frozen in plastic bags and taste as good as freshly baked when heated.

Dough temperature 27°C (81°F)
Sits 1 hour

For 60 30-gram buns
400 grams (1½ cups) milk
170 grams (¾ cup) water
35 grams (8¾ teaspoons) yeast
500 grams (3½ cups) wheat flour high in
    protein, preferably stone ground
500 grams (2½ cups) Durum wheat, prefer-
    ably stone ground
20 grams (5 teaspoons) granulated sugar
40 grams (3 tablespoons) olive oil
50 grams (6 tablespoons) pine nuts, roasted
25 grams (4 teaspoons) sea salt
175 grams (3¼ cups) sundried tomatoes,
    quite finely chopped
50 grams (1¼ cups) Basil Genovese, finely
    chopped

2 basil plants, for decoration

Brushing with egg
1 egg
1 egg yolk
a pinch of salt

1. Dissolve the yeast with a whisk in the milk and water, and add the other ingredients except for the salt, tomatoes, and basil. Knead at lowest speed for about 13 minutes.
2. Add the salt, increase the speed, and knead the dough for another 7 minutes. It should be elastic and it should pass a gluten test (see page 35).
3. Mix the tomatoes and basil into the dough. Put it in a lightly oiled plastic container covered with a lid and let it rest for 30 minutes.
4. Put the dough on a floured board and push it together (see page 36). Put it back in the container with the seam facing downward and repeat the process after another 30 minutes. Put it back in the plastic container and let it relax for 10 minutes.
5. Shape 30-gram (10.6-ounce) round buns and let them relax for 5 minutes.
6. Roll the dough into oblong buns, brush them with egg, and put a basil leaf on top of each bun. Let them rise in a warm place until doubled in size.
7. Preheat the oven to 250°C (482°F).
8. Put the trays with the buns in the oven and spray in a little bit of water with a squirt bottle to make the bread crispy. Bake for about 8–10 minutes until golden brown. Let cool on a rack.

Pesto buns

Pestosnurror

You can also use this recipe for making tapenade. Serve with soups, cold cuts, and *vitello tonnato*, which is thinly sliced veal in tuna sauce with capers and olives—fantastically simple and delicious.

Dough temperature 28°C (82°F)
Sits about 45–60 minutes

For about 35 buns
Sweet bread dough (Smörbullsdeg)
½ batch pesto (see page 108)
300 grams (1¼ cups) milk
25 grams (6¼ teaspoons) yeast
500 grams (3½ cups) wheat flour high in protein,
    preferably stone ground
200 grams (1 cup) butter
20 grams (1½ tablespoons) granulated sugar
15 grams (2 teaspoons) honey
10 grams (1¾ teaspoons) sea salt

1. Dissolve the yeast in the milk with a whisk, pour it over the other ingredients in the bowl, and knead the dough for about 18 minutes until it is elastic. Make a gluten test (see page 35). Put the dough in a lightly oiled plastic container to rise until tripled in size.
2. Push together the dough to release the air (see page 36) and put it in the refrigerator to stiffen for 1 hour.
3. Roll out the dough with a little bit of wheat flour, 3 millimeters (about ⅛ inch) thick, 43 centimeters (about 17 inches) wide, and 50 centimeters (about 20 inches) long. Spread the pesto over the dough and brush the edge at the bottom with a little bit of egg. Twist together like shells (see page 209) and put the roll with the seam facing downward.
4. Cut into 40-gram (1.4-ounce) shells and put them on a tray with baking parchment. Brush them with a little bit of egg and sprinkle with a little coarse Durum wheat. Leave them to rise for about 45–60 minutes until doubled in size.
5. Preheat the oven to 230°C (446°F).
6. Bake the pesto buns until golden brown for about 10–12 minutes. Let them cool on a rack. ➤

Pesto

This sauce is known in France as *Pistou*, but this excludes the roasted pine nuts. I always make it with a mortar for smaller batches. It is important to always blanch the basil leaves quickly in boiling water first and then cool them in cold water. This intensifies the basil taste, makes the sauce greener and prettier, and also helps it last much longer.

60 grams (½ cup) pine nuts
240 grams (6 cups) fresh basil leaves, chopped
8 grams (1 tablespoon) garlic cloves
200 grams (2 cups) grated Parmesan cheese, preferably aged 4 years
fleur de sel
fresh ground black pepper
2½ deciliters (10½ cups) extra virgin olive oil, light in color

1. Preheat the oven to 200°C (392°F).
2. Put the pine nuts on a tray and roast them until golden brown for about 5 minutes.
3. Boil 1 liter (4¼ cups) of water, put the basil leaves in a strainer, and blanch for 1 minute. Cool under running water.
4. Squeeze the liquid out of the leaves and crush them in the mortar with the garlic cloves, roasted pine nuts, and a little salt and pepper into an even paste. Add the Parmesan cheese and work until smooth.
5. Add the oil drop by drop, just like when making mayonnaise, until all of the oil is absorbed.
6. Pour into small jars with a little bit of oil on top. Keep it in a jar in the refrigerator. Keeps for about 1 month.

Tapenade

500 grams (2 cups) black olives, pitted
100 grams (7 tablespoons) anchovies
50 grams (3½ tablespoons) capers, drained
3 grams (1 teaspoon) garlic cloves, crushed
¾ deciliter (3 cups) extra virgin olive oil

1. Crush all of the ingredients except for the olive oil together in a mortar.
2. Add the oil gradually while continuously working the mixture.
3. Pour it into small jars with lids. Pour a little bit of oil on top to help it preserve better. Keep it in the refrigerator. Keeps for about 3 months.

St. Gallen Bürli bread

St Gallen Bürli-bröd

I could never tire of Handgemachte Bürli, nor can the Swiss. Max Hürliman is a baker outside of Basel and makes better Bürli bread than anyone else.

 This bread is originally from St Gallen outside of Zürich and is typical for its region. The bakers breach it by hand, and each piece should weigh 90 grams (3.2 ounces). You put them directly onto a floured cloth to rise in pairs and sift with fine rye flour. They should be baked hard and crispy, and the crumb should be light and airy. A good table bread.

Dough temperature 26°C (79°F)
Sits 2 hours

For 14 loaves
DAY 1
Pre-dough (Fördeg)
135 grams (¾ cup) spelt wholemeal, preferably stone ground
45 grams (½ cup) coarse rye flour, preferably stone ground
150 grams (⅔ cup) water
22 grams (5½ teaspoons) yeast
2 grams (⅓ teaspoon) salt

Pour all of the flour, water, yeast, and salt into a bowl and knead for 15 minutes. Immediately put the dough in a lightly oiled plastic container covered with a lid. Let it sit at room temperature for 2 hours and then put it in the refrigerator until the next day.

DAY 2
Combining (Bortgörning)
335 grams (11.8 ounces) pre-dough
315 grams (2⅓ cups) wheat flour high in protein
100 grams (1 cup) fine rye flour, preferably stone ground
350 grams (1½ cups) water
15 grams (3¾ teaspoons) yeast
15 grams (2½ teaspoons) sea salt

1. Take the pre-dough out 1 hour before baking so that it is not too cold.
2. Pour the pre-dough into a bowl with all the flour. Dissolve the yeast in the water with a whisk and pour it in.
3. Knead the dough for 7 minutes at lowest speed. Add the salt and knead for another 8–10 minutes. Make sure that the dough is elastic (see gluten test, page 35).
4. Put the dough in a lightly oiled plastic container covered with a lid. Let sit for 45 minutes.
5. Push together the dough (see page 36) on a floured table and fold it like an envelope. Put it back into the container with the seam facing downward and let it rest for 45 more minutes.
6. Push the air out of the dough again, put the dough back in the container, and let it rest for another 30 minutes.
7. Roll the dough into one long piece in fine rye flour, break off about 90 grams (3.2 ounces) for each piece, and put them 2 and 2 together on a floured cloth. Let rise for about 45 minutes.
8. Preheat the oven to 250°C (482°F) and place a baking stone or tray inside.
9. Put the bread in the oven with a baker's peel and spray in a generous amount of water with a squirt bottle. After 15 minutes, vent the oven by briefly opening the door to make the bread crispy. Bake them for about 10 minutes until dark and let cool on a rack.

Grissini with extra virgin olive oil

Grissini med extra virgin olivolja

Good with antipasto, cheese, soups, and salads. For tomato grissini, replace the water with tomato juice.

Dough temperature 28°C (82°F)
Sits 30 minutes

For about 35 grissini
275 grams (1 cup + 2½ tablespoons) water
25 grams (6¼ teaspoons) yeast
500 grams (2½ cups) Durum wheat,
    preferably stone ground
15 grams (2 teaspoons) honey
35 grams (2½ tablespoons) extra virgin
    olive oil
10 grams (1¾ teaspoons) sea salt

1. Dissolve the yeast in the water with a whisk, and pour it over the flour along with the honey and oil. Knead the dough at lowest speed for 12 minutes. Add the salt, increase the speed, and knead for another 8 minutes. Make a gluten test (see page 35).
2. Put the dough to rest in a lightly oiled plastic container covered with a lid for 30 minutes.
3. Roll out the dough about 5 millimeters (about ¼ inch) thick with a rolling pin and a little bit of Durum wheat. Cut out long rolls and put them on a tray lightly coated with olive oil. Let rise in a warm place for about 45 minutes until doubled in size.
4. Preheat the oven to 210°C (410°F).
5. Bake the bread 10–12 minutes until golden brown and spray in a little water with a squirt bottle at the beginning.
6. Turn off the oven and let them dry inside of it.

Pain de mie au beurre

This buttery-tasting bread is excellent for breakfast as well as for lunch and dinner. I had it for breakfast at the chef Michel Guérard's in Eugénie-les-Bains at his fantastic place. He was one of the co-founders of the new French cuisine in the 1970s.

Dough temperature 28°C (82°F)
Sits 1 hour

For about 44 buns
500 grams (2 cups) water
30 grams (7½ teaspoons) yeast
100 grams (½ cup) milk
1,000 grams (7⅓ cup) wheat flour, extra
    strong
22 grams (3¾ teaspoons) sea salt
25 grams (6 teaspoons) granulated sugar
120 grams (½ cup) unsalted butter

For brushing
50 grams (¼ cup) melted butter

1. Dissolve the yeast in water and milk with a whisk. Add the other ingredients except for the butter and work the dough at lowest speed for 13 minutes.
2. Add the butter, increase speed, and work the dough for about 5 minutes until elastic. Make a gluten test (see page 35) and pull a thin film off of the dough. If it is not thin enough, just work it a little bit more. Put the dough in a lightly oiled plastic container covered with a lid to rest for 30 minutes.
3. Push together the dough (see page 36) on a floured table and let it rest for 30 more minutes.
4. Divide the dough into 40-gram (1.4-ounce) pieces and roll round buns. Let them rest under a floured cloth for 10 minutes.
5. Shape the buns into ovals, put them on a floured cloth, and brush them on top with melted butter. Press on the middle with a rolling pin so that the dough is thin in the middle. Cover them with a cloth for about 1 hour until doubled in size.
6. Preheat the oven to 240°C (464°F).
7. Put the buns on 2 trays. Bake them for about 15 minutes until golden brown. Move them onto a rack to cool.

Grissini with extra virgin olive oil and grissini baked with risotto dough.

Top: Pain de mie au beurre

Bottom: Pain Écossais

Pain Écossais

This soft French bread of Scottish origin is good for breakfast with jam and marmalade or as a neutral table bread. Roger Vergé served it for breakfast at his fantastic restaurant Moulin de Mougins in Provence with his apricot marmalade with freshly harvested almonds and spiced with lavender flowers and vanilla. Unfortunately Roger is no longer at the stove, but I have heard that his heirs in the kitchen are still cooking food at a high level of quality.

Here, too, are the recipes for fig and raspberry marmalade that go excellently with this bread.

Dough temperature 28°C (82°F)
Sits 45 minutes

For about 36 buns
20 grams (5 teaspoons) yeast
250 grams (1 cup) water
250 grams (1 cup) milk
790 grams (5½ cups) wheat flour high in
    protein, preferably stone ground
20 grams (1 tablespoon) sea salt
35 grams (3 tablespoons) granulated sugar
75 grams (⅓ cup) butter

Topping
milk
wheat flour

2 baking trays with an edge
50 grams (¼ cup) butter for the trays

1. Dissolve the yeast in water and milk with a whisk. Add the other ingredients and work the dough at lowest speed for 13 minutes.
2. Increase the speed and work the dough for about 7 more minutes until elastic and smooth. Make a gluten test (see page 35) to make sure you can pull the dough very thinly.
3. Put the dough in a lightly oiled plastic container covered with a lid to rest for 45 minutes.
4. Divide the dough into 40-gram (1.4-ounce) pieces and roll them into buns.
5. Brush the trays with melted butter on the surface and on the sides. Put 9 buns spaced apart a little on each tray. Brush them with milk and sift on a little wheat flour.
6. Put the trays in a turned-off oven to rise for 2 hours until doubled in size.
7. Take the buns out of the oven and preheat the oven to 240°C (464°F).
8. Spray a little bit of water in the oven and bake the buns for about 15 minutes. Check in the middle of the buns with a thermometer that the internal temperature is 98°C (208°F). Put them on a rack to cool.

Fig and raspberry jam

Fikon- och hallonmarmelad

This wonderful marmalade is good not only with toast but also with a duck liver terrine with roasted brioche or ripe cheese.

500 grams (3⅓ cups) dried figs
500 grams (2 cups) red wine, preferably from the Rhône Valley
500 grams (2 cups) frozen raspberries

DAY 1
Cut the figs into small pieces and let them marinate in the wine for 12 hours or overnight.

DAY 2
1. Cook the figs in the wine with the thawed raspberries and remove any potential foam.
2. Mix the marmalade with a hand blender into a paste and pour it into warm jars that have been heated in the oven to 100°C (212°F). Close the lids immediately and put them upside down until the next day.
3. Keep the marmalade in the refrigerator.

Envelope Bread

Kuvertbröd

This bread was always served at nice restaurants when I was a boy. The restaurants often ordered them with the pastry chef and baker. The rolls were to weigh no more than 20–30 grams (0.7–1 ounce), and were always served heated and wrapped in a napkin for the meal. At the Savoy Hotel in Malmö, they were very popular, along with mini-croissants that were served with lobster soup.

Many people use regular French bread dough for these rolls, which makes them dry and uninteresting after an hour. The dough has to contain milk and butter, which makes it soft and lasting.

Dough temperature 27°C (81°F)
Sits 1 hour

For about 50 rolls
600 grams (4⅓ cups) wheat flour high in
    protein, preferably stone ground
15 grams (3½ teaspoons) granulated sugar
330 grams (1⅓ cups) milk
40 grams (10 teaspoons) yeast
70 grams (5 tablespoons) butter
12 grams (2 teaspoons) sea salt

Decoration
Seeds, such as blue and yellow sesame
    seeds, sunflower seeds, rye flakes,
    pumpkin seeds

1. Pour the flour and sugar into a bowl. Dissolve the yeast in the milk with a whisk and pour it into the bowl. Knead the dough for 5 minutes at lowest speed. Add the butter and knead for another 8 minutes. Add the salt, increase the speed, and knead the dough for 7 minutes until completely elastic. Make a gluten test (see page 35).

2. Put the dough in a lightly oiled plastic container covered with a lid to rest for 30 minutes.

3. Put the dough on a floured table and push it together (see page 36). Put it back in the container with the seam facing downward and let it rest another 30 minutes.

4. Push together the dough one more time. Then let it relax for 10 minutes.

5. Divide the dough into 300-gram (10.6-ounce) sized pieces and divide each piece into 10 parts. Roll them into round buns, put them on a cloth, and roll the pieces into various shapes such as pretzels, double buns, and knots, as in the photograph. Put them on a tray with baking parchment and brush them with egg. Pick up and dip them in different kinds of seeds as in the photograph. Let rise under a cloth for 45–60 minutes until doubled in size.

6. Preheat the oven to 230°C (446°F).

7. Put the buns in the oven. Spray in a little bit of water with a squirt bottle after 2–3 minutes.

8. Bake the bread until golden brown for about 12–15 minutes. Let cool on a rack.

Envelope bread in different shapes and toppings.

Mailand bread

Mailandbröd

A good, neutral bread with almost any food. Bäckerei Baumann, across from the railroad station in Basel, makes fantastic Mailand bread and naturally perfect Basel bread, which are two loaves attached together and baked very hard.

Dough temperature 27°C (81°F)
Sits 30 minutes

For 4 loaves
Poolish
250 grams (1 cup) water
5 grams (1¼ teaspoons) yeast
250 grams (2 cups) wheat flour high in protein, preferably stone ground

Dissolve the yeast with a whisk in the water and whisk in half of the flour to a pancake-like consistency. Whisk in the rest of the flour until the dough feels slightly tough. Cover with plastic wrap and let sit at room temperature for 3 hours until it starts to collapse.

Combining (Bortgörning)
505 grams (1 pound 1.8 ounces) poolish
zest from one washed lemon
5 grams (¾ teaspoon) honey
300 grams (2 cups + 3 tablespoons) wheat flour high in protein, preferably stone ground
10 grams (2½ teaspoons) yeast
25 grams (2 tablespoons) extra virgin olive oil
12 grams (2 teaspoons) sea salt

1. Put the poolish in a bowl with the lemon zest, honey, flour, and yeast. Knead at lowest speed for 10 minutes. Add the oil and salt and knead for another 8 minutes at higher speed until very elastic. Make a gluten test (see page 35).
2. Put the dough in a lightly oiled plastic container covered with a lid to rest for 30 minutes.

Top: French sourdough batarde, see page 72
Bottom: Mailand bread

3. Divide the dough into 4 equal pieces and roll them into round buns. Cover with a cloth and let them relax for 5 minutes.

4. Roll the buns into long, tight rolls. Dust on a little wheat flour and put them on a cloth to rise until doubled in size, which usually takes about 60–90 minutes. Cut a deep incision in the middle of the loaves with a sharp knife.

5. Preheat the oven to 230°C (446°F).

6. Put all of the loaves in the oven with a baker's peel. Spray in generously with water using a squirt bottle after 2 minutes. Lower the heat to 200°C (392°F) after 10 minutes. After 20 minutes, vent the oven by briefly opening the door.

7. Bake the bread until fairly light brown, for about 30 minutes. Put them on a rack to cool.

Lemon sandwich bread

Citronsandwichbröd

This recipe comes from the famous Pâtissérie Wittamer in Place de Sablon in Brussels. Do not miss the antique market there on Saturdays when in Brussels.

These light and airy buns go perfectly with seafood salad and shrimp boats, or as pockets filled with Skagen salad. When making neutral sandwiches, omit lemon zest and juice and replace the lemon juice with 50 grams (¼ cup) of milk. When making a coarser version, you can use 250 grams (2 cups) of graham flour, 100 grams (¾ cup) of coarse rye flour, and 650 grams (4¾ cups) of wheat flour instead of only rye and dip the buns in coarse rye flour before leavening and baking them.

Dough temperature 27°C (81°F)
Sits 45 minutes

For 30 loaves
450 grams (2 cups) milk
40 grams (10 teaspoons) yeast
3 ripe lemons (peel) and 50 grams (¼ cup) pressed juice
1,000 grams (7⅓ cups) wheat flour high in protein, preferably stone ground
180 grams (1 cup) butter
50 grams (4 tablespoons) granulated sugar
120 grams egg yolk (about 6 yolks)
20 grams (3⅓ teaspoons) sea salt
coarse Durum wheat

For the egg
1 egg and a pinch of salt

1. Dissolve the yeast in the milk with a whisk. Wash the lemons, zest off the outer peel with a grater, and press out the juice. Mix the other ingredients in a bowl and pour in the yeast mixture.

2. Knead the dough at low speed for about 15 minutes. Make a gluten test and make sure that the dough is completely elastic (see page 35). If not, increase the speed and knead until the dough is fully developed.

3. Put the dough in a lightly oiled plastic container covered with a lid and let it rest for 20 minutes. Push it together on a floured table and fold it together like an envelope. Put the dough back in the container with the seam facing downward and let it rise for 25 more minutes.

4. Put the dough on a floured table, measure 80-gram (2.8-ounce) pieces, roll them into tight buns, and put a cloth on top. Let them relax for 5–10 minutes.

5. Roll out the buns like tight hot dog bread, brush them carefully all over with egg, and dip them in coarse Durum wheat. Put them on a tray with baking parchment, preferably in a turned-off oven, and let them rise for about 45 minutes until doubled in size. Make an incision across the middle with a sharp knife.

6. Preheat the oven to 230°C (446°F).

7. Bake the buns for about 12 minutes until golden brown. Take them out and let cool on an oven rack.

To make pockets instead of buns, roll the buns out like saucers, brush one side with oil, and fold the dough over. Brush with egg and powder with Durum wheat. Bake in the same way as for buns.

When cooled, open the pocket and fill it with seafood salad, such as Skagen, or with shrimp, egg, and mayonnaise. Delicious and practical for bringing on outings.

See photograph on page 119.

Wholegrain sandwich bread

Fullkornssandwichbröd

These flavorful buns go well with good cheese and cold cuts and for breakfast with jam and marmalade. You can also mix 200 grams (1½ cups) of roasted and coarsely chopped nuts into the dough. You can also split them in half with a fork and roast them until golden brown at 150°C (302°F) into whole grain biscuits.

Dough temperature 27°C (81°F)
Sits 1 hour

For about 34 buns
Pre-dough (Fördeg)
500 grams (4 cups) graham flour, preferably
    stone ground
25 grams (3½ teaspoons) honey
25 grams (6¼ teaspoons) yeast
275 grams (1 cup + 2 tablespoons) milk
250 grams (1 cup) water

Pour the flour and honey into a bowl. Dissolve the yeast in the milk and water and pour it over the flour. Knead the dough at lowest speed for 10 minutes. Put it in a lightly oiled plastic container covered with a lid and let it rise for about 30–45 minutes at room temperature until doubled in size.

Combining (Bortgörning)
1,050 grams (2 pounds 5 ounces) pre-dough
100 grams (3.5 ounces) rye sourdough (see
    page 27)
250 grams (2 cups) graham flour, preferably
    stone ground

150 grams (⅔ cup) butter, soft
20 grams (3⅓ teaspoons) sea salt

Topping
250 grams (2 cups) sunflower seeds

1. Put the pre-dough, sourdough, and flour in a bowl and knead at low speed for 5 minutes. Add the butter and knead for another 7 minutes. Add the salt and knead at higher speed for about 5 minutes.
2. Make a gluten test (see page 35). If the dough does not feel elastic enough, just keep kneading until it feels right. Put the dough in a lightly oiled plastic container covered with a lid and let it rest for 30 minutes.
3. Put the dough on a lightly floured table. Push the air out of it (see page 36) and fold it together like an envelope. Put it back in the container with the seam facing downward and let it rest for another 30 minutes.
4. Divide the dough into 80-gram (2.8-ounce) pieces. Roll them into round buns, cover with a cloth so that the dough does not get dry on the surface, and let them relax for 5 minutes.
5. Roll the buns into oblong loaves about 12 centimeters (about 5 inches) long. Brush them with water and dip them in sunflower seeds. Put them on baking parchment and let them rise at room temperature until doubled in size, which usually takes 30–45 minutes.
6. Preheat the oven to 250°C (482°F).
7. Put the buns in the oven and spray generously with cold water with a squirt bottle. Bake for about 12 minutes, until they are golden brown and feel light and airy. Put them on a rack to cool. If you do not want to use them all at once, put them in the freezer as soon as they have cooled.

Oat and rye sandwich buns

Havre- och rogsandwichbullar

These delicious, airy buns go with most toppings, and it feels healthy to eat them, too. Also great as biscuits—split them in half with a fork and roast them until golden brown at 150°C (302°F).

Dough temperature 27°C (81°F)
Sits 1 hour

For about 20 buns
Pre-dough (Fördeg)
350 grams (2¾ cups) coarse rye flour,
    preferably stone ground
150 grams (1 cup) oat grains
25 grams (1 tablespoon) honey

25 grams (6¼ teaspoons) yeast
275 grams (1 cup + 2 tablespoons) milk
250 grams (1 cup) water

Mix the flour, oat grains, and honey in a bowl. Dissolve the yeast in the milk and water with a whisk and pour it into the bowl. Knead the dough at lowest speed for about 10 minutes.

    Put the dough in a lightly oiled plastic container covered with a lid to rise to double its size, for about 30–45 minutes depending on the temperature of the room.

Combining (Bortgörning)

925 grams (1 pound 0.6 ounce) pre-dough

250 grams (1¾ cups + 1 tablespoon) wheat flour high in protein, preferably stone ground

100 grams (3.5 ounces) rye sourdough (see page 27)

150 grams (⅔ cup) butter, at room temperature

30 grams (5 teaspoons) sea salt

oat grains

1. Put the pre-dough in a bowl, add the wheat flour and rye sourdough, and knead the dough for 5 minutes. Add the butter, increase the speed a little, and add the salt. Knead the dough carefully for about 5–7 more minutes (be careful, it is easy to work the dough too much when it contains rye and oat grains). Make a gluten test (see page 35).

2. Put the dough in the plastic container again and let it rise for 30 minutes.

3. Put the dough on a floured table and push it together (see page 36). Fold it like an envelope, put it back in the container, and let it rest another 30 minutes.

4. Divide the dough into 80-gram (2.8-ounce) pieces and roll them into round buns. Let them rest under a cloth for 5 minutes to relax.

5. Roll into oblong buns, 12 centimeters (about 5 inches) long. Brush them with water, turn them in oat grains, and put them on 2 trays with baking parchment. Let them rise at room temperature until doubled in size, which usually takes 30–45 minutes.

6. Preheat the oven to 250°C (482°F).

7. Put the tray in the oven and spray generously with water using a squirt bottle.

8. Bake the loaves for about 12–15 minutes until golden brown. Put them on a rack to cool. If you do not want to use them all at once, put them in the freezer immediately in plastic bags.

Top from left: Whole grain sandwich bread, hot dog bread with pumpkin seeds, oat and rye sandwich buns
Bottom from left: Lemon sandwich bread, hot dog bread with sesame seeds, hot dog bread

Hamburger/Hot dog buns

Hamburgerbröd/Korvbröd

When I was 7 years old, we were told to write an essay about what we would do with 100 crowns, a gigantic amount in the 1950s. I wrote that I would buy a hot dog stand and then eat all of the hot dogs, and if there was any money left I would buy a bandy stick. These days, my interest in eating hot dogs (and bandy) is not quite as strong, but I am still passionate about gastronomy.

This bread should be lightly grilled on the surface before it is filled with a juicy, freshly grilled hamburger of ground beef that has been seasoned only with salt and pepper. It should be about 1 centimeter (about ½ inch) high and shaped with a circular cutter.

On the Caribbean island of St. Thomas, which I often visited during my cruise ship years, there is a place close to the famous Reese Liquor Shop where they make fantastic hamburgers. They top their burgers with homemade hot ketchup and grated cheddar cheese and let it melt a little. They add guacamole with plenty of tomato cubes and a big pile of crispy, fried onion rings. This is served with the best French fries of the Caribbean, light and crispy. Joe Allen's in London and New York also makes great hamburgers. A properly made burger is a delicacy, but they should be grilled.

Hot dog bread made from the same recipe should always be warm, light, and airy with a good grilled hot dog inside and hot mustard. For a healthier bread, you can replace a quarter of the wheat flour with spelt wholemeal or graham flour, but the result will not be as light and airy.

Dough temperature 28°C (82°F)
Requires no time to rise

For about 20 hamburger buns or
27 hot dog buns
900 grams (6½ cups) wheat flour high in
    protein, preferably stone ground
50 grams (4 tablespoons) granulated sugar
15 grams (2⅛ teaspoons) honey or light
    malt
500 grams (2 cups) milk
40 grams (10 teaspoons) yeast
125 grams (½ cup) butter, at room
    temperature
20 grams (1 tablespoon) sea salt
1 egg for brushing
1 egg yolk
a pinch of salt
sesame seeds

Pre-dough (Fördeg)
Mix 750 grams (5½ cups) of the flour in a bowl with the sugar and honey/malt. Dissolve the yeast in the milk with a whisk. Pour the yeast mixture into the bowl. Knead the dough for 10 minutes, put it in a lightly oiled plastic container covered with a lid, and let it rise at room temperature for about 30 minutes until doubled in volume.

Combining (Bortgörning)
1. Put the dough back in the bowl, add the rest of the flour, and knead for 5 minutes. Add the butter and increase the kneading speed. Add the salt and knead for about 10 minutes until the dough is tough and very elastic. Make a gluten test (see page 35).
2. Immediately divide into 80-gram (2.8-ounce) pieces, roll them into tight buns, and let them relax for 10 minutes.
3. Put the buns on baking parchment, sprinkle lightly on top with wheat flour, cover with a second sheet of baking parchment on top, and then press the buns flat with another tray.
4. Whisk together an egg mixture consisting of an egg, an extra yolk, and a little bit of salt. Brush the bread with the egg mix. Repeat brushing after 30 minutes and sprinkle immediately with a generous amount of sesame seeds.
5. When the buns feel airy and light, preheat the oven to 250°C (482°F).
6. Bake the buns in batches for about 12 minutes until golden brown. Put them on a rack to cool. Put them in the freezer immediately if they are not to be used all at once.
7. Split the buns and grill on the sectioned surface to warm them up before adding the meat.

For hot dog buns
1. Divide the dough into 40-gram (1.4-ounce) pieces and roll them into round buns. Let them relax for 5 minutes.
2. Roll short, narrow buns and put them on baking parchment. Brush them immediately with egg mix, wait for 30 minutes, and repeat brushing.
3. Bake the buns in the same way as the burger buns but only for about 7–8 minutes until golden brown. Let cool on a rack. Immediately put them in the freezer if they are not to be used all at once. Thaw the buns in the plastic bag in a microwave oven to make them warm and soft.

See photograph on page 119.

Lauge sandwich bread

Lauge-sandwichbröd

In Switzerland, Germany, and Austria, this flavorful bread is popular for making sandwiches, but you hardly ever see it in Sweden. The sandwich dough is excellent for making nice, airy *Lauge* sandwiches. At Honold Confiserie in Zürich, we made hundreds of these every day.

   Note: Lye is corrosive, so be careful when handling the dough, as it may irritate your skin. Use gloves and goggles and you will not have any problems. Otherwise, this is the only recipe in this book that requires safety equipment.

For about 28 buns or pretzels
Soda solution
100 grams (6 tablespoons) Food-Quality
   Lye
2,000 grams (8½ cups) water

WARNING: Lye is poisonous and can cause severe burns or blindness if contact is made with skin or the eyes. When working with lye, always wear protective goggles and gloves and only use glass or stainless steel containers. Do not allow children near lye. The poisonous properties of lye will disappear once the bread is properly baked.

Pour the soda into a stainless pot with half of the water, and boil it. Add the rest of the cold water. Any leftover liquid can be kept in a jug with a clear warning label and heated only when needed.

Lauge-dough (Lauge-deg)
Dough temperature 26°C (79°F)
Sits 30 minutes

Pre-dough (Fördeg)
250 grams (1 cup) water
20 grams (5 teaspoons) yeast
375 grams (2¾ cups) wheat flour high in protein, preferably stone ground

Dissolve the yeast in the water with a whisk. Measure the flour into a baking bowl and pour it into the liquid. Knead the dough at lowest speed for 10 minutes. Put it in a lightly oiled plastic container covered with a lid and let it rise for 3 hours.

Combining (Bortgörning)
250 grams (1 cup) milk
25 grams (6¼ teaspoons) yeast
645 grams (1 pound 6.8 ounces) pre-dough
750 grams (5½ cups) wheat flour high in protein, preferably stone ground
10 grams (1½ teaspoons) Swedish honey
50 grams (3¾ tablespoons) sunflower oil
10 grams (½ tablespoon) sea salt

1. Dissolve the yeast in the milk with a whisk and pour it over the pre-dough. Add the other ingredients except for the oil and salt. Knead the dough for 3 minutes at low speed and add the oil. Knead for another 5 minutes and add the salt. Increase the speed and knead the dough for another 10 minutes until tough and elastic. Make a gluten test (see page 35). ➤

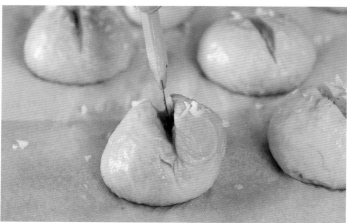

2. Put the dough in a lightly oiled plastic container covered with a lid, and let it rest for 30 minutes.

3. For salty pretzels: Cut up 60–80-gram (2–3-ounce) pieces. Roll them like hot dog buns, cover with a cloth, and let them rest for 5 minutes.

4. Roll out the buns into 45–50-centimeter (17½–20-inch) long pieces, a little thicker around the middle. Shape them into pretzels and put them on a cloth. Cover with a cloth and let them rise for about 45 minutes until doubled in size.

5. For round buns: Cut up 60-gram (2-ounce) pieces. Roll them into buns, put them on a cloth, cover with a cloth, and let rise for about 45 minutes.

6. Preheat the oven to 230°C (446°F). Check the temperature of the liquid; it should be 40°C (104°F).

7. Put on kitchen gloves and a pair of goggles and dip the buns in the liquid. Put them on a greased tray. Cut the pretzels with a sharp knife like in the photograph and sprinkle with flake salt. Cut the buns deeply in the middle and sprinkle with a little bit of flake salt after dipping them in the liquid.

8. Bake the buns until golden brown for about 12–15 minutes. Let cool on a rack.

Different variations of Lauge sandwich bread

For sandwiches

Cut the cold buns with a sharp knife and brush them with a thin layer of whipped butter. Put on a slice of Italian salami and then put the other half of the bun on top. Decorate with a couple of cornichons on the side, or fill with coppa and tapenade or pastrami with mustard, pickles, and grated horseradish. Serrano ham with peppers marinated in olive oil or slices of mortadella is also delicious.

Italian spinach sandwich bread with Parmesan cheese

Italienskt spenatbröd med parmesan till sandwich

This dough is not only good for making sandwiches, but also pockets that can be filled in different ways.

Dough temperature 28°C (82°F)
Sits 30 minutes

For 3 loaves or 12 pockets
2 2-liter (½-gallon) aluminum pans
25 grams (3 tablespoons) butter for greasing
the pans

Poolish
150 grams (1 cup) wheat flour high in protein,
preferably stone ground
75 grams (5 tablespoons) milk
20 grams (5 teaspoons) yeast
3 grams (¾ teaspoon) raw sugar

Whisk everything together into a pancake-like
batter. Cover with plastic wrap and let rise at
room temperature for 30 minutes.

Combining (Bortgörning)
248 grams (8.7 ounces) poolish
175 grams (¾ cup) milk
25 grams (6¼ teaspoons) yeast
650 grams (4¾ cups) wheat flour high in
protein, preferably stone ground
15 grams (2½ teaspoons) sea salt
15 grams (2 teaspoons) honey
100 grams egg (about 2 eggs)
125 grams (1 cup) spinach, chopped
75 grams (¾ cup) aged Parmesan cheese,
grated
125 grams (9 tablespoons) butter
a little bit of grated nutmeg

1. Put the poolish in a bowl, dissolve the yeast
   in the milk with a whisk, and pour it in
   along with the flour, salt, honey, and egg.
2. Knead the dough at lowest speed for 10
   minutes. Add the spinach, cheese, butter,
   and nutmeg and knead for about 8 minutes
   until very elastic. Make a gluten test (see
   page 35).

3. Put the dough in a lightly oiled plastic container to rise for 30 minutes.
4. Push together the dough on a floured table (see page 36). Let it relax for
   10 minutes. Butter the pans with soft butter with a brush.
5. Divide the dough into 3 equal pieces, tear them into round buns, cover
   with a cloth, and let them relax for 5 minutes.
6. Divide each bun with a scraper into 4 parts. Roll them into oval buns and
   put 4 buns together in each form. Let them rise under a cloth in a warm
   place until doubled in volume.
7. Preheat the oven to 230°C (450°F) and place a baking stone or tray inside.
8. Put the bread in the oven and spray generously with water using a squirt
   bottle. Lower the temperature to 180°C (350°F) after 5 minutes. After 20
   minutes, vent the oven by briefly opening the door. Bake for about 40
   minutes. Make sure with a thermometer that the internal temperature of
   the bread is 98°C (208°F).
9. Move the buns from the pans to a rack and put them in the oven again,
   this time without a pan. Let them sit for 5 minutes; this way they will hold
   together better.
10. Let the bread cool on a rack. Put them in the freezer in plastic bags when
    they have cooled.

Tomato sandwich bread with parmesan cheese

Tomatbröd med Parmesan till sandwich

**The same recipe as for spinach bread, but replace the spinach with 125
grams (¾ cup) of mixed small preserved Italian cherry tomatoes and
add 15 grams (3 teaspoons) of tomato puree.**

How to make sandwich pockets with this dough:

1. Divide the dough into 80-gram (2.8-ounce) pieces and tear them into
   buns. Cover over with a cloth and let them relax for 5 minutes.
2. Roll out the buns with a little wheat flour, saucer size. Brush one half with
   a little sunflower oil and fold over the other half. Put them on a tray with
   baking parchment to rise for about 45–60 minutes until doubled in
   volume.
3. Preheat the oven to 250°C (482°F).
4. Bake the buns for about 12 minutes until light and beautiful. Put them on
   a rack to cool immediately.
5. Open the pockets and fill them with various goodies like in the photograph.

The sandwich supposedly originates from the fourth Earl of Sandwich. He was
a card player who had a hard time taking a break, so he ordered 2 bread slices
with a filling in the middle so that he could eat with one hand and play with
the other. Thanks to this clever invention, his name will live forever.

Scalded Emmer bread

Skållat emmerbröd

Whole wheat bread must consist of 70% whole wheat flour containing all parts of the shell. This moist and flavorful bread quickly turns into a breakfast favorite with cheese. Emmer flour is popular in the USA, and when in New York and craving something sweet you should visit François Payard on 1032 Lexington Avenue. You will not regret it.

Dough temperature 27°C (81°F)
Sits 1 hour and 30 minutes

For 4 loaves

DAY 1
Scalding (Skållning)
250 grams (1 cup) water
125 grams (¼ cup + 2 tablespoons) whole Emmer wheat
25 grams (4 teaspoons) sea salt

Boil the water and pour it into the flour and the salt. Work until the dough is smooth. Cover with plastic wrap and let sit at room temperature until the next day.

DAY 2
Combining (Bortgörning)
500 grams (2 cups) milk
50 grams (12½ teaspoons) yeast
400 grams (14 ounces) *skållning*
600 grams (3 cups + 2 tablespoons) whole Emmer wheat
300 grams (2 cups) wheat flour high in protein
25 grams (3½ teaspoons) Swedish honey
150 grams (1⅓ sticks) butter, soft

1. Dissolve the yeast in the milk with a whisk and pour it over the *skållning*, all the flour, and the honey. Knead the dough at lowest speed for 5 minutes and add the butter in batches. Knead for another 10 minutes at lowest speed. Make a gluten test (see page 35) and knead for about another minute (but be careful).

2. Put the dough in a lightly oiled plastic container covered with a lid and let it rest for 45 minutes.

3. Put the dough on a lightly floured table and push it together (see page 36). Put the dough back in the container with the seam facing downward. Let it rest for 45 minutes.

4. Push the air out of the dough again and let it relax for 10 minutes.

5. Divide the dough into 4 equal pieces and tear them into round buns. Put them on a cloth and let them relax for 5 minutes.

6. Dust on a little bit of Emmer flour and roll out ⅓ of the bun with a rolling pin. Make an incision in the rolled-out dough with a knife and fold it over the bun. Put the bread on a floured cloth to rise at room temperature for 45–60 minutes.

7. Preheat the oven to 250°C (482°F) and place a baking stone or tray inside. Put 2 of the loaves in the refrigerator to stop the leavening.

8. Put 2 of the loaves in the oven with a baker's peel and spray generously with water using a squirt bottle. Lower the heat to 200°C (392°F) after 5 minutes. After 20 minutes, vent the oven by briefly opening the door. Repeat once more while the bread is baking.

9. Bake the loaves for about 40–45 minutes, making sure with a thermometer that their internal temperature is 98°C (208°F). Put the bread on a rack to cool. Repeat the same process with the bread in the refrigerator.

Scalded graham bread with walnuts and raisins

Skållat grahamsbröd med valnötter och russin

This moist bread is great with cheese and for breakfast as an energy boost with marmalade or jam. You can replace the raisins with prunes or apricots. I remember a bread at Restaurant le Train Bleu on Gare de Lyon in Paris. It was served with a perfect ripe St. Marcellin cheese, which tasted fantastic. This beautiful railroad restaurant is always worth a visit, if not for the food, then for the environment.

Dough temperature 27°C (81°F)
Sits 1 hour and 30 minutes

For 4 loaves or 45 buns, 60 grams/piece

DAY 1
Scalding (Skållning)
250 grams (1 cup) water
125 grams (1 cup) graham flour, preferably
   stone ground
25 grams (4 teaspoons) sea salt

Boil the water, pour it over the flour and the salt, and stir until smooth. Cover with plastic wrap and let it sit until the next day at room temperature.

DAY 2
Combining (Bortgörning)
300 grams (2 cups) raisins
400 grams (14 ounces) *skållning*
900 grams (6½ cups) graham flour
25 grams (3½ teaspoons) honey
500 grams (2 cups) milk
50 grams (4 tablespoons) yeast
150 grams (1⅓ sticks) butter, at room
   temperature
450 grams (4½ cups) walnuts

1. Soak the raisins in cold water for about 30 minutes.
2. Combine the *skållning* in a bowl with the flour and honey. Dissolve the yeast in the milk with a whisk and pour it into the bowl. Knead the dough for 5 minutes at lowest speed and add the butter in batches. Knead for another 10 minutes at lowest speed, and make a gluten test (see page 35). Perhaps knead the dough for a little longer.
3. Drain the raisins and knead them into the dough along with the walnuts. Put the dough in a lightly oiled plastic container covered with a lid to rest for 45 minutes.
4. Put the dough on a floured table, push the air out of it (see page 36), and fold it together like an envelope. Put it back into the container with the seam facing downward. Let it rest for another 45 minutes.
5. Push together the dough one more time and let it relax for 20 minutes.
6. Divide the dough into 4 equal pieces, tear them into 4 tight buns, cover them with a cloth, and let them relax for 10 minutes.
7. Shape the buns into 4 oblong loaves and put them with the seam facing up on a floured cloth, slightly bent. Pull up the cloth between the loaves to keep them rising upward (see photograph on page 54). Let rise for about 45–60 minutes until doubled in size. Or shape 60-gram (2-ounce) buns with the dough and let them rise on a tray.
8. Preheat the oven to 250°C (482°F) and place a baking stone or tray inside. Put 2 of the loaves in the refrigerator to stop the leavening.
9. Put the 2 other loaves on a baker's peel, put them in the oven, and spray generously with water using a squirt bottle. Lower the heat to 200°C (392°F) after 5 minutes and vent the oven by briefly opening the door after 20 minutes. Vent once more while the bread is in the oven.
10. Bake the loaves for about 50 minutes, and make sure with a thermometer that their internal temperature is 98°C (208°F). Put them on a rack to cool and repeat the process with the 2 loaves in the refrigerator.
11. When making buns, let them bake for about 12–15 minutes at 250°C (482°F) until golden brown. Spray in water with a squirt bottle at the beginning. Let the buns cool on a rack.

Seed bread

Kärnbröd

This healthy bread leaves no one unaffected, and it is highly addictive, with a lovely texture and strong aroma and flavor. It only requires a little bit of butter, and maybe a good cheese. Master pastry chef and teacher Hans Herman at the trade school in Munich treated me to a similar bread once when I was guest lecturing on Swedish specialties.

Dough temperature 26°C (79°F)
Sits 90 minutes

For 4 loaves

DAY 1
Poolish
180 grams (¾ cup) water
3 grams (¾ teaspoon) yeast
65 grams (½ cup) wheat flour high in protein, preferably stone ground
120 grams (¾ cup + 2 tablespoons) graham flour, preferably stone ground

Dissolve the yeast in the water with a whisk. Add half of the flour and whisk into a pancake-like batter. Add the rest of the flour and whisk until the dough gets tough. Let it sit at room temperature for 1 hour and then for 24 hours in refrigerator.

Soaking (Blötläggning)
450 grams (2 cups) water
145 grams (⅔ cup) pumpkin seeds
100 grams (6¼ tablespoons) sunflower seeds
50 grams (5½ tablespoons) sesame seeds
50 grams (5 tablespoons) linseeds
130 grams (¾ cup) cut rye

Heat up the water to 50°C (122°F), pour it over the seeds, and let it sit in the refrigerator until the next day. Take the soaked mixture out of the refrigerator 2 hours before baking.

DAY 2
Combining (Bortgörning)
235 grams (2¾ cups + 2 tablespoons) coarse rye flour, preferably stone ground
115 grams (¾ cup + 2 tablespoons) wheat flour high in protein, preferably stone ground
368 grams (13 ounces) poolish
925 grams (1 pound 0.6 ounces) *blötläggning*
525 grams (2¼ cups) water

25 grams (6¼ teaspoons) yeast
70 grams (5 tablespoons) sunflower oil
60 grams (3 tablespoons) sea salt
25 grams (1 tablespoon) honey

1. Pour both kinds of flour, the poolish, and the soaked mix into a bowl. Dissolve the yeast in the water and pour it in. Knead the dough at lowest speed for about 5 minutes. Add the oil and knead for another 5 minutes.
2. Add the salt and knead at lowest speed for 5 more minutes. Increase the kneading speed for about 2 minutes. Make a gluten test (see page 35).
3. Put the dough in a lightly oiled plastic container covered with a lid and let it rest for 45 minutes.
4. Put the dough on a floured table and push it together (see page 36). Fold it like an envelope and put it back into the container with the seam facing downward.
5. Push the air out of the dough again after another 45 minutes, put it back again, and let it relax for 10 minutes.
6. Put the dough on a floured board and divide it into 4 equal pieces. Tear/roll 3 round or oblong loaves. Brush them all over with water and dust with graham flour.
7. Put the bread in round or oblong baskets to rise for about 45–60 minutes until doubled in size.
8. Preheat the oven to 250°C (482°F) and place a baking stone or tray inside. Put 2 of the loaves in the refrigerator to stop the leavening.
9. Put 2 loaves in the oven with a baker's peel. Spray in generously with water using a squirt bottle. Lower the heat to 200°C (392°F) after 5 minutes. Vent the oven after 20 minutes by briefly opening the door. Repeat once more while baking.
10. Bake the loaves for about 50 minutes, and make sure with a thermometer that their internal temperature is 98°C (208°F). Put the bread on a rack to cool. Repeat the whole process with the last batch.

Spelt wholemeal bread

Dinkelfullkornsbröd

The advantages of scalding include better kneading abilities, a strong aroma and flavor, and making the bread more durable. The disadvantage is a slightly smaller size, though it yields moist slices. This bread tastes very healthy and reminds me of a good bread that I had at Stadt Bäckerei in Hamburg.

Dough temperature 26°C (79°F)
Sits 1 hour and 10 minutes

For 3 loaves

DAY 1
Scalding (Skållning)
750 grams (3 cups) water
500 grams (2¾ cups + 2 tablespoons) spelt
    wholemeal
35 grams (2 tablespoons) sea salt

Boil the water and pour it over the flour and salt in a bowl. Knead the dough well and let it cool covered with plastic in the refrigerator overnight.

DAY 2
Combining (Bortgörning)
1,285 grams (2 pounds 13.3 ounces) *skållning*
100 grams (3.5 ounces) white sourdough
    (see page 27)
800 grams (4½ cups + 2 tablespoons) spelt
    wholemeal
325 grams (1⅔ cups) water
50 grams (4 tablespoons) yeast
olive oil

1. Let the *skållning* come to room temperature 1 hour before you start combining it with other ingredients.
2. Put the *skållning*, sourdough, and flour into a bowl. Dissolve the yeast in the water with a whisk and pour it in. Knead at lowest speed for about 13–15 minutes. Make a gluten test (see page 35) and check the gluten development in the dough.
3. Put the dough in a lightly oiled plastic container covered with a lid to rest for 40 minutes.
4. Put the dough on a floured table. Push it together (see page 36) and fold it like a pillow. Put it back in the container with the seam facing downward and let it rest for another 30 minutes.
5. Push the air out again and let the dough relax for another 10 minutes.
6. Divide the dough into 3 equal pieces. Roll them on a lightly oiled baking table, not too tight, and roll them in a generous amount of spelt wholemeal. Put them in floured baskets with the floured side facing up. Let rise for about 1 hour until increased by ¾ in volume.
7. Preheat the oven to 250°C (482°F) and place a baking stone or tray inside. Put 1 loaf in the refrigerator to stop the leavening.
8. Put 2 loaves in the oven with a baker's peel, and spray generously with water using a squirt bottle. Lower the heat to 200°C (392°F) after 5 minutes. Vent the oven after 20 minutes by briefly opening the door. Repeat once more while baking to get a crispy crust.
9. Make sure with a thermometer that the internal temperature of the loaves is 98°C (208°F) after 55–60 minutes. Put them on a rack to cool. Repeat the process with the loaf in the refrigerator.

Scalded spelt wholemeal bread with sunflower seeds

Skållat dinkelbröd med solrosfrön

This bread both feels and tastes healthy and goes excellently with cheese, jam, and marmalade. We used to bake it at the Richemont school in Lucerne, the baking academy of Switzerland with students from around the world.

Dough temperature 26°C (79°F)
Sits 1 hour and 30 minutes

For 3 loaves

DAY 1

Scalding (Skållning)

460 grams (2 cups) water
290 grams (1²/₃ cups) spelt wholemeal,
    preferably stone ground
25 grams (1⅓ tablespoons) salt

Boil the water, pour it over the flour and the salt, and mix into a smooth batter. Cover with plastic wrap and let sit at room temperature until the next day.

DAY 2

Combining (Bortgörning)

300 grams (2⅓ cups) sunflower seeds,
    roasted
750 grams (1 pound 10.5 ounces) *skållning*
315 grams (1⅓ cups) water
25 grams (2 tablespoons) yeast
200 grams (1 cup + 2 tablespoons)
    spelt wholemeal, preferably
    stone ground
460 grams (3⅓ cups) white sifted spelt
    wheat flour, preferably stone ground
10 grams (2 teaspoons) apple cider vinegar
15 grams (2 teaspoons) honey

1. Preheat the oven to 200°C (392°F), pour the sunflower seeds onto a tray with edges, and roast them for about 10 minutes until golden brown.
2. Pour the *skållning* into the bowl and dissolve the yeast with a whisk in the water. Pour it over the flour, vinegar, and honey. Knead the dough at lowest speed for about 15 minutes. Make a gluten test (see page 35) and maybe knead a little more.
3. Knead the sunflower seeds into the dough. Put it in a lightly oiled plastic container covered with a lid to rest for 45 minutes.
4. Put the dough on a floured table and push it together (see page 36). Put it back in the container with the seam facing downward and let it rest for 45 minutes.
5. Push the air out of the dough again and let it relax for 10 more minutes.
6. Divide the dough into 3 equal pieces and tear them into round buns. Cover with a cloth and let them rest for 5 minutes.
7. Roll into short, oblong shapes. Place them with the seam facing downward on a floured cloth and pull up the cloth between the loaves (see page 54). Let them rise until doubled in volume.
8. Preheat the oven to 250°C (482°F) and place a baking stone or tray inside.
9. Put the bread in the oven with a baker's peel. Spray in water with a squirt bottle. Lower the temperature to 200°C (392°F) after 5 minutes. Vent the oven after 20 minutes by briefly opening the door. Repeat once more while baking.
10. Bake the loaves for about 45–50 minutes, making sure with a thermometer that the internal temperature is 98°C (208°F). Lift them onto an oven rack to cool.

Whole Kamut wheat bread

Fullkornskamutbröd

This bread can also be baked in greased bread pans. It is flavorful yet neutral and goes with most foods. Kamut flour has a strong original taste that does not compare to any other flour. I had brick-oven-baked Kamut bread in Alexandria in Egypt, served with baked dove in grape leaves, a specialty from Kairo, and they tasted delicious together.

Dough temperature 27°C (81°F)
Sits 30 minutes

For 4 loaves

DAY 1

1,000 grams (4¼ cups) water
500 grams (2⅔ cups) Kamut seeds

Boil the water, pour in the Kamut seeds, and let them simmer for about 45 minutes until soft. Let cool and put them in the refrigerator until the next day. Drain them in a sieve or strainer before using.

Pre-dough (Fördeg)
330 grams (1⅔ cups) water
425 grams (2¼ cups) Kamut flakes
1 gram (¼ teaspoon) yeast

Mix everything into a paste and let it sit at room temperature for 12–15 hours.

DAY 2

Combining (Bortgörning)
755 grams (1 pound 10.6 ounces) pre-dough
150 grams (5.3 ounces) rye sourdough (see page 27)
1,000 grams (5½ cups) whole Kamut wheat
550 grams (2⅓ cups) water
30 grams (2½ tablespoons) yeast
40 grams (2 tablespoons) sea salt
750–800 grams (4–4⅓ cups) cooked, drained Kamut seeds

1. Knead all of the ingredients into a dough for about 15 minutes. Cover with plastic wrap and let rest for 30 minutes.
2. Divide the dough into 4 parts and shape round loaves. Brush them all over with water and powder them with whole Kamut wheat with a sieve. Let them rise for 20–30 minutes at room temperature on a floured cloth.
3. Preheat the oven to 250°C (482°F) and place a baking stone or tray inside. Put 2 of the loaves in the refrigerator for baking later.
4. Put 2 of the loaves in the oven with a baker's peel and spray generously with water using a squirt bottle. Lower the temperature to 180°C (356°F) after 5 minutes. Vent the oven after 20 minutes by briefly opening the door. Repeat once more while baking to get a crispy crust.
5. Bake for about 1 hour, making sure with a thermometer that the internal temperature is 98°C (208°F). Let the bread cool on a rack. Repeat the process with the bread in the refrigerator.

Wort bread

Vörtbröd

This traditional Swedish Christmas bread comes in many local variations. The mixture of spices and amount of syrup and wort varies; sometimes it contains raisins, sometimes not. In my previous book about bread, there is a recipe for heavier wort bread, which I love for Christmas, but this is lighter and at least as good. At Blekingsborg's pastry shop in Malmö, we used to make this delicious wort bread and buns. We shaped the bread like saddles, which was an old tradition in Gothenburg, according to the legendary baker and pastry chef teacher Birger Lundgren. We used to cut the buns in half and top with butter, a big slice of light smoked ham, lots of Skåne mustard, and a tablespoon of cold red cabbage.

This Christmas sandwich was well liked by most customers at the café. Wort bread with *gubbröra* (a Swedish potato and anchovy specialty) is also good, or with pickled onion herring with a classic Swedish "1–2–3" sauce (1 part vinegar, 2 parts sugar, and 3 parts water), red onion, and allspice.

If you cannot get ahold of wort, ask for it at a pastry shop or bakery. Otherwise, cook down 1 liter (¼ gallon) of light beer to 150 grams (⅔ cup); it is almost as good as real wort.

Wort bread can be put in the freezer in plastic bags. Thaw carefully in a microwave oven in the plastic bag.

Dough temperature 28°C (82°F)
Sits 1 hour

For 5 loaves or about 45 buns
Quick-dough (Raskdeg)
500 grams (1½ cans) light beer
100 grams (8⅓ tablespoons) yeast
750 grams (5½ cups) wheat flour high in protein, preferably stone ground

Heat the light beer to 35°C (95°F). Dissolve the yeast in the beer with a whisk and pour it over the flour. Knead for about 10 minutes at lowest speed. Cover with a cloth and let it rise for about 30 minutes until doubled in volume.

Combining (Bortgörning)
400 grams (2½ cups) raisins (soaked weight)
1,350 grams (3 pounds) quick-dough
150 grams (⅔ cup) liquid wort
50 grams (3½ tablespoons) rapeseed oil
210 grams (¾ cup) dark syrup
30 grams (5 teaspoons) sea salt
15 grams (8½ teaspoons) ground ginger
15 grams (7½ teaspoons) ground bitter orange peel
10 grams (5 teaspoons) freshly ground cardamom
5 grams (2⅓ teaspoons) ground cloves
500 grams (3 cups) sifted rye, preferably stone ground

For buns
1. Soak the raisins in cold water for about 30 minutes and drain them in a sieve.
2. Mix all the ingredients except for the raisins and knead into a dough at lowest speed for about 13 minutes. Increase the speed and knead the dough for another 7 minutes until very elastic. Make a gluten test (see page 35).
3. Knead in the drained raisins.
4. Put the dough in a lightly oiled plastic container covered with a lid and let it rest for 30 minutes.
5. Put the dough on the baking table and push it together (see page 36). Put it back in the plastic container and let it rest for another 30 minutes.
6. Push the air out of the dough one more time, divide it into 60-gram (2-ounce) pieces and roll round buns. Put them on a tray and let them rise in a warm place for about 45 minutes until doubled in volume.
7. Preheat the oven to 250°C (482°F).
8. Bake the buns for about 12–14 minutes, until beautifully brown. Brush them with glaze (see page 40) directly after they come out of the oven. Let cool on a rack.

For bread
1. Divide the dough into 5 540-gram (19-ounce) pieces. Tear the loaves round, cover them with a cloth, and let them relax for 10 minutes.
2. Flatten the bread lightly and fold in the sides like a bicycle seat. Leave them to rise on a floured cloth in a warm place until doubled in size.
3. Preheat the oven to 250°C (482°F) and place a stone or tray inside. Put 2 of the loaves in the refrigerator to stop the leavening.
4. Put the bread in the oven with a baker's peel. Spray in a little bit of water with a squirt bottle and lower the heat to 200°C (392°F) after 5 minutes.
5. Bake the loaves for 45 minutes until golden brown, making sure with a thermometer that their internal temperature is 98°C (208°F). Take them out of the oven and brush them with a glaze immediately. Let cool on a rack. Repeat the process with the 2 loaves in the refrigerator.

Old-time syrup loaf

Gammaldags sirapslimpa

Syrup in bread is not one of my personal favorites, but sometimes it is fun to make bread that evokes nostalgic memories from childhood. Syrup loaf should be soft and moist and not too spicy. The seasoning will be more elegant and less dominant if the spices are not finely ground. In the old days, they sometimes added ground bitter orange peel to the dough, and it became a bitter orange loaf instead. The baker Erik Olofsson is famous for his delicious bitter orange loaf, in which he uses dried, soaked, and cooked bitter orange peel.

Dough Temperature 27°C (81°F)
Sits 1 hour

For 3 loaves
Quick-dough (Raskdeg)
500 grams (2 cups) water
100 grams (½ cup) yeast
750 grams (7⅓ cups) sifted rye, preferably
    stone ground
10 grams (1½ tablespoons) whole anise
    seeds
10 grams (5 teaspoons) whole fennel seeds

Dissolve the yeast in the water and pour it over the sifted rye and spices. Knead at lowest speed for 5 minutes. Cover the dough with a cloth and let it rise for about 30 minutes until doubled in volume.

Combining (Bortgörning)
1,370 grams (3 pounds) quick-dough
400 grams (3 cups) wheat flour high in
    protein
250 grams (¾ cup) light syrup
25 grams (1¾ tablespoons) butter
25 grams (4 teaspoons) salt

1. Add the flour, syrup, butter, and salt to the pre-dough. Knead at lowest speed for 12 minutes. Increase the speed and knead the dough until elastic for about 8 more minutes. Make a gluten test (see page 35).
2. Put the dough in a lightly oiled plastic container covered with a lid to rise for 30 minutes.
3. Put the dough on a floured table and push it together (see page 36). Fold it like an envelope and put it back in the plastic container to rest for another 30 minutes.
4. Divide the dough into 3 equal pieces and tear them into round shapes. Cover with a cloth and let them relax for 5 minutes.
5. Roll out 3 oblong loaves (see shaping of bread on page 37). Put them to rise until doubled in volume on a tray and brush them with egg mixture (see page 40).
6. Preheat the oven to 250°C (482°F).
7. Put the bread into the oven, spray generously with water, and bake for 5 minutes.
8. Lower the temperature to 200°C (392°F) and vent the oven after another 10 minutes. Bake the loaves for a total of 45 minutes, making sure with a thermometer that their internal temperature is 98°C (208°F).
9. For extra old-time gloss you can brush the warm bread with glaze (see page 40).

Dark rustic Skåne bread

Skånskt mörkt lantbröd

We used to bake this classic scalded bread at Blekingsborg's pastry shop in Malmö. It is rich in flavor and well worth the effort. I bake it a lot harder than most Skåne bakers, because I want a stronger crust; that is where the flavor is.

This bread is great for cold cuts such as *spickekorv* (a salty Swedish salami) and Skåne onion sausage or a slice of veal brawn with beets.

Dough temperature 28°C (82°F)
Sits 2 hours

For 4 loaves

DAY 1

Scalding (Skållning)
500 grams (2 cups + 2 tablespoons) water
250 grams (2½ cups) fine rye flour
20 grams (1 tablespoon) sea salt

Boil the water and pour it over the flour and salt. Work the dough heavily until properly mixed. Cover with plastic wrap and let it sit at room temperature until the next day.

DAY 2

Quick-dough (Raskdeg)
770 grams (1 pound 11 ounces) *skållning*
100 grams (½ cup) water
50 grams (4 tablespoons) yeast
200 grams (2 cups) fine rye flour
150 grams (5.3 ounces) rye sourdough
    (see page 27)

Knead all the ingredients for 8 minutes at lowest speed into a dough. Put it in a lightly oiled plastic container covered with a lid and let it rise 2 hours.

Combining (Bortgörning)
1,270 grams (2 pounds 12.7 ounces) quick-dough
150 grams (½ cup) light syrup
400 grams (3 cups) extra-strong wheat flour
250 grams (2½ cups) fine rye flour

1. Add the syrup, wheat flour, and rye flour to the quick-dough. Knead for about 15 minutes at low speed until elastic. Make a gluten test (see page 35). The dough should be very smooth.
2. Put the dough back in the lightly oiled plastic container to rest for 1 hour.
3. Divide the dough into 4 equal pieces and tear them into round loaves. Brush them all over with soft butter and put them next to each other in a greased baking pan. Let them rise in a warm place until doubled in volume.
4. Preheat the oven to 250°C (482°F).
5. Put the bread in the oven and spray in a little bit of water with a squirt bottle. Lower the heat to 180°C (356°F) after 5 minutes.
6. Vent the oven after 15 minutes by briefly opening the door. Repeat venting twice while baking.
7. Bake for a total of about 45 minutes, making sure that the bread's internal temperature is 98°C (208°F). Put the bread on a rack to cool.

Coarse Skåne bread

Skånskt grovt bröd

Adding cooked potato makes this bread moist and good. Also, it is easy to slice because it is scalded. This is a good bread for herring and *nubbe*, or snaps. My mother and Aunt Gullan were specialists at making Skåne herring. When it is really good and the bone slides out easily when you clean it, it is one of my favorites. Head cold buffet Inga at the Savoy Hotel in Malmö and herring-Elsa always taught their students to pickle Skåne herring and Baltic herring, which is also really good. Onion herring with the classic "1–2–3" sauce (a Swedish specialty), chopped red onion, and crushed allspice is always the journeyman test that proves if you know how to pickle herring. Below is a fantastic recipe for this homemade preserve that goes well with this tasty bread or with a proper *kavring*.

Dough temperature 28°C (82°F)
Sits 1 hour

For 4 loaves

DAY 1

Scalding (Skållning)
500 grams (2 cups) water
250 grams (2 cups) coarse rye flour
20 grams (3⅓ teaspoons) sea salt

Boil the water and pour it over the flour and salt. Stir with a ladle into a smooth porridge, cover with plastic wrap, and let it sit at room temperature until the next day.

DAY 2

Quick-dough (Raskdeg)
770 grams (1 pound 11 ounces) *skållning*
25 grams (6¼ teaspoons) yeast
200 grams (14 tablespoons) water
350 grams (2¾ cups) coarse rye flour
250 grams (8.8 ounces) rye sourdough (see page 27)

Mix the *skållning* with the yeast, water, flour, and rye sourdough. Knead for 8 minutes into a dough and let it rise for 3 hours in a lightly oiled plastic container covered with a lid.

Combining (Bortgörning)
1,595 grams (3 pounds 8.3 ounces) quick-dough
350 grams (1 cup) dark syrup
150 grams (1¼ cups) coarse rye flour
200 grams (1¼ cup) cooked mashed potatoes
about 350 grams (3½ cups) fine rye flour
soft butter for brushing

1. Mix the quick-dough with the other ingredients. Knead for about 8 minutes at lowest speed into a dough. Increase the speed and knead for another 2 minutes. The dough should form small creases on the surface when ready, which is typical for rye dough.
2. Let it rest for 1 hour in a lightly oiled plastic container covered with a lid.
3. Divide the dough into 4 equal pieces and tear them into round loaves. Brush them all over with butter and put them in a greased baking pan to rise in a warm place until doubled in volume.
4. Preheat the oven to 250°C (392°F).
5. Put the bread in the oven and spray in water with a squirt bottle. Lower the temperature to 180°C (356°F) after 5 minutes.
6. Vent the oven after 15 minutes by briefly opening the door. Repeat twice while baking.
7. Bake for a total of 45–50 minutes. Make sure with a thermometer that the bread's internal temperature is at least 98°C (208°F). Let them cool on a rack.

Pickled herring

Kryddsill

1 kilogram (about 2 pounds) fresh tiny herring

Liquid
1 cup vinegar essence for 1 liter (4¼ cups) water
1 tablespoon salt

Spice mixture
4 deciliters (1⅔ cups) granulated sugar
1 deciliter (½ cup) salt
2 tablespoons crushed allspice
1 teaspoon crushed white pepper
10 bay leaves

1. Clean the herring and remove the fins and head, but leave the backbone. Rinse it well.
2. Mix the liquid and pour it over the herring. Let it sit in a cool place with a weight on top for 2 days.
3. Take out the herring and drain it. Place the herring, with the back facing down, and the spice mixture on top of each other in layers in a spacious pot. Let it sit in a cool place for 2 days under pressure.

Barley crispbread

Kornknäckebröd

A crispbread dough should be quite firm. If it feels loose, add a little more flour, but be careful not to make it too firm.

Dough temperature 28°C (82°F)
Sits 1 hour

For about 60 rounds
300 grams (1¼ cups) water
10 grams (2½ teaspoons) yeast
100 grams (¾ cup) wheat flour high in
    protein, preferably stone ground
170 grams (1⅔ cups) fine rye flour
95 grams (¾ cup) coarse rye flour
90 grams (½ cup + 2 tablespoons) barley
    flour
18 grams (3 teaspoons) sea salt
20 grams (1½ tablespoons) butter

Egg mixture
1 egg
a pinch of salt

For sprinkling
sunflower seeds
sesame seeds
lentils
pumpkin seeds

1. Dissolve the yeast in the water with a whisk and pour it over all the other ingredients. Knead at lowest speed for 15 minutes.
2. Put the dough in a lightly oiled plastic container covered with a lid to rest for 1 hour.
3. Push together the dough and divide it into 2 equal pieces. Roll them out with a little flour as thinly as possible on 2 sheets of baking parchment. Prick the dough with a fork.
4. Brush with egg and sprinkle with seeds, lentils, and pumpkin seeds. Roll over with a rolling pin to make them stick in the dough.
5. Divide the dough using a ruler and a pastry wheel into 10 x 10-centimeter (4 x 4-inch) squares. Let them rise for 30 minutes.
6. Preheat the oven to 175°C (347°F) and bake the bread until golden brown for about 20–30 minutes. Break them apart and keep them dry.

See photograph on page 146.

Honey and oat crispbread

Honungs- och havreknäcke

A very tasty and aromatic crispbread with a mild flavor.

Dough temperature 28°C (82°F)
Sits 1 hour

For 11 rounds
Poolish
250 grams (1 cup) water
5 grams (1¼ teaspoons) yeast
50 grams (1.8 ounces) rye sourdough
    (see page 27)
25 grams (3½ teaspoons) honey
125 grams (1 cup) coarse rye flour, preferably
    stone ground

Mix all the ingredients and whisk into a very thick
batter. Let it rest at room temperature for 2 hours.

Combining (Bortgörning)
455 grams (1 pound) poolish
20 grams (5 teaspoons) yeast
15 grams (2½ teaspoons) sea salt
75 grams (5½ tablespoons) butter
250 grams (1¾ cups + 2 tablespoons) wheat flour high in protein
125 grams (1 cup) oat grains

1. Pour the poolish into a bowl, add the yeast, and whisk until dissolved. Add the other ingredients and knead into a dough for about 15 minutes at lowest speed.
2. Put the dough in a lightly oiled plastic container covered with a lid and let it rest for 1 hour.
3. Divide the dough into 80-gram (2.8-ounce) pieces. Tear them into round buns, cover with a cloth, and let them relax for 5 minutes.

4. Roll out the buns barely 2 millimeters (about ¹⁄₁₆ inch) thick with coarse rye flour and oat grains on trays covered with baking parchment. Prick the rounds well with a fork and let them rise for 30 minutes at room temperature.

5. Preheat the oven to 175°C (347°F).

6. Bake the rounds for about 10 minutes until golden brown. Keep them in an airtight container to keep from getting soft.

Top: Caraway crispbread with spelt wholemeal
Bottom left: Honey and oat crispbread
To the right: Rye crispbread with sourdough and fennel

Caraway crispbread with spelt wholemeal

Kumminknäcke med fullkornsdinkel

This delicious crispbread tastes of classic caraway.

Dough temperature 28°C (82°F)
Sits 1 hour

For 18 squares
Pre-dough (Fördeg)
500 grams (2 cups) milk
50 grams (4 tablespoons) yeast
375 grams (2 cups + 2 tablespoons) spelt wholemeal,
   preferably stone ground
10 grams (1½ tablespoons) whole caraway

Dissolve the yeast in the milk with a whisk and pour it over the spelt wholemeal and caraway. Knead for 8 minutes at lowest speed and put the dough in a lightly oiled plastic container covered with a lid. Let it rest for 30 minutes.

Combining (Bortgörning)
935 grams (2 pounds 1 ounce) pre-dough
25 grams (3½ teaspoons) honey
20 grams (3½ teaspoons) sea salt
5 grams (1 teaspoon) cloudberry salt
125 grams (9 tablespoons) butter
375 grams (2¾ cups) sifted spelt wheat flour, preferably stone-ground

1. Knead the pre-dough with the other ingredients for 12 minutes and put it back in the container to rise for 1 hour.
2. Divide the dough into 80-gram (2.8-ounce) pieces, tear them into buns, and cover them with a cloth. Let them relax for 5 minutes.
3. Roll out the buns into 24-centimeter (9½-inch) round wheels. Prick them with a patterned rolling pin and make a small hole in the middle with a cookie cutter. Let them rise on a floured cloth or table for 30 minutes.
4. Preheat the oven to 175°C (347°F) and place a baking stone or tray inside.
5. Bake the crispbread directly on the stone or tray for about 8 minutes until quite dark. You can also turn them while baking. See photograph on page 145.

Lemon crispbread with Kamut flour and olive oil

Citronknäcke med kamutmjöl och olivolja

Mediterranean-inspired bread with the fresh taste of lemon. Good for dipping in hummus, guacamole, or tapenade.

Dough temperature 28°C (82°F)
Sits 1 hour

Top: Barley crispbread
Bottom: Lemon crispbread

For about 60 squares
Poolish
500 grams (2 cups) milk
50 grams (4 tablespoons) yeast
375 grams (2¾ cups) whole Kamut wheat
  flour
10 grams (1½ tablespoons) whole anise
  seeds

Dissolve the yeast in the milk with a whisk. Add half of the flour and whisk into a pancake-like batter. Add the rest of the flour and whisk until a little bit tough. Add the anise. Let rest and rise for 2 hours at room temperature.

Combining (Bortgörning)
935 grams (2 pounds 1 ounce) poolish
25 grams (3½ teaspoons) honey
20 grams (2⅓ teaspoons) sea salt

2 lemons, only zest (about 10 grams)
100 grams (½ cup) olive oil
5 grams (1 teaspoon) cloudberry salt
375 grams (2¾ cups) wheat flour high in protein
200 grams (1⅔ cups) polenta

Egg mixture
1 egg
a pinch of salt

1. Mix all the ingredients except for the polenta and knead for about 12 minutes at lowest speed. Put the dough in a lightly oiled plastic container. Let it rest for 1 hour.
2. Divide the dough in half and roll it out as thinly as possible on 2 sheets of baking parchment. Brush with the egg mix, sprinkle with polenta, and divide the dough with a ruler and a pastry wheel into 10 x 10-centimeter (4 x 4-inch) squares. Let them rise at room temperature for 30 minutes.
3. Preheat the oven to 175°C (347°F).
4. Bake the squares for about 25–30 minutes until golden brown. Keep them dry in an airtight jar.

Rye crispbread with sourdough and fennel

Rågknäcke med surdeg och fänkål

A slightly acidic crispbread with the perfect amount of seasoning. Bake it well until quite dark.

Dough temperature 28°C (82°F)
Sits 1 hour

For about 20 rounds
Poolish
500 grams (2 cups) milk
50 grams (12½ teaspoons) yeast
375 grams (2¾ cups) coarse rye flour,
  preferably stone ground
10 grams (5 teaspoons) whole fennel seeds

Dissolve the yeast in the milk with a whisk. Add half of the flour and whisk into a pancake-like batter. Add the rest of the flour and fennel, and whisk until the batter gets a little bit tough. Let it rest at room temperature for 2 hours.

Combining (Bortgörning)
935 grams (2 pounds 1 ounce) poolish
25 grams (3½ teaspoons) honey

20 grams (2⅓ teaspoons) sea salt
5 grams (1 teaspoon) cloudberry salt
100 grams (7 tablespoons) butter
150 grams (5.3 ounces) rye sourdough (see page 27)
450 grams (4½ cups) sifted rye, preferably stone ground

1. Mix all the ingredients and knead into a dough at lowest speed for 12 minutes.
2. Put the dough in a lightly oiled plastic container covered with a lid and let it rest for 1 hour.
3. Divide the dough into 80-gram (2.8-ounce) pieces and tear them into round buns. Cover with a cloth and let relax for 5 minutes.
4. Roll out the buns into round loaves, 24 centimeters (9½ inches) in diameter, with a coarse rye flour. Put them on a floured board and let them rise for 30 minutes.
5. Preheat the oven to 175°C (347°F) and place a baking stone or tray inside.
6. Put the rounds directly onto the hot stone or tray with a baker's peel and bake them for about 8–10 minutes until quite dark.
7. When all rounds are baked, put them in a turned-off oven to dry. Store them dry in jars with lids to keep them from getting soft.
   See photograph on page 145.

Classic brioche dough

Klassisk briochedeg

This dough was named after the region Brie in France. Brioche buns should taste good from the butter without feeling greasy. It is important to work the dough until it is completely elastic before adding the butter and that the dough temperature does not go above 25°C (77°F). A proper brioche is characterized by an airy inside with a textured crumb, achieved by allowing the dough to rise for a long time, as well as pushing the air out of the dough. It is interesting to compare the 2 methods and see which dough you like the best. Personally I cannot make my mind up.

For classic brioche buns, brush 20 ruffled baking tins (you can get them in kitchenware stores) with butter. For a brioche loaf, use a classic 2-liter (½ gallon) brioche pan.

Dough temperature 23–24°C (73–75°F)
Sits 2 hours + 12–15 hours in refrigerator

250 grams egg (about 5 eggs)
20 grams (5 teaspoons) yeast
500 grams (3⅔ cups) wheat flour high in protein
20 grams (3⅓ teaspoons) *fleur de sel*
60 grams (5 tablespoons) granulated sugar
375 grams (3⅓ sticks) unsalted butter

DAY 1

1. Dissolve the yeast in the eggs with a small whisk. Pour the flour, salt, and sugar into a bowl and pour in the egg mixture. Knead into a tough and elastic dough at lowest speed for 15 minutes or by hand for 20 minutes. You should be able to stretch out a thin film of the dough between your fingers. Test the dough and make sure that it does not burst but that the gluten stretches well. Keep kneading until it does.
2. Add the butter a little at a time in 4 turns. Knead the dough until it is shiny and smooth between the turns.
3. Increase the speed and knead into a smooth and elastic dough.
4. Pour the dough into a lightly oiled plastic container covered with a lid and let it rise until doubled in size in the kitchen heat for about 2 hours.

5. Push together the dough (see page 36) and work it until shiny again with your hands. Put the dough back in the container and put it in the refrigerator for at least 12–24 hours (15 hours is ideal).

DAY 2

1. *For brioche buns:* Measure 800 grams (1 pound 12 ounces) of dough, roll it out with wheat flour into a long piece, and divide it into 40-gram (1.4-ounce) pieces. Roll into round buns. Put them on their sides and roll with your palm until ⅔ of the whole bun turns into a ball. Press the dough into the tins with the big ball facing down. Press the tiny ball down, or it will fall over in the oven.
   For a brioche loaf: Divide 600 grams (1 pound 5 ounces) of brioche dough into 4 equal pieces and roll into big round buns. Brush a big pan with soft butter, put 3 balls in the bottom, and press 1 more down in the middle. Or take ⅓ of the dough and roll it into a ball (called the head or *tête*). Turn the rest of the dough into a bigger bun and put it in the pan. Make a deep dent with your fingers and put in the little ball.
2. Brush the brioche with beaten egg with a pinch of salt. Do not brush so much that it runs into the pans causing the brioche to stick and not rise as much in the oven. Let it rise at room temperature or in a turned-off oven until doubled in size, for about 90 minutes for a big brioche and 1 hour for the buns.
3. Preheat the oven to 220°C (428°F) and brush the brioche lightly with egg again. Make 6 cuts with scissors around the big brioche. Do not cut the buns. Put a tray in the oven so that it is warm when the breads are put in; this way they will rise more evenly.
4. Bake the brioche until golden brown, the big loaf for 45–50 minutes and the buns for 8–9 minutes (make sure with a thermometer that the large brioche keeps an internal temperature of 98°C / 208°F so that it is completely baked and does not collapse). Turn the bread out of the pan immediately and let cool on a rack.

Alsace Brioche

Brioche på Alsacevis

The region of Alsace keeps its traditions, even if the brioche comes from a different region, namely Brie. I remember a visit to the restaurant Le Crocodile in Strasbourg where Emile Jung served a fantastic warm brioche with pilgrim oysters and foamy champagne sauce topped with Russian caviar. Brioche bread can be used in many ways. It is a classic accompaniment for goose or duck liver with Sauternes jelly on the side.

Remember to use eggs from free-range hens who have had a good life. Butter becomes airiest when stirred at 20°C (68°F) and creates the most volume in dough at room temperature. A brioche dough must not become warmer than 25°C (77°F), and in the summer you might have to use refrigerated eggs and sometimes cooled flour.

Because of the large amount of eggs in the dough, you can use a lot of butter without it feeling or tasting greasy. The lecithin in the yolk makes the egg capable of binding so much butter.

Adding a yolk at the end improves the distribution of fat and makes the dough become velvet smooth. This dough is a little lighter than a classic brioche dough.

Dough temperature 23–24°C (73–75°F)
Sits 2 hours + 12–15 hours in refrigerator

25 grams (1²⁄₃ tablespoons) milk
20 grams (5 teaspoons) yeast
500 grams (3²⁄₃ cups) wheat flour high in
    protein
20 grams (3½ teaspoons) *fleur de sel*
50 grams (4 tablespoons) granulated sugar
275 grams egg (about 5–6 eggs)
500 grams (4½ sticks) unsalted butter
20 grams egg yolk (about 1 yolk)

DAY 1

The same preparation as for classic brioche, except the yeast is dissolved in milk and is mixed with the eggs at the end. Add a yolk after the butter has been worked in.

DAY 2

Put the dough on a lightly floured table and fold it together like a package. Continue as with classic brioche.

Pan bread or Brioche Nanterre

Formbröd eller Brioche Nanterre

The best toast in the world! A classic breakfast, and an absolute must with duck liver terrine.

Each loaf requires 400 grams (1¾ cups) of dough, and both versions are good. Butter ordinary sponge cake pans (23 x 9 centimeters / 9 x 3½ inches) or aluminum pans with soft butter. Divide the dough into 4 100-gram (3.5-ounce) pieces and roll them like hot dog buns. Put them in the pans and let them rise like a regular brioche.

Brush with the egg mixture and make a cut in the middle to keep the dough from splitting open. Bake for 35 minutes and make sure that the bread's internal temperature is 98°C (208°F).

You can make buns or braid the loaves into pan bread to break up the gluten strings. This way the bread becomes softer inside than a bread in which all the gluten strings run in the same direction.

Mayonnaise

Majonnäs

Keep in mind that the oil and egg yolk should be kept at room temperature, otherwise the mayonnaise will curdle. If it curdles anyway, whisk in another yolk. A shrimp sandwich with a good bread, proper mayonnaise with a boiled egg, lemon, and fresh dill is a real treat for any sandwich lover. You can also make good mayonnaise with half light, mild olive oil and half rapeseed oil.

40 grams egg yolk (about 2 yolks)
1 teaspoon light Dijon mustard
fleur de sel and freshly ground white pepper
250 milliliters (1 cup) rapeseed oil
1 teaspoon white wine vinegar
1 teaspoon pressed lemon juice

Whisk the yolks with the mustard and a little bit of salt and pepper into an even batter. Put the bowl on a wet towel and add the oil drop by drop while constantly whisking until all the oil is absorbed. Add the vinegar and lemon juice and salt and pepper to taste. Keep in a jar in the refrigerator.

My version of Toast Skagen with homemade mayonnaise

Toast Skagen på mitt sätt med hemgjord majonnäs

Werner Vögeli and Tore Wretman, who created this popular toast, have been incredibly important to Swedish food culture. Everybody likes this great toast. I always cut a slice of brioche bread, fry it until golden brown in clarified butter, and let it drain a little on a paper towel.

Mix fresh newly peeled shrimp with a little bit of mayonnaise to hold it together and season with a little bit of finely chopped dill and grated horseradish. Put a healthy spoonful of shrimp on the warm bread and a big spoonful of well-drained white fish roe on top. Garnish with dill and a piece of lemon (never with twisted lemon slices; they are impossible to press). With this meal I prefer to drink Jubileum snaps and a cold beer.

Brioche *feuilletée*

Rolled brioche dough can be used for many delicious breads. Here I have chosen to use it as a garnish for lobster soup.

250 grams (2¼ sticks) unsalted butter, cold
900 grams (4 cups) classic brioche dough, cold
sesame seeds
flake salt

1. Beat the butter until smooth. Put greaseproof paper on top and hit it with a rolling pin. Roll out the brioche dough until it is twice as large as the butter.
2. Fold in the butter and roll out the dough about 8 millimeters (about ⅓ inch) thick with wheat flour and a rolling pin. Brush away any excess flour and quadruple-fold it: Roll out the dough like when triple-folding (see page 183). Fold in the dough from both sides so that it meets in the middle. Press down a little bit on the middle and fold the dough double. Wrap the dough in plastic wrap and put it in the refrigerator to rest for 30 minutes.
3. Roll out the dough the same way one more time and let rest in the refrigerator again for 30 minutes.
4. Roll the dough 20 millimeters (¾ inch) thick and cut it into 60-gram (2-ounce) pieces, 1½ centimeters (½ inch) wide. Twist them with both hands like in the photograph and brush them with the egg mixture. Sprinkle with sesame seeds and flake salt. Put them on baking parchment and let them rise for 1½–2 hours at 25°C (77°F) (room temperature).
5. Preheat the oven to 220°C (428°F).
6. Bake the brioche for about 12–15 minutes until golden brown. Let cool on rack.

Apple brioche

Äppelbriocher

1 recipe classic brioche dough

Almond cream (see page 199)

Apple slices

Egg mixture
1 egg
1 egg yolk
a pinch of salt

Cinnamon sugar (see page 158)

Apricoture
100 grams (5 tablespoons) apricot jam,
    strained
25 grams (6 teaspoons) granulated sugar
25 grams (1½ tablespoons) water
25 grams (5 teaspoons) lemon juice

Cook on low heat until it starts to turn into jelly. Pour a little bit onto a plate, test, and see that the jam stiffens and does not stick when you touch it.

1. Tear 50-gram (1.8-ounce) buns from the brioche dough and put a cloth over them. Let relax for 10 minutes.
2. Flatten the buns with your hand and press down a hollow with a spice jar. Put them on a tray covered with baking parchment. Pour 10 grams (2 teaspoons) almond cream in each bun with a piping bag or with a teaspoon. Brush all over with the egg mixture.
3. Put on 5-millimeter (¼-inch) thick peeled apple slices, preferably Belle de Boskoop or Gravensteiner. Sprinkle a little bit of cinnamon sugar on top and let them rise in a warm place until doubled in size for about 1–1½ hours.
4. Preheat the oven to 225°C (437°F).
5. Bake the bread until golden brown for about 12–15 minutes. Brush them right after baking with warm apricoture. Let cool on a rack. Preferably served with a glass of calvados.

Raspberry brioche

Follow the directions for apple brioche, but put in 4–5 raspberries instead of the apple slice. Brush with cooked red currant jelly immediately after baking.

Walnut caramel brioche

Follow the directions for apple brioche, but sprinkle 4 walnut halves over the almond cream and a teaspoon of cassonade sugar on top. Let rise and bake in the same way until walnut caramel starts to form on top.

Asian brioche

My good friend Eric Rowcliffe came to visit from the USA and was full of ideas, contributing enthusiastically to this book. Eric is a clever gastronomist with a great understanding of baking and cooking.

These recipes are inspired by pastries served in China and Japan, often with tea. Eric recommends them with a red pu'er tea. The black sesame filling goes with a stronger tea, like Lapsang Souchong.

Fillings:

Lotus flowers

You can find lotus seed puree in jars at assorted Asian stores. Alternatively, you can soak dried lotus seeds, cook them until soft, and then mix them in a food processor with equal parts Chinese brown sugar or light Muscovado sugar.

Black sesame seeds

Grind black sesame seeds in an electric crush grinder into a fine paste. Mix it with equal parts Chinese brown sugar or Muscovado sugar.

Adzuki (sweet red beans)

You can find ready-made Adzuki puree in Asian stores.

Roll out 400-gram (14-ounce) pieces of brioche dough and cut them into 10 pieces. Tear them into round buns, put them on a cloth, and let portions relax for 5 minutes.

Roll out the pieces to the size of saucers with a little bit of wheat flour. Put a ball of 10 grams (about 2 teaspoons) of the filling in the middle and pinch around the dough like a bun. Put them with the seam facing downward on a tray with baking parchment. Brush with egg mixture and make cuts in the dough with scissors like in the photograph on page 155. Let them rise like regular brioche buns, bake them in the same way, and serve them a little bit warm with a good tea.

In the photograph on page 155, the round one is filled with lotus flowers and cut all the way around like a lotus flower. One of the long ones contains a black sesame seed paste and is also garnished with black sesame seeds. The other one is filled with adzuki puree.

Asian brioche

On the plate from the left: Raspberry brioche, walnut caramel brioche, apple brioche, in the middle natural brioche

pastries

Kaffebröd (coffee bread) is the common Swedish term for sweet bread, Karlsbader pastries, Danish breads (*Wiener/Viennoiserie*), doughnuts, and other pastries that are consumed with good, freshly brewed coffee.

During the late 17th century, coffee became popular in Europe. Coffee was first imported to Sweden in 1685, and it soon became a trendy high society beverage. The ready-roasted coffee became popular in the 1920s, and many pastry shops and cafés opened around this time. Home bakeries mostly made pastries and soft French rolls (since they had no steam in their ovens) in addition to rolls, biscuits, French bread, and "hole cakes."

Berliner doughnuts

Berlinermunkar

When I was a boy, I loved Berliner doughnuts. My mother and grandmother usually bought them at Rosberg's home bakery. These classic deep-fried pastries, known as *Boule de Berlin* in France and *Berliner Pfannkuchen* in Germany, should always contain a lot of egg yolk for the dough to become light and airy. At Confiserie Zoo, we added a little dark rum to the dough. Nobody could make better Berliner doughnuts than these, I assure you. You can fill them with raspberry jam, apricot marmalade, or with applesauce, which is the most common in Sweden. It is important to make a pre-dough to get the nice brim around it and to make them light and airy.

These were the pastries that President John F. Kennedy unintentionally referred to in Berlin when he exclaimed *"Ich bin ein Berliner."*

For about 30 doughnuts
DAY 1
Raspberry jam
1,000 grams (4 cups) raspberries
800 grams (4 cups) granulated sugar
1 lemon, yellow and ripe, about 60 grams (4 tablespoons) juice

Mix the raspberries and sugar with the lemon juice and cook it up in a spacious pot (preferably copper). Pour it into a plastic bucket and let cool. Put it in the refrigerator until the next day.

DAY 2
1. Cook the berry paste at as high a heat as possible for about 20 minutes. Stir occasionally. Brush the brim down every now and then with a brush dipped in cold water and take any foam off of the surface with a cream ladle.
2. Make a jam test on a cold plate: Run your finger through a pat of jam without it flowing out. Raspberry jam is usually

ready at 105–107°C (221–225°F), depending on whether the berries are ripe (preferably use frozen berries). It is usually ready at 105°C (221°F). Pour it immediately into jars heated in the oven to 80–100°C (176–212°F). Fill them to the brim and immediately shut the lids. Turn the jars upside down and let them sit until the next day. This is 3 times as much as you need for the doughnuts, but when you have tried it you will be glad that you made as much as you did at once.

DAY 3
Dough temperature 28°C (82°F)
Sits 50 minutes

For about 28–30 doughnuts
Pre-dough (Fördeg)
175 grams (¾ cup) milk
25 grams (4 teaspoons) yeast
250 grams (1¾ cups) wheat flour high in protein

Heat the milk lightly to 35°C (95°F). Crumble in the yeast and whisk until dissolved. Stir in the flour and work for at least 5 minutes into an elastic dough, by hand or with a machine. Cover it with plastic wrap and put it in a draft-free place at room temperature to rise until doubled in size. It takes about 30–40 minutes.

TIP: For an even wider white brim around the doughnuts, you can mix the pre-dough with cold milk and let it sit for 12 hours in the refrigerator instead of at room temperature. The master pastry chef Georg Maushagen in Düsseldorf always used this method.

Combining (Bortgörning)
450 grams (1 pound) pre-dough
250 grams (1¾ cups) wheat flour high in
    protein
150 grams egg yolk (about 7 yolks)
50 grams (¼ cup) granulated sugar
10 grams (2½ teaspoons) real vanilla sugar
4 centileter (2 ⅔ tablespoons) dark rum
zest of 1 lemon
150 grams (1⅓ sticks) unsalted butter
10 grams (1⅔ teaspoons) *fleur de sel* or
    sea salt

1 fryer or a 4-liter (1-gallon) pot
1 liter (4½ cups) frying oil

raspberry jam for filling

Cinnamon sugar
100 grams (½ cup) granulated sugar
5 grams (1¼ teaspoons) real vanilla sugar
10 grams (3¾ teaspoons) cinnamon

1. Mix the pre-dough with all the other ingredients for about 20 minutes into an elastic and tough dough. You should be able to stretch the dough thinly when it is ready.
2. Put the dough in a lightly oiled plastic container covered with a lid and let it rise for 30 minutes.
3. Push the dough on the baking table so that the air comes out (see page 36). Fold it together like a pillow, with the seam facing downward in the plastic container and let rest for another 20 minutes.
4. Push out the air one more time and let the dough relax for 10 minutes. (In Switzerland we always pushed the dough twice to make it completely elastic and shiny.)
5. Roll out the dough with a little wheat flour and cut it into buns with a dough scraper. They should weigh 40 grams (1.4 ounces) each. Roll them into round buns.
6. Sift a little wheat flour over a tray covered in baking parchment. Put the buns on it, cover them with a baking cloth, and let them rise for about 1 hour to double their size.
7. Heat the oil to 180°C (356°F). Always use a thermometer when frying to make sure that you do not burn the fat.
8. Put in 3–4 doughnuts at a time. Fry them for 2 minutes on one side until golden brown. Turn with a fork and fry the other side. Take them out with a cream ladle and let them drain on paper towels or an oven rack. To make sure that they are done all the way through, put in a thermometer and check that the internal temperature is 97–98°C (207–208°F).
9. Fill a piping bag with the jam and fill the doughnuts by pushing the cornet into one side.
10. Mix the sugar and vanilla sugar with the ground cinnamon and turn the doughnuts in it. Serve as freshly baked as possible. If you have any doughnuts left, freeze them in a plastic bag. Heat frozen doughnuts carefully in a microwave oven, and keep in mind that the jam is warm so that you do not burn your tongue. Strong good coffee or a glass of German sweet *Eiswein* goes well will this.

Pine cones

Grankottar

Variation of Berliner doughnuts
For Christmas I usually season the dough with 3 grams (1½ tablespoons) of crushed saffron, shape the buns into cones, and roll them into little pieces that are long and narrow. Let them rise until 75% bigger in volume and cut them with scissors to make them look like pinecones. Let them leaven, and fry and fill them with the same jam, but dust them lightly with powdered sugar instead of cinnamon sugar. They become both tasty and beautiful.

Cramique and Craquelin

Cramique och Craquelin

These Belgian specialties taste excellent for breakfast with a *café au lait*, and preferably in Brussels at Hotel Metropols cafe, which is great for sitting and people-watching. The hotel is old with a lovely atmosphere.

Cramique is filled with juicy raisins, and with a layer of extra-salted butter it becomes a perfect bread for breakfast. *Craquelin* is made from the same dough, but with crackly sugar crumbs inside, which makes it a true delicacy at the breakfast table or for afternoon coffee.

Pâtisserie Wittamer in Place du Sablon with Paul Wittamer makes the best *Cramique* and *Craquelin* in Brussels. When you are there, try their almond-financier. Great quiche with various fillings and fresh salads are served on the second floor.

Dough temperature 28°C (82°F)
Sits 1 hour

For 2 loaves
480 grams (2 cups) milk
50 grams (8⅓ teaspoons) yeast
1,000 grams (7⅓ cups) wheat flour high in
    protein, preferably stone ground
120 grams egg yolk (about 6 yolks)
20 grams (1 tablespoon) sea salt
40 grams (3 tablespoons) granulated sugar
300 grams (2⅝ sticks) regular salted butter,
    at room temperature

For cramique
450 grams (3 cups) Californian raisins,
    soaked for 30 minutes in cold water and
    drained

For craquelin
400 grams (2¼ cups) sugar cubes, coarsely
    crushed with a rolling pin
50 grams (3½ tablespoons) melted butter

Egg mixture
1 egg
1 egg yolk
a pinch of salt

1. Dissolve the yeast in the milk with a whisk. Add 750 grams (5½ cups) of the flour and the egg yolks and mix the dough at lowest speed for 4 minutes. Cover the dough with plastic wrap and let it sit and rise in a warm place for 30 minutes.
2. Add the rest of the flour and the salt, sugar, and butter. Mix the dough at lowest speed for another 6 minutes. Add sugar and butter when making *craquelin*. Increase the speed and run it for about 6 more minutes. Make a gluten test (see page 35) and see if the dough is elastic and stretches without breaking.
3. For *cramique*, knead the raisins into the dough. Put the dough in an oiled plastic container covered with a lid and let it sit for 30 minutes.
4. Put the dough on a floured baking table and push the air out of it (see page 36). Fold the dough together and put it in the plastic container for another 30 minutes.
5. Divide the dough into 450-gram (15.9-ounce) pieces, tear them into round buns, cover them with a cloth, and let them rest for 10 minutes.
6. Shape into long loaves. Brush them with the egg mixture and put them in greased long 2-liter (½-gallon) pans. Let rise at maximum 28°C (82°F) until they run over the edges of the pans. Preheat the oven to 190–200°C (374–392°F).
7. Brush the loaves carefully one more time with the egg mixture. Let them sit for 5 minutes and make a few incisions with a sharp knife.
8. Bake for about 35–40 minutes until golden brown. Loosen them from the pans and put them in the oven without a pan for 5 minutes so that they do not collapse in the sides, which pan-baked bread tends to do. Let cool on an oven rack.

Gâteau de Savoie

I usually include a soft cake in my books because it reminds me of grandmother and mother, and emits a certain sense of security. This one is a light, soft French sponge cake that is very dear to me. It is both tasty and easy to make. It freezes well too, which we often take advantage of at my house.

Madame Perlia at the Coba school in Basel, married to the principal Julius Perlia, often baked this cake on Fridays for our strong afternoon coffee to keep us awake during classes in writing and drawing. At Julius Perlia's house, it was often served with a cold *crème anglaise* and a little compote of, for example, strawberries.

For 8 portions

a 2-liter (½-gallon) round pan, 20 centimeters (8 inches) in diameter (the classic model has ruffled edges)

25 grams (1¾ tablespoons) soft butter, to butter the pan

wheat flour, to flour the pan

150 grams (1 cup) wheat flour (regular wheat flour, not enriched)

1 ripe yellow lemon

1 ripe orange

120 grams egg yolk (about 6 yolks)

110 grams (½ cup) granulated sugar

1 gram (2 or 3 dashes) *fleur de sel*

10 grams (2½ teaspoons) real vanilla sugar

180 grams egg white (about 6 whites)

10 grams (2 teaspoons) pressed lemon juice

30 grams (2½ tablespoons) granulated sugar

1. Preheat the oven to 190°C (374°F). Butter the pan with the soft butter using a brush. Flour it inside and shake out excess flour.
2. Sift the wheat flour through a fine sieve on a baking sheet. Wash and grate lemon and orange peel with a fine grater.
3. Pour the egg yolk, sugar, salt, and vanilla sugar into an absolutely clean metal bowl. Add the orange and lemon peel. Whisk with a mixer into a firm foam at medium speed or by hand with a strong balloon whisk. Put aside.
4. Clean a metal bowl with vinegar and salt to get rid of any lingering fat, rinse it out with cold water, and let the water run off without drying the bowl. Pour the egg whites and lemon juice into it. Whisk at medium speed with a mixer or with manual force using a balloon whisk. When the egg white rises and the foam starts to get firm, add the sugar, increase the speed, and whisk into a firm foam.
5. Fold the egg yolk foam gently into the meringue with a spatula. Add the wheat flour and fold it in carefully so that the foam keeps its air.
6. Pour the batter into the pan and pull it toward the edge to straighten the cake.
7. Put the cake in the oven and bake it for 20–25 minutes, and check it by poking it with a stick to see if it is ready. If the stick is dry, the cake is done.
8. Take it out of the oven and let it sit for 5 minutes to set. Turn it onto an oven rack to cool.

Bremer Butterkuchen

I recently spoke with pastry chef Hans Eichmüller about this cake. I had it served warm like a petit four at the nice restaurant Fischereihafen in Hamburg after attending a lecture about Olof Viktor's bakery in Glemminge. Hans told me that during his time as an apprentice at the pastry chef Stecker's in Bremen, he was famous in all of Germany for his *butterkuchen*. He started as an apprentice at age 13 and passed his journeyman exam when he was 19. Those were different times, I can assure you.

This cake is good for freezing. Heat it up just before serving. If you do not have any pans, simply roll the dough onto a tray covered in baking parchment and make them square instead.

For 2 cakes
Dough temperature 27°C (81°F)
Sits 1 hour

Fondant
100 grams (½ cup) water
250 grams (1¼ cups) granulated sugar
50 grams (2¼ tablespoons) glucose

1. Pour the water and sugar into a small pot. Whisk the sugar until dissolved. Put the pot on low heat. Let it sit until the syrup is boiling.
2. Dip a brush in cold water and brush down the crystals that stick to the inside of the pot. Skim off any foam with a tea strainer. Add the glucose and keep cooking while constantly brushing down the inside of the pot.
3. Cook until 118°C (244°F) or make an alternative test, a ball test or caramel test: Dip your fingers in cold water, grab some of the caramel, and put it in cold water until you can shape a loose ball. But if you are not inclined, I recommend that you get a sugar thermometer.
4. Pour the syrup water out onto a covered surface, preferably a marble plate or a thoroughly cleaned counter. Sprinkle cold water onto the surface to keep the syrup from forming a crust.
5. After 5 minutes, when the fondant has cooled, you can start working it with a spatula until the glaze starts to whiten.
6. Put the glaze in a bowl, and splash a little water on the surface. Put on a tight lid and keep it in the refrigerator. If it hardens too much, just heat it in a microwave oven until soft.

Butter filling
500 grams (4½ sticks) butter, room temperature
300 grams (1⅓ cups) fondant

Stir the butter into the fondant until light and foamy.

German sweet bread dough, called *süssteig* (lighter consistency than our Swedish sweet bread dough):

Pre-dough (Fördeg)
250 grams (1 cup) milk
40 grams (10 teaspoons) yeast
350 grams (2½ cups) wheat flour high in protein

Dissolve the yeast in the milk with a whisk and pour it over the flour. Knead at lowest speed for about 10 minutes. Put the dough in a lightly oiled plastic container covered with a lid and let it rise in a warm place for about 30–35 minutes until doubled in volume.

Combining (Bortgörning)
640 grams (1 pound 6.6 ounces) pre-dough
50 grams eggs (about 1 egg)
225 grams (1⅔ cups) wheat flour high in protein
1 lemon, only the zest
40 grams (3 tablespoons) granulated sugar
10 grams (1⅔ teaspoons) sea salt
65 grams (4½ tablespoons) butter
2 baking trays with an edge or 2 pans, 24 centimeters (9½ inches) in diameter
50 grams (3½ tablespoons) butter, for buttering the pans
50 grams (4 tablespoons) granulated sugar, to sprinkle on top of cakes
50 grams (½ cup) almond shavings

Egg mixture
1 egg
1 egg yolk
a pinch of salt

1. Put the pre-dough in a bowl and add the eggs, flour, lemon zest, sugar, and salt. Knead at low speed for 5–6 minutes. Add the butter in small pieces, increase the speed, and knead the dough for about another 10 minutes until elastic. Make a gluten test (see page 35).

2. Put the dough in a lightly oiled plastic container covered with a lid and let it rise for 30 minutes.

3. Put the dough on a floured baking table, push it together (see page 36), and fold it like a pillow. Put it back in the container to rise for another 30 minutes.

4. Divide the dough in half, fold it together into 2 square pieces, and let it relax for 10 minutes.

5. Butter the trays or pans with soft butter using a brush. Flour them inside and shake out any excess flour.

6. Roll the dough into the size of the pan with a rolling pin and a little wheat flour. Roll up the dough on a rolling pin, roll it out over the pan, and push until it sits evenly in the pan. Repeat the process with the other half of the dough.

Brush with the egg mixture.

7. Put the butter filling in a piping bag with a small, smooth tulle, or cut a small hole in the front with scissors. Push the tulle into the dough and distribute all of the filling in pats throughout all of the dough. Sprinkle with sugar and almond shavings.

8. Leave the cakes to rise in a warm place for about 1 hour until doubled in volume.

9. Preheat the oven to 230°C (446°F).

10. Bake the cakes for about 15–18 minutes until golden brown. Let them cool a little, divide them into squares, and serve immediately with good coffee.

Buchteln

We made this Austrian specialty every week for our Bavarian nights with fried suckling and *Sauerkraut*, *Knödeln*, and *weisswürst* aboard the cruise ships *Vista/Fjord* and *Saga/Fjord*. Afterward we always served warm *Kaiserschmarren* with plum sauce and *Topfenknödel* and *Buchteln* filled with apricot jam, and finally fresh-baked *Apfelstrudel* with vanilla sauce.

   These light, tart, warm delicacies with cold vanilla sauce work nicely after horseradish meat, known as *Tafelspitz* in Austria, or a good *Wienerschnitzel*. Austrian desserts are often delicious but sometimes need to be lightened a little for our time and taste. This light and delicious dough is a result of this. When in Vienna, try to visit Kur-Café Oberla, where you will have fantastic pastries by Karl Schumacher. Alhough Karl is no longer participating in the production, his legacy still lives.

Dough temperature 27°C (81°F)
Sits 1 hour in room temperature +
   12 hours in the refrigerator

For 27 buns (9 portions)
DAY 1
Apricot jam, strained (also known in Austria as Marillen Marmelade and also used to apricoture pastries)
For about 1,500 grams (6²/₃ cups) jam

1 decileter (about ½ cup) water
6 bitter almonds
2 liters (about ½ gallon) water
1,200 grams (34) fresh apricots, fully ripe
3 deciliters (about 1¼ cups) water
60 grams (¼ cup) pressed lemon juice
1 vanilla bean, preferably bourbon
800 grams (4 cups) granulated sugar

1. Fill a saucepan with the water and bring to a boil. Blanch/scald the almonds. Put them immediately in cold water and remove the peel. Crush them into a paste in a mortar.
2. Boil 2 liters (½ gallon) of water and scald the apricots for about 1 minute. Put them immediately in cold water and remove the peel with a knife. Divide them in half and pick out the pits.
3. Boil the water and add the scalded apricots, lemon juice, and bitter almond paste. Cook for about 10 minutes under a lid until the apricots are completely soft.

4. Pour into a mixer and mix the fruit paste in batches. Use a strainer to drain into a smooth puree.
5. Pour the puree back into the jam pot. Divide the vanilla bean lengthwise, scrape out the marrow with a small knife, and put it and the bean into the pot.
6. Add the sugar and keep cooking while constantly stirring. Skim off any foam with a spoon while cooking. Brush the edge inside the pot with a brush dipped in cold water to prevent sugar crystals from forming. Cook until 105°C (221°F), or make a jam test (see page 157). Immediately pour into sterilized jars and close the lids right away. Turn the jars upside down. Keep opened jars in the refrigerator.

Vanilla sauce (known as Kanariemilch in Vienna)
For about 7 deciliters (3 cups) sauce

1 vanilla bean, preferably Tahiti or bourbon from Madagascar
500 grams (2 cups) milk
120 grams egg yolk (about 6 yolks)
125 grams (½ cup + 2 tablespoons) granulated sugar

1. Divide the vanilla bean lengthwise. Scrape the seeds into a pot. Put in the bean, pour in the milk, and cook. Let it sit next to the stove for 10–15 minutes to absorb the flavor. Take out the bean.
2. Whisk the egg yolk and sugar for 4–5 minutes until thick and airy. Pour it into the warm milk, and stir thoroughly.
3. Pour the mixture back into the pot. Heat carefully while constantly stirring with a wooden ladle. Stir until the sauce starts to thicken; its temperature should be 85°C (185°F).
4. Strain the sauce into a cold bowl and cool the sauce in a cold water bath while stirring it. Cover with plastic wrap and keep in the refrigerator until served.

Pre-dough (Fördeg)
65 grams (¼ cup) milk
15 grams (3¾ teaspoons) yeast
100 grams (¾ cup) wheat flour high in protein, preferably stone ground

Dissolve the yeast in the milk at room temperature with a whisk. Add the flour and knead for 10 minutes at low speed. Cover with plastic wrap and let it rise at room temperature for 30 minutes.   ➤

Combining (Bortgörning)
180 grams (6.3 ounces) pre-dough
80 grams (6½ tablespoons) granulated sugar
10 grams (1⅔ teaspoons) sea salt
40 grams egg yolk (about 2 yolks)
200 grams eggs (about 4 eggs)
200 grams (¾ cup + 2 tablespoons) butter, at room
    temperature
400 grams (3 cups) wheat flour high in protein, preferably
    stone ground

1. Add the other ingredients to the pre-dough and knead the
   dough for about 12 minutes at low speed. Increase the
   speed and knead the dough for about another 5 minutes
   until completely elastic. Make a gluten test (see page 35).
2. Cover the dough with plastic wrap and let it sit at room
   temperature for 1 hour.
3. Put the dough on a floured baking table and push it
   together (see page 36). Fold it like an envelope and put it
   in a lightly oiled plastic container covered with a lid to rest
   in the refrigerator for 12 hours or until the next day.

DAY 2
50 grams (3½ tablespoons) butter to butter the pan

1. Weigh up the dough into 300-gram (10.6-ounce) pieces,
   divide them into 10 portions, and tear round buns and put
   them on a floured cloth. Cover with a cloth and let them
   relax for 10 minutes.
2. Dust the buns lightly with flour and roll them out like
   saucers with a rolling pin and a little wheat flour. Pipe with
   apricot jam using a paper cornet, about 15 grams (0.5
   ounce) on each saucer.
3. Pinch them together into buns and put them in a greased
   pan (about 25 x 32 centimeters/10 x 12½ inches) with the
   seam facing downward. Cover with plastic wrap and let
   them rise until doubled in size.
4. Bake at 190°C (374°F) for about 20 minutes, until the
   internal temperature is at 98°C (208°F). Dust with powdered
   sugar and serve 3 per person with vanilla sauce on plates.

Wiener Mohn-Beugel (poppy croissants)

Wiener Mohn-Beugel (vallmogifflar)

**These classic croissants are light and delicious and can
be varied with a nut filling (see page 192).**

**Served in the afternoon in Vienna, the best are made
at Hofsückerbäckerei Demel in Kohlmarksgasse. Do not
miss a visit there when you are in Vienna. At 4 PM it is
Jause, the Austrians' equivalent to British afternoon tea.**

**You can make them with this classic dough or a
Karlsbader or brioche dough instead.**

Dough temperature 26°C (79°F)
Sits 1 hour

For 35 croissants
Poppy filling
100 grams (⅔ cup) black poppy seeds
20 grams (3 tablespoons) bread crumbs
5 grams (2½ teaspoons) grated lemon peel
20 grams (2½ tablespoons) ground cinnamon
120 grams (½ cup) milk
40 grams (3 tablespoons) granulated sugar
15 grams (1 tablespoon) butter

1. Grind the poppy seeds in an electric coffee grinder or in a
   food processor with a jagged knife. Mix the poppy seeds
   and bread crumbs with the lemon peel and cinnamon.

2. Cook the milk, sugar, and butter and pour it over the poppy mixture. Scrape the paste back into the pot and cook while constantly stirring. Pour it into a mixer and make into a paste. Cover with plastic wrap and let it swell until the next day.

Dough (Deg)

500 grams (3⅔ cups) wheat flour high in protein, preferably stone ground
15 grams (2½ teaspoons) sea salt
50 grams (4 tablespoons) granulated sugar
60 grams egg yolk (about 3 yolks)
250 grams (1 cup) milk
25 grams (6¼ teaspoons) yeast
150 grams (⅔ cup) butter, at room temperature

Egg yolk mixture

80 grams egg yolk (about 4 yolks)
1 pinch of salt

1. Pour the flour, salt, sugar, and egg yolks into a bowl. Dissolve the yeast in the milk with a whisk and pour it into the bowl.
2. Knead at low speed for 5 minutes. Increase the speed, add the butter one portion at a time, and knead for about 10 minutes into a tough and elastic dough. The dough should be quite stiff.
3. Put the dough in a lightly oiled plastic container covered with a lid and let it rest for 30 minutes.
4. Put the dough on a floured baking table, push it together (see page 36), and fold it like an envelope. Put it back in the plastic container with the seam facing downward and let it rest for another 30 minutes.
5. Push together the dough one more time and let it relax for 10 minutes.
6. Divide the dough into 30-gram (1-ounce) pieces and tear them into round buns.
7. Divide the poppy paste into equal pieces like the buns (30 grams/1 ounce) and roll them into cylinders. Roll out the dough onto plates, 15 x 10 centimeters (6 x 4 inches), put one cylinder on each rolled-out piece, and roll them together into croissants. Roll them into 12–15-centimeter (4¼ x 6-inch) long peices, bend them as in the photograph, and put them on baking parchment.
8. Whisk the egg yolks with the salt and brush the croissants carefully with the egg yolk mixture. Let them dry for 15 minutes and brush them one more time. Let them rise until doubled in size, for 45–60 minutes, until they crackle properly.
9. Preheat the oven to 240°C (464°F).
10. Bake the croissants for about 12–15 minutes until golden brown. Let them cool on an oven rack and serve warm with Vienna coffee.

Almond panettone like at Honold's in Zürich

Mandel-panettone som hos Honold i Zürich

Swiss panettone is very popular in Lugano and Trieste. For Easter we used to bake panettone even in Zürich, and it went like hotcakes. For Christmas we used to make lots of Dresdner *Weihnachtsstollen* instead. Otherwise, rice-cake with butter dough was the pastry of choice in Switzerland for Easter.

Preferably use Italian yellow wheat flour, otherwise you will not get the bread as airy and light as the bread in Italy. You can usually find it in Italian gourmet stores, even in Sweden.

Dough temperature 28°C (82°F)
Sits 2 hours

For 20 portions
400 grams (2¾ cups) raisins
zest of 1 orange
zest of 1 lemon
300 grams (3 cups) chopped preserved
    orange peel
300 grams (3¼ cups) chopped peeled
    almonds

Soak the raisins in plenty of cold water for 30 minutes. Let them drain and mix with the citrus zest, orange peel, and almonds.

Pre-dough (Fördeg)
500 grams (2 cups) milk
75 grams (6 tablespoons) yeast
700 grams (5 cups) wheat flour high in
    protein, preferably stone ground
15 grams (2 teaspoons) honey

Dissolve the yeast in the milk with a whisk and pour it over the flour and honey. Knead at lowest speed for 8 minutes. Put the dough in a lightly oiled plastic container covered with a lid to rise for 30 minutes or until doubled in volume, depending on the temperature of the room.

Combining (Bortgörning)
125 grams (⅔ cup) granulated sugar
1 vanilla bean, bourbon
1,290 grams (2 pounds 13.5 ounces) pre-dough
350 grams (2½ cups) wheat flour high in protein, preferably stone ground
20 grams (3½ teaspoons) salt
100 grams egg yolk (about 5 yolks)
150 grams (10½ tablespoons) butter, at room temperature

1. Grind the sugar with the vanilla bean into a powder in a food processor and pour it into the pre-dough. Add all the other ingredients except the butter and knead at lowest speed for about 8 minutes.
2. Add the butter in batches and knead the dough at a higher speed for about 10 more minutes. Make a gluten test (see page 35). The dough should be completely tough and elastic.
3. Carefully knead the fruit mixture into the dough. Put it in a lightly oiled plastic container covered with a lid and let it rise for 1 hour.
4. Put the dough on a floured baking table and push it together (see page 36). Put it back into the container with the seam facing downward and let it sit for 1 hour.
5. Push out the air again and let the dough relax for 10 minutes.
6. Oil the table with a little rapeseed oil. Divide the dough into 150-gram (5.3-ounce) pieces and tear them into round buns. Put a cloth on top and let the dough relax for another 30 minutes.
7. Tear the dough into buns again and put them in 1½-deciliter (5-ounce) panettone pans or large muffin tins. Leave them to rise in a warm place until the dough starts to rise over the edges of the pan. Brush once with egg yolk and let them dry. Repeat the brushing and cut a cross with a sharp knife, and fold back the edges a little bit.
8. Preheat the oven to 170°C (338°F).
9. Put the tray with the panettone in the oven and bake them for about 30–35 minutes, checking with a thermometer that their internal temperature is 98°C (208°F). Let cool on an oven rack in the pans, lying on their sides to keep their volume.

Chocolate panettone

Choklad-panettone

This Italian specialty is fantastic, and I learned how to make it with apple yeast at Pasticceria Motta in Milan. Yellow Italian wheat flour makes the dough even more elastic, if you can get ahold of it, and makes the bread lighter and airier. The chocolate version is not too sweet. You can use any leftover starter for bread. It is not possible to make a smaller amount and get a good result.

Naturally, you can use levain made of raisins, apple, or sourdough instead. When in Brescia, do not miss a visit to Igino Massari on Via Salvo d'Aquisto 8. He is the best pastry chef in Italy.

Dough temperature 28°C (82°F)
Sits many hours

For 13 portions
DAY 1
Levain—natural starter
(This is more apple yeast than you need, but you cannot make a smaller amount because the fermentation activity would be too low)

100 grams (6½ tablespoons) raw apple
    puree
300 grams (2 cups) finely sifted graham
    flour
140 grams (½ cup + 2 tablespoons) water,
    30°C (86°F)

Blend the apples into a puree in a juicer or use a food processor and strain in a sieve until you have 100 grams (6½ tablespoons). Add the flour and water and mix into a dough. Put it in a plastic container covered with a lid and let it sit at room temperature until tripled in volume, which usually takes about 16 hours.

For the first kneading
260 grams (1 cup) water
110 grams (4 ounces) levain
500 grams (3⅔ cups) enriched wheat flour,
    or ideally yellow
Italian wheat flour
125 grams (½ cup + 2 tablespoons) granu-
    lated sugar
125 grams (1 stick) unsalted butter

Mix the water with the levain, flour, and sugar. Work at lowest speed for 2 minutes. Add the butter and work the dough at highest speed for 5 minutes. The dough should be completely smooth and dry. Let it rise at ideally 28°C (82°F) or in a turned-off oven for about 8 hours until tripled in volume.

DAY 2
Second kneading
50 grams (2½ tablespoons) Swedish honey
50 grams (4 tablespoons) granulated sugar
50 grams (3½ tablespoons) unsalted butter
5 grams (1¼ teaspoons) real vanilla sugar
240 grams egg yolk (about 12 yolks)
4 grams (⅔ teaspoon) salt, preferably *fleur de sel*
325 grams (1½ cups) chopped dark chocolate, 70% preferably
    Valrhona Grand Cru Guanaja
100 grams (7 tablespoons) chopped pickled orange peel

1. Mix all the ingredients except the chocolate and the orange peel with the first dough into a smooth and completely elastic dough, which takes about 10 minutes. You should be able to stretch out a very thin film of the dough. Then work in the chocolate and orange peel.
2. Oil the table with a little rapeseed oil and divide the dough into 150-gram (5.3-ounce) pieces. Tear into buns and cover them with a baking cloth for 30 minutes and let the dough relax.
3. Roll into buns again and put them in panettone pans or big muffin tins with the seam facing downward. Let them rise for about 3 hours at 28°C (82°F) or in a turned-off oven until the dough has come up to edge of the pan.
4. Preheat the oven to 170°C (338°F).
5. Bake for 30–35 minutes, checking with a thermometer that the bread's internal temperature is 98°C (208°F). Let cool on an oven rack, lying on their sides to keep their volume.

This dough is delicious. It has nothing to do with Karlsbad, however. It is much like the case of Finnish Sticks—they do not exist in Finland. But the practice of mixing short dough with sweet bread dough is common in Germany as a base for *Bleckkuchen*. Long Karlsbader buns with butter and a slice of aged cheese with coffee are good for breakfast or a snack. The consistency is light, and the bread tastes like butter and melts in your mouth.

Classic Karlsbader pastries are long and unfilled buns, and croissants filled with almond remonce. You can use the dough in the same way as sweet bread dough for wreaths, braids, and buns.

When I started working in bakeries and pastry shops, we often made Karlsbader dough by mixing equal parts Danish dough, sweet bread dough, and short dough. A little baking powder or cloudberry salt was added, and possibly an egg for the dough to become airy and light.

If you would like to try this, knead into a smooth dough and let it relax for 10 minutes before you shape it into loaves or buns. Keep in mind that egg yolks lump together when in contact with sugar, flour, or salt. Whisk or knead the dough immediately, otherwise you will have a lumpy dough that is impossible to work with.

Karlsbader dough

Karlsbaderdeg

This dough is amazingly light and airy and, more importantly, good.

Dough temperature 28°C (82°F)
Sits 30 minutes

Pre-dough (Fördeg)
375 grams (2¾ cups) wheat flour high in
   protein, preferably stone ground
25 grams (½ tablespoon) granulated sugar
250 grams (1 cup) milk
50 grams (4 tablespoons) yeast

Pour the flour and sugar into a bowl. Dissolve the yeast in the milk with a whisk and pour it over the flour. Work the dough at low speed for 10 minutes. Put it in a lightly oiled plastic container covered with a lid and let it rise in a warm place for about 30–45 minutes until doubled in volume.

Combining (Bortgörning)
700 grams (1 pound 8.7 ounces) pre-dough
55 grams (4½ tablespoons) granulated sugar
10 grams (1⅔ teaspoons) sea salt
80 grams egg yolk (about 4 yolks)
200 grams (¾ cup + 2 tablespoons) milk

500 grams (3⅔ cups) wheat flour high in protein, preferably stone ground
125 grams (9 tablespoons) butter, at room temperature

1. Put the pre-dough in the bowl with the sugar, salt, egg yolk, milk, and flour.
2. Knead the dough at low speed for 5–6 minutes. Add the butter in small pieces, increase the speed, and knead for another 10 minutes until the dough is completely elastic. Make a gluten test (see page 35).
3. Put the dough in a lightly oiled plastic container covered with a lid and let it rest for 30 minutes.

How we used to make Karlsbader dough when I was a boy

Vetekarlsbader
500 grams (1 pound 1.6 ounces) sweet bread dough (see page 201)
500 grams (1 pound 1.6 ounces) short dough (see page 215)
50 grams eggs (about 1 egg)
15 grams (1 tablespoon) baking powder

Wienerkarlsbader
500 grams (1 pound 1.6 ounces) Danish dough (see page 183)
500 grams (1 pound 1.6 ounces) short dough (see page 215)
10 grams (1⅔ teaspoons) cloudberry salt

Roll 40-gram (1.4-ounce) buns, cover with a cloth, and let them relax for 5 minutes. Roll them out like hot dog buns and put them on a tray with baking parchment. Brush with the egg mixture and let them rise in a warm place for about 45 minutes until doubled in volume. Preheat the oven to 230°C (446°F). Brush one more time with the egg mixture and bake for about 10–12 minutes until golden brown.

Now you have classic Karlsbader buns. If you wish to make biscuits instead, divide them with a fork when cooled. Preheat the oven to 150°C (302°F) and roast them until golden brown. Store them in an airtight jar to keep them from getting soft.

Apple groves

Äppelgömmor

For 16 pieces
Apple compote
Pour leftover compote into warm jars, sterilized for 20 minutes in a water bath at 80°C (176°F) in the oven. Keep in the refrigerator when cooled. However, do not add butter if you intend to preserve the compote. Also good on toast for breakfast.

1,200 grams (about 5½) apples, preferably Cox Orange
1 vanilla bean, preferably bourbon
60 grams (¼ cup) pressed lemon juice
200 grams (¾ cup + 2 tablespoons) dry French apple cider
200 grams (1 cup) granulated sugar
60 grams (4¼ tablespoons) unsalted butter

1. Peel and pit the apples and cut them into cubes, or mix them coarsely in a food processor. Divide the vanilla bean lengthwise and scrape out the marrow with a knife.
2. Cook the apples, vanilla, lemon juice, apple cider, and sugar in a pot. Put on a lid and let simmer until the apples become soft. Take out the vanilla bean and add the sugar.
3. Cook on high heat until almost all the liquid is gone and the compote feels firm. Put the compote in a vegetable mixer until it becomes a chunky puree.
4. Whisk in the butter. Pour the compote into a bowl and let cool. Keep in the refrigerator until ready to use.

1,000 grams (2 pounds 3.3 ounces) Karlsbader dough
160 grams (1 cup) almond remonce (see page 209)
320 grams (3 cups) apple compote

Egg mixture
1 egg
1 egg yolk
a pinch of salt

almond shavings

1. Roll out the dough 4 millimeters (⅛ inches) thick and cut into squares of 10 x 10 centimeters (4 x 4 inches).
2. Pipe 10 grams (1 tablespoon) of almond remonce and 20 grams (3 tablespoons) of apple compote onto each piece. Sprinkle with cinnamon sugar (see Berliner doughnuts, page 158). Fold together like for *Spandauer* (see page 185) and put them in big paper cups. Brush with the egg mixture and let them rise in a warm place for about 45 minutes until doubled in size.
3. Preheat the oven to 230°C (446°F). Brush the groves with the egg mixture one more time, sprinkle with almond shavings, and bake for about 12–15 minutes until golden brown. Let cool on an oven rack.

Karlsbader croissants with nut remonce

Karlsbadergifflar med nötremonce

For about 16 pieces

1. Make half a batch of nut remonce (see page 192).
2. Measure 1,000 grams (2 pounds 3.3 ounces) of Karlsbader dough, and roll it out, 3 millimeters (⅛ inch) thick and 16 centimeters (2¼ inches) wide. Cut out 60-gram (2-ounce) triangles with a 9-centimeter (3½-inch) base. Make a cut in the base with a pastry wheel to release the tension in the croissant.
3. Fill a piping bag with the nut remonce, cut a small hole in the front with scissors, and pipe 15 grams (1½ tablespoons) of remonce onto each piece of dough. Roll them together into croissants, put them on a tray with baking parchment, brush with the egg mixture, and let them dry for 10 minutes.
4. Brush the croissants once more and let them rise for about 45 minutes in a warm place, until they have doubled in volume and they feel light when you lift them.
5. Preheat the oven to 230°C (446°F).
6. Bake the croissants for about 12–15 minutes until golden brown. Let cool on an oven rack.

Pistachio bows

Pistaschbågar

1,000 grams (2 pounds 3.3 ounces) Karlsbader dough

Pistachio remonce
100 grams (¾ cup) pistachio nuts
100 grams (½ cup) peeled sweet almonds
200 grams (1 cup) granulated sugar
150 grams (¾ cup) vanilla cream (see page 211)

Egg mixture
1 egg
1 egg yolk
a pinch of salt

1. Blend the peeled almonds with the sugar into a smooth paste in a food processor with a jagged knife.
2. Mix the paste with the vanilla cream into a smooth paste, adding the cream a little at a time to avoid lumps in the filling.
3. Roll out the dough 3 millimeters (⅛ inch) thick and 16 centimeters (6 inches) wide. Cover with pistachio remonce with a kitchen palette and roll up the dough from both sides into a tight bun. Cut 75-gram (2.6-ounce) pieces and put them on a tray with baking parchment.
4. Brush with the egg mixture and let rise in a warm place for about 45 more minutes until doubled in size.
5. Brush one more time. Preheat the oven to 230°C (446°F).
6. Bake the bows for about 8–10 minutes until golden brown. Let cool on an oven rack.

Karlsbader buns with blueberries

Karlsbaderbullar med blåbär

Delicious and healthy buns that I count among my own favorites. Blueberries are fantastic, but avoid the big flavorless ones. These buns are just as delicious with lingonberries.

For 20 buns
1,200 grams (2 pounds 10.3 ounces) Karlsbader dough
200 grams (1⅓ cups) blueberries
300 grams (1⅓ cups) cream paste (see page 210)

Egg mixture
1 egg
1 egg yolk
a pinch of salt

Sprinkles
25 grams (1¾ tablespoons) butter
25 grams (2 tablespoons) granulated sugar
25 grams (3 tablespoons) almond flour
25 grams (3 tablespoons) wheat flour

1. Mix all the ingredients for the sprinkles by hand into a crumbly paste.
2. Shape 60-gram (2.1-ounce) buns with the dough, put them on a baking tray covered in baking parchment, brush with the egg mixture, and let them rise in a warm place for about 45 minutes until doubled in size.
3. Brush with the egg mixture one more time. Pipe 15 grams (1 tablespoon) of cream paste into each bun with a piping bag. Add on blueberries and cover with sprinkles. Preheat the oven to 230°C (446°F).
4. Bake the buns for about 8–9 minutes until golden brown. Let cool on an oven rack and serve them preferably with vanilla sauce for dessert or just as something sweet with coffee.

Karlsbader twist with apple

Karlsbaderkrans med äpple

We used to make this delicious twist all the time when I was young. Peeling apples was a part of everyday life, especially for butter dough baked apples, also known as queen apples, or *Apfel in Hemd* ("apples in robe," in German) with cinnamon paste inside. Served warm with vanilla sauce.

For 8–10 portions
1 round or long baking pan, 26 centimeters (10¼ inches) in diameter

150 grams (5.3 ounces) short dough (see page 215)
20 grams (1½ tablespoons) butter for the pan
400 grams (14 ounces) Karlsbader dough
200 grams (1½ cups) almond remonce (see page 209)
1 tart green apple, preferably Cox Orange or *Belle de Boskoop*
cinnamon sugar (see Berliner doughnuts, page 158)
1 recipe apricoture (see page 153)

Egg mixture
1 egg
1 egg yolk
a pinch of salt

1. Roll out the short dough with a little wheat flour into a round shape 26 centimeters (10¼ inches) in diameter. Put it in a greased pan and prick the bottom with a fork.
2. Roll out the Karlsbader dough 3 millimeters (⅛ inch) thick and 24 centimeters (9½ inches) long with a rolling pin and a little wheat flour. Cover it with the almond remonce and fold it over 3 times.
3. Put the twist in the pan with the seam facing up and put a cookie cutter in the middle.
4. Peel the apple and cut it into about 12 slices. Brush the twist with the egg mixture, garnish it all the way around with apple slices, and sprinkle with cinnamon sugar. Let it rise in a warm place for about 45 minutes, until the dough has risen properly and doubled in volume.
5. Preheat the oven to 190°C (374°F).
6. Put the twist in, lower the temperature to 180°C (356°F) right away, and bake the twist for about 25–30 minutes until golden brown. Let cool and brush with apricoture.

Upper plate clockwise from the left: Karlsbader bun with blueberries, karlsbader croissant with nut remonce, pistachio bows, apple grove
Lower plate: Karlsbader twist with apple

Bienstich

This old German specialty should not be eaten too cold. Let it warm up to room temperature first, and it will taste much better. When in Karlsruhe, visit Olivier et Dieter Endle on Kaiserstrasse 241 and and you will get a perfect *Bienstich*.

For 8 portions
1 circular pan, 22 centimeters (8½ inches) in
    diameter, or preferably heart-shaped as
    in the photograph, or a long baking pan

20 grams (1½ tablespoons) butter for the
    pan
400 grams (14 ounces) Karlsbader dough

Tosca paste
25 grams (1½ tablespoons) butter
25 grams (3½ teaspoons) Swedish honey
25 grams (2 tablespoons) granulated sugar
25 grams (½ cup) whipped cream
25 grams (¼ cup) shaved almond
5 grams (1¾ teaspoons) wheat flour

Filling, diplomat crème
2 grams gelatin (about 1 leaf)
300 grams (1½ cups) vanilla cream
    (see page 211)
100 grams (1⅔ cups) whipped cream
possibly 10 grams (2 teaspoons)
    Kirschwasser

1. Butter the pan and roll out the dough to fit into it. Put it in the pan and prick with a fork.
2. Cook the butter, honey, sugar, and cream at 115°C (239°F). Check with a sugar thermometer or make a caramel test by dipping your fingers in cold water and grabbing some of the batter; it should form a soft ball. Usually you can tell Tosca paste is ready when the batter starts to come off the edges of the pot.
3. Stir in the almonds mixed with the wheat flour and spread the paste over the dough with a kitchen palette. Let it rise in a warm place for about 45 minutes, until the pan is ¾ of the way filled.
4. Preheat the oven to 190°C (374°F).
5. Bake the cake for about 20–25 minutes until golden brown. Lower the temperature to 170°C (338°F) after 5 minutes so that the cake does not brown too much. Check with a thermometer that its internal temperature is 98°C (208°F). Take off the pan and let the cake cool on an oven rack.
6. Divide the cake in half with a sharp knife and lift off the top half.
7. For the filling: Put the gelatin leaf to soak in plenty of cold water for at least 10 minutes.
8. Drain the cold cooked vanilla cream through a sieve. Whisk the cream into a foam in a cold bowl.
9. Lift the gelatin leaf out of the water, and pour in the remaining water, too. Melt the leaf in a pot or in a microwave oven at 45–50°C (113–122°F), whisk in a couple of spoons of vanilla cream, and heat it up until the cream is melted.
10. Mix the gelatin solution into the cream with a whisk. Pour in the whipped cream with a spatula. Possibly flavor with *Kirschwasser* (it tastes exquisite, I think).
11. Pour the cream into a piping bag, pipe it out onto the bottom half, and put the top half back on. Put the cake in the refrigerator and let the cream stiffen.
12. Bring the cake out into room temperature about 30 minutes before serving so that it is not too cold.

Top: Windsor cake
Bottom: Bienstich

Windsor cake

Windsorkaka

This variation of *Strusselkuchen* is made from Karlsbader dough instead of sweet bread dough. The filling is a *crème mousseline* with vanilla. Serve the cake after it has been at room temperature for 30 minutes for the best taste.
Hans Werner Fassbender on Mittelstrasse 12 in Cologne bakes perfect *Strusselkuchen*.

For 8 portions
1 circular pan, 22 centimeters (8½ inches) in
    diameter, or a long baking pan

400 grams (14 ounces) Karlsbader dough
20 grams (1½ tablespoons) butter for the
    pan

Egg mixture
1 egg
1 egg yolk
a pinch of salt

For sprinkles
25 grams (1½ tablespoons) butter
25 grams (2 tablespoons) granulated sugar
25 grams (3 tablespoons) almond flour
25 grams (3 tablespoons) wheat flour

Crème mousseline
2 grams gelatin (about 1 leaf)
½ vanilla bean, preferably Tahiti
250 grams (1 cup) milk
20 grams (2½ tablespoons) cornstarch
60 grams egg yolk (about 3 yolks)
80 grams (6½ tablespoons) granulated
    sugar
125 grams (9 tablespoons) unsalted butter
possibly 10 grams (2 teaspoons)
    Kirschwasser or dark rum

1. Mix the ingredients for the sprinkles by hand into a crumbly paste.
2. For the cream: Put the gelatin leaf to soak in plenty of cold water for at least 10 minutes. Divide the vanilla bean lengthwise and scrape out the seeds with a small, sharp knife.
3. Put the vanilla seeds and vanilla bean in a small pot with the milk. Cook and put aside to brew for 10–15 minutes.
4. Stir the cornstarch with the egg yolks and sugar until lightly foamy. Pour in some of the vanilla milk and whisk together into a sauce.
5. Pour it back into the pot and cook while constantly stirring, but do not let it boil. Whisk in half of the butter until melted.
6. Strain the cream using a sieve and let it cool under plastic wrap.
7. Whisk the cream with remaining cold butter into a light and airy cream with a mixer at low speed. Flavor preferably with *Kirschwasser* or rum.
8. Butter the round cake form or pan. Roll out the dough to the size of the pan and prick the bottom with a fork. Brush with the egg mixture, cover with sprinkles, and put in a warm place and let rise to about ¾ of the pan.
9. Preheat the oven to 220°C (428°F).
10. Put the cake in the oven on a baking tray and lower the temperature to 190°C (374°F) after 5 minutes. Bake the cake for about 20–25 minutes until golden brown, and check with a thermometer that its internal temperature is 98°C (208°F). Take off the pan and let the cake cool on an oven rack.
11. Divide the cake in half with a sharp knife and take off the top half. Pour the cream into a piping bag, distribute it across the bottom half, and put the top half back on. Put in the refrigerator to stiffen.

See photograph on page 180.

Danishes are a Nordic specialty, and the Danish are especially famous. In Denmark they always weighed the base dough and then rolled in 50% rolling margarine. Some roll in as much as 60% butter, but I think 50% is the best. Personally I never use margarine for anything you are supposed to eat, but only natural butter, which is much better. The melting point for butter is around 27–30°C (81–86°F), in other words below body temperature, which is what makes it melt so pleasantly in the mouth. Try our Danishes next time when you visit Olof Viktor's Bakery in Glemminge!

Danishes should be crispy and freshly baked. I remember the first time I rolled Danish dough like it was yesterday, and how nervous I was, but it went well. When I passed my journeyman test, knowing how to bake fine Danishes was very important, much like when I passed my master exam in both bread and pastry making.

All ingredients for the dough should be properly cooled to keep from rising before baking. If it starts to rise before shaping the dough, the layers will be destroyed. Do not work the base dough for too long and always use frozen flour high in protein.

The base dough and the butter should be as similar as possible in consistency. If the butter is too hard it can break during the rolling process and thereby form lumps in the dough, resulting in bad layering. The dough contains 27 butter layers and 28 dough layers.

The rolling is very important to the Danishes' appearance. If rolled too little, the butter will run during baking. If rolled too thinly, there will not be any layers, and the dough becomes dense instead. Use a ruler and be careful when rolling, and I promise you will be fine. Appropriate rolling is 3 x 3, which means 3 triple foldings (see below).

When shaping the dough, use clean and sharp knives to protect the dough layers. Brush off excess flour from the dough pieces. Let them rise at room temperature until doubled in volume.

Danish dough expands both from the carbon dioxide developed during the fermentation process and from the increasing steam pressure developed inside the dough from the water.

Danishes

Wienerbröd

For about 30

600 grams (4⅓ cups) wheat flour high in protein, preferably stone ground
250 grams (1 cup) water
50 grams (12½ teaspoons) yeast
100 grams eggs (about 2 eggs)
40 grams egg yolk (about 2 yolks)
35 grams (3 tablespoons) granulated sugar
10 grams (1⅔ teaspoons) sea salt
625 grams (5½ sticks) unsalted butter

1. Prepare the dough by putting the flour in the freezer 1 hour before you mix the dough.
2. Pour the water into a baking bowl and dissolve the yeast with a whisk. Add the eggs, egg yolks, sugar, salt, and frozen wheat flour. Work the dough for 2–3 minutes in a machine, or by hand until it releases the edges of the bowl. Fold in the dough in plastic wrap and freeze it for 15 minutes.

3. Put the dough on a floured baking table and roll it out into 35 x 20 centimeter (14 x 8 inch) pieces.
4. Beat the cold butter with the rolling pin several times so that it softens but stays cold. Spread it on one side of the dough. Fold the corners over the butter so that it is completely covered. Wrap the dough in plastic wrap and let it sit in the refrigerator for 30 minutes so that the dough and butter are at the same temperature.
5. Flour the baking table lightly and carefully roll out the dough, from the inside out, into a rectangle of 45 x 75 centimeters (18 x 30 inches). Fold in the ends to triple-fold. This is the first round, or the first folding.
6. For the second folding, the rectangle is turned a quarter circle on the lightly floured table. Carefully roll out the dough again, from the inside out, into a rectangle of 45 x 75 centimeters (18 x 30 inches) and fold it in 3 parts. Put the dough in plastic wrap and let it stiffen in the refrigerator for 30 minutes.
7. Roll out the dough in the same way again and triple-fold it for the last time. Now the Danish dough is ready to use.
8. Cut up the pieces according to weight. Put them in plastic wrap and back into the refrigerator to keep from rising, or the layers will be destroyed.

NOTE: Be careful when brushing off the flour in between folding not to interfere with the rising.

Upper plate clockwise from the left: Blonde bread, combs, Spandauer, Danish croissant
Lower plate clockwise from the left: Cut Danishes, Danish envelopes, a variation of Spandauer, Danishes with vanilla cream

Strawberry *Spandauer*

Jordgubbs-spandauer

Our customers love strawberry Danishes throughout the summer.

For about 30

1,710 grams (3 pounds 12.3 ounces) Danish dough
375 grams (2⅓ cups) almond remonce (see page 209)
1 recipe vanilla cream (see page 211)
1 kilogram (7 cups) fresh strawberries

1. Roll out the dough about 4 millimeters (⅛ inch) thick, and flour very lightly underneath and on top. Polish the edges with a knife and cut up square pieces with a ruler, 9 x 9 centimeters (3½ x 3½ inches).
2. Pour the almond remonce into a piping bag, cut a small hole in the front, and pipe 10 grams (1 tablespoon) of remonce onto each square. Fold the corners into an envelope and push your thumb down hard to keep the Danishes from opening during leavening.
3. Brush all the pieces carefully with the egg mixture and put them on trays with baking parchment, 12 per tray, to rise for about 45 minutes at room temperature. They should increase in volume by ¾.
4. Brush carefully one more time with the egg mixture.
5. Pour the vanilla cream into the piping bag and pipe 20 grams (1½ tablespoons) of cream onto each Danish.
6. Preheat the oven to 220°C (428°F).
7. Bake the Danishes for about 12–15 minutes. Let them cool.
8. Rinse the strawberries in cold water, dry them with paper towels, and snip them. Make sure that they are dry, as not to wet the Danishes, which would then become tough instead of crispy.
9. Pipe 10 grams (2 teaspoons) of vanilla cream onto each Danish, decorate with a couple of strawberries, and sift over a little bit of powdered sugar.

Raspberry Danish

Hallonwienerbröd

It can hardly get better than fresh raspberries on crispy Danishes.

For about 30

Roll out the dough like for *Spandauer*. Divide the dough into squares and cut a square in the middle with a sharp knife. Fold through the outer dough like in the photograph, brush the bread with the egg mixture, and let them rise in the same way as for *Spandauer*. Pipe with vanilla cream and bake in the same way as for *Spandauer*. Pipe with 10 grams (2 teaspoons) of vanilla cream when cooled, decorate with raspberries, and sift with a little powdered sugar.

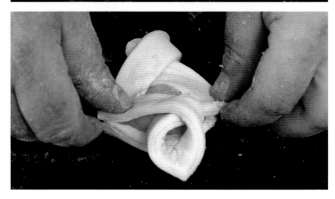

Cut Danishes

Skurna wienerbröd

These sticky, sweet Danishes were one of my favorites when I was a child, and just thinking about these delicacies is a sensual pleasure. Mother always bought them at the Danish pastry shop in Malmö, where they also made wonderful pistachio pastries. We always used to make them with leftover Danish dough.

For about 18
2 300-gram (10.6-ounce) pieces Danish dough
300 grams (2 cups) almond remonce (see page 209)
250 grams (1¼ cups) vanilla cream (see page 211)
125 grams (6 tablespoons) raspberry jam
almond shavings
water glaze with rum (see below)

1. Roll out the dough pieces 20 centimeters (8 inches) wide and the same length as the tray with a rolling pin and little wheat flour.
2. Cover the middle of both dough pieces with the almond remonce and fold them together toward the middle in 3 layers.
3. Turn them upside down with the seam facing downward. Roll over them in the middle to make deeper. Brush with the egg mixture.
4. Pour the vanilla cream in a plastic piping bag, cut a hole in the front, and pipe vanilla cream onto the pastries. Repeat piping with the raspberry jam.
5. Sprinkle with almond shavings and leave them to rise in a warm place for about 45 minutes until doubled in volume.
6. Preheat the oven to 210°C (410°F).
7. Bake for about 20 minutes until golden brown. Glaze with water glaze as soon as cooled and cut into 70-gram (2.5-ounce) big Danishes.

See photograph on page 184.

Pistachio twist

Pistaschsnurra

This Danish dough specialty is moist and crispy at the same time. With real pistachio nuts in the filling, it will taste like it should, and not like it usually does in less scrupulous bakeries and pastry shops.

For 6–8 portions
400 grams (14 ounces) Danish dough
200 grams (1⅓ cups) pistachio remonce (see page 176)

Egg mixture
1 egg
1 egg yolk
a pinch of salt

Water glaze with rum
75 grams (⅔ cup) water
25 grams (5¼ teaspoons) dark rum
200 grams (1⅔ cups) powdered sugar

Mix everything into the glaze with a ladle and cover with plastic wrap. To make it firmer, just add more powdered sugar.

1. Roll out the dough 20 centimeters (8 inches) long and 16 centimeters (6 inches) wide with a rolling pin and a little wheat flour.
2. Pour the pistachio remonce into a piping bag and pipe a string on each long side of the dough. Roll the dough together from both sides to close in the remonce.
3. Bend the dough like a horseshoe on a baking tray covered with baking parchment and brush it with the egg mixture. Let it rise for about 45 minutes until increased by ¾ in volume.
4. Preheat the oven to 220°C (428°F). Brush the dough once more with the egg mixture.
5. Put the tray in the oven. Lower the temperature to 190°C (374°F) after 5 minutes.
6. Bake the twist for about 15–20 minutes until golden brown. Glaze with water glaze when cooled.

See photograph on page 190.

Apple Danish

Äppelwienerlängd

This classic combination tastes especially good in the fall when the apples are best. Danishes with apple jam are also always good if the jam is tart and not too sweet.

For 6–8 portions
400 grams (14 ounces) Danish dough
150 grams (2/3 cup) cream paste
    (see page 210)
150 grams (1¼ cups) apple compote
    (see page 175)
10 grams (2½ teaspoons) cinnamon sugar
    (see page 158)

Egg mixture
1 egg
1 egg yolk
a pinch of salt

water glaze with rum (see page 186)

1. Roll out the dough 20 centimeters (8 inches) long and 16 centimeters (6 inches) wide with a rolling pin and a little wheat flour.
2. Pipe a string of cream paste on the Danish and one string of apple compote next to it with a piping bag. Sprinkle with cinnamon sugar.
3. Fold together the dough in 3 layers and put it on a baking tray covered with baking parchment with the seam facing downwards.
4. Make deep incisions in the dough with a sharp knife and bend it like in the photograph on page 188. Brush with the egg mixture and let it rise for about 45 minutes until increased by ¾ in volume.
5. Preheat the oven to 220°C (428°F). Brush the dough with the egg mixture one more time.
6. Put the tray in the oven and lower the temperature to 190°C (374°F) after 5 minutes.
7. Bake for about 20–25 minutes until golden brown. Glaze with water glaze when cooled.

See photograph on page 188.

Danish Envelopes

Wienerkuvert

In a properly rolled Danish dough, you can see all of the layers in the cake and it gets crispy and moist after baking. This is a delicious specialty that I always bake when I make Danish dough. Baking master Ingvar Larsson at Pastry shop Hollandia in Malmö was a specialist at making Danish envelopes and great at making any butter dough pastries.

For 6–8 portions
1 circular or long baking pan, 26 centimeters
    (10¼ inches) in diameter
20 grams (1½ tablespoons) butter for the pan

400 grams (14 ounces) Danish dough
200 grams (2/3 cup + 1½ tablespoons) cream
    paste (see page 210)
5 grams (2½ teaspoons) ground cardamom
5 grams (2 teaspoons) ground real cinnamon
150 grams (¾ cup) vanilla cream
    (see page 211)
10 grams (2 teaspoons) almond shavings

Egg mixture
1 egg
1 egg yolk
a pinch of salt

water glaze with rum (see page 186)

1. Cut out a 400-gram (14-ounce) square of Danish dough and roll it out with a rolling pin and a little wheat flour from the middle to make the corners thick and the dough thinner in the middle. Pipe the cream paste in the middle and sprinkle with cinnamon and cardamom.
2. Fold together like a big *Spandauer* (see page 185), brush with the egg mixture, and leave it to rise in a round or a long baking pan on a tray for about 45 minutes until increased by ¾ in volume.
3. Brush one more time with the egg mixture. Pour the vanilla cream into a plastic cornet, pipe it into the middle of the cake, and sprinkle with almond shavings.
4. Preheat the oven to 220°C (428°F).
5. Put the tray in the oven and lower the heat to 190°C (374°F). Bake for about 25–30 minutes until golden brown. Glaze with water glaze when cooled.

See photograph on page 188.

Danish Bows with farine remonce

Wienerkrok med farinremonce

This delicious pastry was a specialty at Conditori Desirée in Copenhagen. It was on the corner at Hotel d'Angleterre in the beginning of Strøget. The store was full of great pastries, petits fours, Danishes, and beautiful Danish French bread that you can no longer find in Copenhagen.

For about 10–12 portions
2 300-gram (10.6-ounce) pieces of Danish dough

Farine remonce
100 grams (7 tablespoons) butter, at room temperature
125 grams (½ cup + 2 tablespoons) farine sugar
25 grams (5¼ teaspoons) wheat flour

Egg mixture
1 egg
1 egg yolk
a pinch of salt

Topping
20 grams (1½ tablespoons) almond shavings
20 grams (1½ tablespoons) granulated sugar

water glaze with rum (see page 186)

1. Whisk the butter with the sugar and flour into a light and airy remonce.
2. Roll out the dough 20 centimeters (8 inches) long with a rolling pin and a little wheat flour. Roll it over the middle to make the dough thicker at the ends.
3. Pour the remonce into a piping bag and cut a big hole in the front. Pipe the filling onto the middle of the dough.
4. Carefully fold in the dough toward the middle and put the other part over without pressing. Brush with the egg mixture and sprinkle with almond shavings and a little sugar.
5. Put the bread slightly bent on a tray with baking parchment. Let it rise for about 45 minutes at room temperature until increased by almost ¾ in volume.
6. Preheat the oven to 220°C (428°F).
7. Bake for 5 minutes and then lower the heat to 190°C (374°F). Bake the bread for about 30 minutes until golden brown. Lift onto an oven rack. Glaze with the water glaze when cooled.

See photograph on page 190.

Danish Twist

Wienerkringla

These twists are popular in both Denmark and Norway, but you rarely see them in Sweden. When properly rolled in nice layers, this birthday twist is a real adornment at the table. Welch twists are the most popular in Norway. They are made of butter dough in the bottom, a *pâte à choux* paste on top, and filled with cream.

For 10–12 portions
500 grams (1 pound 1.6 ounces) Danish dough
200 grams (1⅓ cups) hazelnut remonce, at room temperature (see page 207)
100 grams (½ cup) cream paste (see page 210)
25 grams (2 tablespoons) cinnamon sugar (see page 158)
50 grams (½ cup) almond shavings
25 grams (2 tablespoons) granulated sugar

Egg mixture
1 egg
1 egg yolk
a pinch of salt

water glaze with rum (see page 186)

1. Roll out the dough into a 50-centimeter (20-inch) long and 1½-centimeter (½-inch) wide band with a rolling pin and a little wheat flour. Roll the long pastry in the middle to make the dough band thinner there.
2. Pour the nut remonce into a piping bag, cut a big hole in the front, and pipe out the remonce along the entire twist. Repeat with the cream paste in the same way. Sprinkle with cinnamon sugar.
3. Fold the dough up on the middle from one side and then from the other side without pressing down the dough.
4. Put the twist on a tray with baking parchment as in the photograph. Brush with the egg mixture and sprinkle with almond shavings and sugar. Let it rise for about 45 minutes at room temperature (not above 28°C / 82°F) until increased in volume by about ¾.
5. Preheat the oven to 220°C (428°F).
6. Put the twist in the oven and lower the heat immediately to 190°C (374°F). Bake for about 35 minutes until golden brown. Glaze with the water glaze when cooled.

See photograph on page 191.

Top: Danish Envelope
Bottom: Apple Danish

Top: Danish Bows
Bottom: Pistachio Twist

Top right: Danish Twist
Bottom right: Mayor's Twist

Danish croissants

Wienergifflar

These croissants are especially crispy and flaky.

For about 12
600 grams (1 pound 5 ounces) Danish dough

Nut remonce
10 grams (1⅔ tablespoons) peel of a ripe yellow lemon
150 grams (¾ cup) granulated sugar
180 grams (¾ cup) water
325 grams (4⅓ cups) roasted hazelnuts, finely ground
3 grams (1¼ teaspoons) freshly ground real cinnamon

Wash the lemon and zest off a quarter of the outer peel. Cook the sugar and water and pour it boiling over the ground hazelnuts, cinnamon, and lemon peels. Work the paste until completely smooth. Cover with plastic wrap and let swell in room temperature until the next day.

Egg mixture
1 egg
1 egg yolk
a pinch of salt

20 grams (1½ tablespoons) almond shavings
20 grams (1½ tablespoons) granulated sugar

water glaze with rum (see page 186)

1. Roll out the dough about 2.5 millimeters (about ⅛ inch) thick with a little wheat flour and a rolling pin into a band, about 12 centimeters (4¾ inches) wide. Polish the edges with a sharp knife, using a ruler to get it right.
2. Mark up 12 triangles; the base should be 12 centimeters (4¾ inches) wide. Make incisions in the base with a sharp knife.
3. Pipe out 15 grams (2 tablespoons) of nut remonce along the base. Roll together into croissants from the base without stretching the dough. Put them on a baking tray with baking parchment and let rise at room temperature for about 45 minutes, until increased in volume by ¾. They should feel light when you lift them.
4. Brush them carefully with the egg mixture and sprinkle with almond shavings and sugar.
5. Preheat the oven to 230°C (446°F).
6. Bake the Danishes for about 18 minutes until golden brown. Lift them onto an oven rack to cool. Glaze with the water glaze.

   See photograph on page 184.

Combs

Kammar

My mother loved combs with lots of chopped almonds on top, and so do I. I like them best when they are a little too brown. Then they do not collapse after baking.

For about 15
500 grams (1 pound 1.6 ounces) Danish dough
½ recipe almond remonce (see page 209)

Almond sugar
100 grams (⅔ cup) raw almonds
50 grams (4 tablespoons) granulated sugar

Egg mixture
1 egg
1 egg yolk
a pinch of salt

1. Grind the almonds coarsely and mix with granulated sugar.
2. Roll out the dough 25 centimeters (10 inches) wide and about 3 millimeters (about ¹/₁₆ inch) thick with a rolling pin and a little wheat flour.
3. Put on a layer of the almond remonce and spread it from the middle with a kitchen palette.
4. Fold over one of the long sides toward the middle, brush with egg mixture, fold up the other side and pinch it in.
5. Powder with a little wheat flour and turn the pastry with the seam facing downward. Brush the top with the egg mixture and sprinkle with almond sugar.
6. Turn it with the almond side facing downward. Measure 15 pieces with a ruler and cut them with a sharp knife. Cut 6 slits on one side of the combs.
7. Put the combs on a tray with baking parchment. Let them rise and bake them in the same way as Danish croissants.

See photograph on page 184.

Blonde bread

Blondebröd

These crispy Danishes with plenty of vanilla cream always taste good. I remember, when I was in school, how we ran to Rosberg's home bakery on Köpenhamnsvägen and bought them on our breaks. They also made a kind of Danish that was known as *Copenhagener*. They were filled with brown almond filling with raisins and cinnamon and were placed on a butter dough plate. The shells were filled with vanilla cream and raspberry jam, and after baking they were glazed and cut into squares.

For 10
600 grams (1 pound 5 ounces) Danish
    dough
½ recipe vanilla cream (see page 211)
20 grams (1½ tablespoons) almond shavings

Egg mixture
1 egg
1 egg yolk
a pinch of salt

water glaze with rum (see page 186)

1. Roll out the dough 1 centimeter (⅓ inch) thick and 25 centimeters (10 inches) long with a rolling pin and a little wheat flour.
2. Cut up 10 60-gram (2.1-ounce) strips (25 centimeters/10 inches) with a sharp knife and a ruler. Twist each strip and shape it into a circle or figure 8. Press it in the seam. Put them on a tray with baking parchment.
3. Brush with the egg mixture and let them rise for about 45 minutes until increased in volume by about ¾.
4. Brush them carefully with the egg mixture again. Pour the vanilla cream into a piping bag and pipe a thick string over each Danish. Sprinkle with almond shavings.
5. Preheat the oven to 230°C (446°F).
6. Bake for about 15–19 minutes until golden brown. Glaze when cooled.

See photograph on page 184.

Danish Tosca

Wienertosca

This Danish dough cake originates from Germany, where it is known as *Bienstich*, but you use German sweet bread dough for that. My sister Gunilla brought home this delicacy and expressed herself most enthusiastically on the phone. The lovely cafe *Flickorna Lundgren* (The Lundgren Girls) in Nyhamnsläge in Skåne always has it, and you can tell from the cake plates that it is a favorite.

For 1 cake (12 portions)
a cake ring pan or long baking pan, 26 centimeters (10¼ inches) in diameter and 3 centimeters (1¼ inches) high
20 grams (1½ tablespoons) soft butter, to butter the ring or pan

Vanilla cream
1 gelatin leaf (about 2 grams)
250 grams (1 cup) milk
½ vanilla bean
60 grams egg yolk (about 3 yolks)
50 grams (4 tablespoons) granulated sugar
20 grams (2½ tablespoons) cornstarch
15 grams (1 tablespoon) butter

300 grams (5 cups) whipped cream

1. Soak the gelatin leaf in plenty of cold water for at least 10 minutes.
2. Divide the vanilla bean lengthwise, scrape out the seeds, and put them in a small pot with the milk. Cook and put the pot aside, put on a lid, and let the milk brew and soak up the vanilla flavor.
3. Whisk the egg yolks and sugar lightly and add the flour. Pour the milk over the mixture and mix everything thoroughly.

4. Pour it back into the pot. Cook the cream while constantly stirring, but do not let it boil. Add the butter and whisk until melted.
5. Take the gelatin leaves out of the water, pour the remaining water into the cream, and stir until the gelatin has melted. Pour into a low bowl, cover with plastic wrap, and let cool in the refrigerator.

400 grams (14 ounces) Danish dough

Tosca
50 grams (3½ tablespoons) butter
50 grams (7 teaspoons) honey
50 grams (4 tablespoons) granulated sugar
50 grams (¼ cup) cream
50 grams (½ cup) almond shavings

1. Butter the round or long baking pan. Roll out the dough with a rolling pin and a little wheat flour into a round plate, turning it over every now and then when rolling. Put the dough in the pan and put the pan in the freezer.
2. Cook the ingredients for the Tosca at 115°C (239°F), or until the batter starts to let go of the edges of the pot. Take the pot off the stove and stir in the almond shavings.
3. Take the cake plate out of the freezer and quickly spread the warm Tosca paste on it with a kitchen palette.
4. Let rise for about 45 minutes at no more than 28°C (82°F) or in a turned-off oven until doubled in volume.
5. Preheat the oven to 180°C (356°F).
6. Bake the cake for about 30 minutes until golden brown. Let it cool completely and cut it in half with a sharp knife. Put the top half on a tray and divide it into 12 cake pieces with a sharp knife.
7. Strain the cold vanilla cream through a sieve with a spatula into a stainless steel bowl.
8. Pour the cream into a cold stainless steel bowl and whisk the cream into a firm foam. Fold it into the vanilla cream with a spatula for an airy filling.
9. Distribute the vanilla cream on the bottom half of the cake with a palette and carefully place the Tosca lid on top of the cream.
10. Dip a sharp knife in warm water and make substantial incisions through the upper and lower halves. Move the cake over to a serving plate.

Mayor's Twist

Borgmästarkrans

We studied this Danish dough specialty very carefully when I was an apprentice. It had to be braided beautifully and then put on the tray with the seams facing downward. We brushed it with egg and sprinkled it with almond shavings. For birthdays and weddings this delicious twist was always on the table.

For 12–15 portions
Mayor's filling
100 grams (½ cup) almond paste 50/50
100 grams (7 tablespoons) butter
100 grams (8 tablespoons) granulated sugar

Mix the almond paste with ¼ of the butter until lump free. Add the sugar and the rest of the butter in batches until the paste is smooth and without lumps. Cool the paste for a couple of hours before using it.

600 grams (1 pound 5 ounces) Danish dough

Egg mixture
1 egg
1 egg yolk
a pinch of salt

water glaze with rum (see page 186)

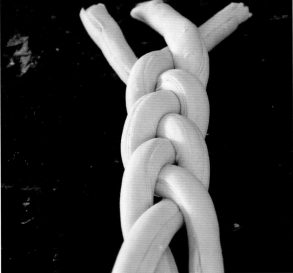

1. Roll out the dough about 50 centimeters (20 inches) long and 20 centimeters (8 inches) wide with a rolling pin and a little wheat flour. Divide it with a pastry wheel into 3 equal long shapes. Brush lightly with the egg mixture at the bottom of the dough strings.
2. Divide the almond paste into 3 equal pieces and roll them out with a little wheat flour into pen-thick long shapes, as long as the lengths of dough.
3. Roll the lengths together tightly with the paste inside. Stretch them out somewhat and check to see that they fit on the tray.
4. Put the lengths of dough with the seams facing upward and braid them together like a 3-part braid (not too hard or tightly, or the twist will burst and lose its shape). Try to finish beautifully and not show the seam in the twist.
5. Shape into a round twist and turn the seams downward. Brush with the egg mixture and sprinkle with almond shavings. Let it rise for about 45 minutes at no more than 28°C (82°F) or in a turned-off oven until doubled in size.
6. Preheat the oven to 190°C (374°F).
7. Bake the twist for about 25 minutes until golden brown. Glaze with water glaze when cooled.

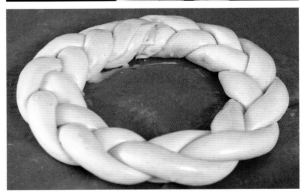

See photograph on page 191.

These French classics are always good, like most French pastries and breads.

The choice of ingredients is important; a good wheat flour high in protein and a good butter with low water content. It is also important to mix the dough until completely smooth without overworking it.

Always brush the croissants twice with egg mixture right before baking for a pretty gloss.

In Switzerland, croissants were known as *gipfeli*, and we baked thousands each morning. The Swiss are just like the French—a day without a croissant or *gipfeli* is unthinkable, and of course lots of strawberry jam to go with it, and a large *café au lait*.

You can get really good croissants at master pastry chef Denis Ruffel's, who runs Pâtissérie Millet at Rue Saint Dominique 103 in Paris.

My classic recipe

Mitt klassiska recept

This is the favorite for classic, unfilled croissants, whereas recipe no. 2 is better for almond croissants, *pain au chocolat*, and *pain au raisin*, since the dough contains more butter and is a little bit airier.

Ideal dough temperature 25°C (77°F)
Sits 8–12 hours

For 16
125 grams (½ cup) water
20 grams (3½ teaspoons) yeast
150 grams (½ cup + 2 tablespoons) milk
500 grams (3⅔ cups) wheat flour extra-high in protein, preferably stone ground
55 grams (4½ tablespoons) granulated sugar
10 grams (1⅔ teaspoons) sea salt

300 grams (2⅔ sticks) unsalted butter, for rolling into the dough
1 egg and a pinch of salt, for brushing

DAY 1

1. Stir out the yeast in the water in a 2-liter (½-gallon) bucket. Whisk in the milk.
2. Pour the flour, sugar, and salt in a bowl and knead until the dough releases the edges of the bowl, for about 5 minutes. Pour the dough into a lightly oiled plastic container covered with a lid and let it rise for about 2 hours until doubled in size.
3. Push together the dough by quickly turning it and pressing out the air. Put it back in the plastic container and let sit in the refrigerator overnight, for at least 8–12 hours. Look in the refrigerator during the first hour, since the dough could start to rise again depending on the temperature of the refrigerator (wild fermentation). If it has started to rise, push it together one more time.

DAY 2

1. Cut a cross on top of the dough. Roll it out in 4 directions on a lightly floured surface. Turn a quarter circle for each time you roll the dough out.
2. Beat the cold butter with the rolling pin to soften it and put it in the middle of the dough. The butter should have the same consistency as the dough to avoid layering.
3. Fold the 4 corners over the dough and make sure that the butter is completely contained and will not leak out.
4. Flour the dough and the table lightly. Roll out the dough into a rectangle, 40 x 70 centimeters (15¾ x 27½ inches), using a ruler. Roll from the inside outward. Brush the flour off the surface.
5. Fold together the dough in 3 parts (see page 183). Wrap in plastic wrap and let it rest for 30 minutes in the refrigerator so that the tension in the dough does not destroy the layers. ➤

6. Repeat the process twice. Then let the dough rest for 30 more minutes to release the tension. You now have 27 butter layers and 28 dough layers in the dough.

7. Roll the dough into a rectangle, 40 x 70 centimeters (15¾ x 27½ inches), flouring the table lightly while rolling. Lift up the dough now and then to prevent it from curling up. Be careful not to destroy the rectangle. The perfect thickness is 2½–3½ millimeters (¹/₁₆–⅛ inch). Polish the edges with a sharp knife, using a ruler to get it right.

8. Mark up 8 triangles. The bases should be 12 centimeters (4¾ inches) wide. First measure with a ruler to get it right and then cut with a sharp knife. Organize the triangles on a lightly floured plate and cover with plastic wrap. Let them stiffen for 30 minutes in the refrigerator to make it easier to roll them together.

9. Roll them together into croissants and put them on 2 trays with baking parchment. Bend the ends in toward the middle to form a crescent. Since the oven is warmest on the sides, the tips should be facing the middle of the tray in order not to burn. Brush them with beaten egg with a pinch of salt. Brush from the inside out so that the dough layers do not stick together, which would prevent them from opening while baking.

10. Let them rise until doubled in size in a turned-off oven, at a maximum temperature of 30°C (86°F), or the butter will melt. The ideal temperature is 24°C (75°F), but a turned-off oven is fine. The leavening takes about 90–120 minutes at 25°C (77°F).

11. Preheat the oven to 220–230°C (428–446°F), or 170°C (338°F) if you use a convection oven.

12. Bake the croissants for about 15 minutes until golden brown. Take them out of the oven and let cool on an oven rack.

NOTE: You can also fold the dough 4 times and get the same result as when folding in, but 3 is traditional in France.

Croissant dough 2

Croissantdeg 2

Dough temperature 25°C (77°F)
Sits 8–12 hours

This base dough is easier to roll than the classic since it contains more butter and becomes a little bit airier. It is best for *pain au chocolat*, *pain au raisin*, and *croissant aux amandes*.

240 grams (1 cup) water
30 grams (5 teaspoons) yeast
500 grams (3²/₃ cups) wheat flour high in protein
60 grams (5 tablespoons) granulated sugar
12 grams (2 teaspoons) sea salt
100 grams (7 tablespoons) butter + 500 grams (4½ sticks) for rolling into the dough

The same preparation as for my classic recipe but add 100 grams (7 tablespoons) of butter to the dough and use 500 grams (4½ sticks) of butter for rolling.

Almond croissant

Mandelcroissant

The same preparation as for classic croissants, but pipe 20 grams (1¼ tablespoons) of almond cream onto each triangle before rolling into croissants. Sprinkle generously with almond shavings.

1 recipe croissant dough 2

Almond cream

Known in French as *crème d'amande*. Remember to keep the eggs and butter at room temperature to make it easier to mix the cream.

¼ recipe (200 grams/1 cup) vanilla cream (see page 211)
50 grams (²/₃ cups) almond flour
50 grams (6 tablespoons) powdered sugar
100 grams (7 tablespoons) butter
20 gramsconr (1½ tablespoons) dark rum
18 grams (2 tablespoons + 1 teaspoon) cornstarch
100 grams eggs (about 2 eggs)

Stir the finely ground almonds with the powdered sugar, butter, rum, and cornstarch into an airy mixture. Add the eggs one at a time and stir into a smooth cream. Strain the vanilla cream through a sieve and stir it in also. ➤

Clockwise from left: Croissant, pain au chocolat, pain au raisin, almond croissant, and in the middle brioche

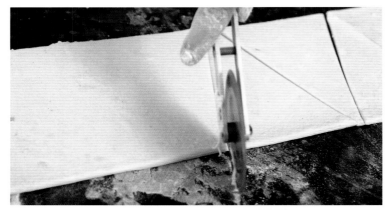

Pain au chocolat

For 16 pieces
1 recipe croissant dough 2
200 grams (7 ounces) dark chocolate, Valrhona Grand Cru
Guanaja 70% (room temperature)

1. Roll out the dough about 3½ millimeters (about ⅛ inch) thick into a rectangle, 40 x 76 centimeters (15¾ x 30 inches), with a rolling pin and a little wheat flour. Polish the edges with a knife and a ruler. Cut the dough into 2 equal lengths and divide each length into 8 equal pieces.
2. Cut the chocolate bars with a sharp knife into 16 pieces.
3. Beat the eggs with a pinch of salt and brush the dough pieces. Put a piece of chocolate in each piece of dough. Fold them together 3 times and put them with the seam facing downward on each baking tray covered with baking parchment. Brush carefully with egg and let rise for almost 2 hours in a warm place.
4. Preheat the oven to 190–200°C (374–392°F) and brush once more with egg.
5. Bake for 12–15 minutes until golden brown and let cool on an oven rack.

Pain au raisin

For about 14–15 croissants
500 grams (1 pound 1.6 ounces) croissant dough 2
100 grams (⅔ cup) raisins
25 grams (2 tablespoons) rum
250 grams (1 cup) almond cream (see page 199)
eggs, for brushing
almond shavings

1. Marinate the raisins in the rum for 1 hour.
2. Roll out the dough 2 millimeters (¹/₁₆ inch) thick and about 45 centimeters (17¾ inches) wide with a rolling pin and a little wheat flour.
3. Cover with the almond cream and sprinkle with the raisins. Brush the edge at the bottom of the dough with egg mixture.
4. Roll the dough together into a tight bun. Cut into 60-gram (2-ounce) shells. Put them with the seam facing downward on a baking tray with baking parchment, about 8 on each tray, and brush them with the egg mixture. Let them rise in a warm place for about 2 hours until doubled in size.
5. Preheat the oven to 220°C (428°F). Brush once more with egg mixture and sprinkle with the almond shavings.
6. Bake for about 12–15 minutes until golden brown and let them cool on an oven rack.

Regular sweet bread dough

Vanlig vetedeg

This Scandinavian specialty is popular in Sweden, Norway, and Finland, and we are the only ones who season the dough with cardamom. Sweet bread dough is prepared in most countries, but not the way we make it.

A sweet bread dough with pre-dough gets a better taste since you do not have to use so much yeast, and the bread gets better volume and becomes more finely pored, airy, and delicious.

Never melt the butter, contrary to what many books and food magazines will tell you, because it makes the dough absorb more flour and become dense and heavy. The butter should be at room temperature when added. Then it is capable of taking up air, which makes the dough light and airy.

It is not traditional to add eggs to sweet bread dough, but it helps to distribute the fat better and gives the dough more volume and makes it airier.

Leaven the bread well and always brush sweet bread dough twice with egg mixture to get a beautiful gloss. Small buns and rolls should have a really warm oven and bigger things like twists somewhat lower temperatures. I do not use pearl sugar on my sweet bread dough since I do not like the modern and hard pearl sugar.

Ideal dough temperature 26–28°C (79–82°F)
Sits 30 minutes

Pre-dough (Fördeg)

700 grams (5 cups) wheat flour high in
    protein, preferably stone ground, or
    white spelt meal
25 grams (2 tablespoons) granulated sugar
500 grams (2 cups) milk
75 grams (4 tablespoons) yeast

Combine the flour and sugar. Dissolve the yeast in the milk and pour it over the flour. Knead the dough at low speed for 5–6 minutes. Put the dough in a lightly oiled plastic container covered with a lid and let it rise in a warm place for about 30–45 minutes until doubled in volume.

Combining (Bortgörning)

1,300 grams (2 pounds 14 ounces) pre-dough
500 grams (3⅔ cups) wheat flour high in
    protein, preferably stone ground
175 grams (¾ cup + 2 tablespoons)
    granulated sugar
20 grams (3⅓ teaspoons) sea salt
20 grams (3½ tablespoons) cardamom,
    crushed in a mortar
50 grams eggs (about 1 egg)
250 grams (2¼ sticks) butter, at room
    temperature

Put the pre-dough in a bowl and pour in the flour, sugar, salt, cardamom, and egg.

Work the dough at low speed for 5–6 minutes. Add the butter in small pieces, increase the speed, and work the dough for about another 10 minutes until completely elastic. Make a gluten test (see page 35). Put the dough in a lightly oiled plastic container covered with a lid and let it rise for 30 minutes.

Wheat biscuits

Veteskorpor

Do not forget this Swedish delicacy with extra salted butter and a good marmalade on it.

Roll 40-gram (1.4-ounce) big buns of sweet bread dough and let them rise until doubled in size. Bake them until golden brown at 230°C (446°F) for about 8–9 minutes, and cut them with a fork when cooled. Put them on a tray with the section surface facing upward and dry until golden brown at 150°C (302°F). Keep the biscuits dry.

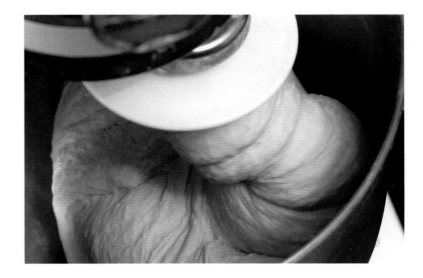

Butter shells

Smörsnäckor

Most people love these light butter shells with a cup of good coffee. Egg and baking powder lighten the dough, and the sugar in the filling carmelizes easily and gives a light caramel tone.

For about 25
1,000 grams (1 pound 3.3 ounces) sweet bread dough
50 grams eggs (about 1 egg)
10 grams (2 teaspoons) baking powder

Butter remonce
250 grams (2¼ sticks) butter
225 grams (2 cups + 2 tablespoons) powdered sugar
25 grams (2 tablespoons) real vanilla sugar

Egg mixture
1 egg
1 egg yolk
a pinch of salt

almond shavings, for decoration

1. Whip the butter until light and airy with the sugars for the remonce.
2. Mix the dough with the egg, the sifted baking powder, and a little wheat flour. Cover with a cloth and let relax for 10 minutes.
3. Roll out the dough in the same way as for cinnamon shells (see page 209) but fill with butter remonce instead. Roll together and cut into shells. Put them in pans, brush with the egg mixture, and sprinkle with almond shavings. Let them rise in a warm place for about 45 minutes until doubled in size.
4. Preheat the oven to 230°C (446°F).
5. Bake the shells until golden brown and glossy for about 8–10 minutes. Let cool on an oven rack.

See photograph on page 213.

Cardamom twist

Kardemummakrans

To me this twist tastes like childhood and Sweden.

For about 6–8 portions
1 ring pan or long baking pan, 26 centimeters (10 inches) in diameter
20 grams (1½ tablespoons) soft butter, for the pan

400 grams (14 ounces) sweet bread dough
200 grams (1 cup) almond remonce (see page 209)
coarsely ground cardamom

Egg mixture
1 egg
1 egg yolk
a pinch of salt

almond shavings, for decoration

1. Butter the pan and put it on a tray with baking parchment. Roll out the dough into a rectangle, 23 x 45 centimeters (9 x 18 inches), with a rolling pin and a little wheat flour.
2. Spread the remonce on the dough and sprinkle generously with cardamom. Roll together into a tight long roll, stretch out the length, and put together like a twist. Check to see that it fits in the pan.
3. Brush the twist with the egg mixture and put it in the circular pan. Let it rise in a warm place for about 45 minutes until doubled in size.
4. Preheat the oven to 210°C (410°F). Brush the twist with egg one more time, cut it with a sharp knife, and sprinkle with almond shavings.
5. Put the twist in the oven. Lower the temperature to 190°C (374°F) after 5 minutes and bake the twist for about 20–25 minutes until golden brown.

See photograph on page 214.

Classic cinnamon twist

Klassisk kanelkrans

This was among the first sweet bread dough specialties I made as an apprentice. It tastes just as good today; you never tire of a good cinnamon twist. Cinnamon twist with apple compote that is folded together is also a classic.

For about 6–8 portions
1 circular pan or long baking pan,
    26 centimeters (10¼ inches) in diameter
20 grams (1½ tablespoons) soft butter, for
    the pan
400 grams (14 ounces) sweet bread dough
200 grams (1 cup) almond remonce (see
    page 209)
cinnamon sugar (see page 158)

Egg mixture
1 egg
1 egg yolk
1 pinch of salt

almond shavings, for decoration

1. Butter the pan and put it on a tray with baking parchment. Roll out the dough into a rectangle, 23 x 45 centimeters (9 x 18 inches), with a rolling pin and a little wheat flour.
2. Cover the dough with almond remonce and sprinkle generously with cinnamon sugar. Roll together into a tight, long roll with the seam facing upward.
3. Divide the length into 2 parallel parts with a pastry wheel or a sharp knife. Braid together both lengths of dough, make the braid into a twist, and put it in the pan. Brush with the egg mixture and let it rise in a warm place for about 45 minutes until doubled in size.
4. Preheat the oven to 210°C (410°F). Brush the dough once more and sprinkle with almond shavings.
5. Put the twist in the oven. Lower the temperature to 190°C (374°F) after 5 minutes. Bake the twist for about 20–25 minutes until golden brown.

See photograph on page 214.

Saffron twist

Saffranskrans

This moist twist is not only good for Christmas, but can be eaten all year round.

For about 12 portions
1 round or long baking pan, 26 centimeters
    (10¼ inches) in diameter
20 grams (1½ tablespoons) soft butter for
    the pan

Egg mixture
1 egg
1 egg yolk
1 pinch of salt

almond shavings, for decoration

Add 3 grams (1½ tablespoons) of crushed saffron for the base recipe for the sweet bread dough and omit the cardamom.

400 grams (14 ounces) saffron dough
100 grams (½ cup) almond remonce
    (see page 209)
100 grams (½ cup) cream paste (see
    almond buns, page 210)

25 grams (2 tablespoons) candied peel
25 grams (2 tablespoons) chopped preserved orange peel
25 grams (2 tablespoons) raisins
cardamom, coarsely ground
cinnamon

1. Butter the pan and put it on a tray with baking parchment.
2. Roll out the dough into a rectangle, 45 x 23 centimeters (18 x 9 inches), with a rolling pin and a little wheat flour. Spread the remonce and cream paste on the dough and sprinkle with the cardamom and cinnamon. Sprinkle with the candied peel, orange peel, and raisins.
3. Roll together into a tight long roll and roll it together to fit in the pan. Put it in the pan, brush with the egg mixture, and cut all the way around with scissors. Let it rise in a warm place for about 45 minutes until doubled in size.
4. Preheat the oven to 210°C (410°F). Brush the twist with the egg mixture one more time and sprinkle generously with almond shavings.
5. Put the twist in the oven. Lower the temperature to 190°C (374°F) after 5 minutes and bake the twist for about 20–25 minutes until golden brown.

See photograph on page 204.

Light saffron Christmas cake

Lätt saffransjulkaka

A Christmas without a saffron Christmas cake on the table is hard to imagine for us Swedes. The Norweigan love their Christmas cakes so much that they bake them all year round instead. The Danes make theirs of Danish dough, fold them round, and fill them with lots of goodies.

There should be plenty of almonds on a Christmas cake. If you do not like saffron, use cardamom instead.

Remember to soak the raisins in cold water for 30 minutes to make them soft, and let them drain in a sieve. You would rather do without hard raisins in sweet bread dough or as garnish on *lussekatter*.

Add 3 grams (1½ tablespoons) of crushed saffron to the base recipe for sweet bread dough and possibly omit the cardamom. Or use both, I like that the best.

When the dough is ready, add:

100 grams (1 cup) chopped peeled
    almonds
100 grams (½ cup) candied peel in cubes
100 grams (¾ cup) raisins

Let the dough rest for 30 minutes in a lightly oiled plastic container covered with a lid.

1. Divide the dough into about 400-gram (14-ounce) pieces (about 8) and tear them into beautiful round buns. Cover them with a cloth and let them relax for 5 minutes.

2. Flatten the buns with your hand and cut all the way around with scissors. Brush with the egg mixture. Or shape them into beautiful breads, about 16 centimeters (6¼ inches) long (see shaping of breads on page 38). Cut all the way around and brush with egg mixture.
4. Put the bread to rise in a warm place for about 45 minutes until doubled in size.
5. Preheat the oven to 220°C (428°F). Brush once more with the egg mixture.
6. Bake for about 15–18 minutes until golden brown and let cool on an oven rack. You can freeze the bread for later, too.

Lussekatter with saffron dough

Lussekatter au saffransdeg

1. Roll the dough into 60-gram (2-ounce) big, tight buns. Cover them with a baking cloth and let them relax for 5 minutes.
2. Roll out and shape the buns like in the photograph. Add soaked raisins to the dough, and push them in hard to keep them from getting dry like at most bakeries. Brush with the egg mixture and let rise heavily for about 45 minutes until a little more than doubled in size.
3. Preheat the oven to 250°C (482°F).
4. Bake the buns for about 8–9 minutes until golden brown and brush them once more with the egg mixture after baking. (Note: Do not brush *lussekatter* that are high in volume with egg a second time before baking, or they will collapse. The same is true for *semlor*/fat Tuesday buns, which are supposed to be light and airy.)

Gosen bread

Gosenbröd

This sweet bread dough specialty is Swedish, and the method of making a cold sweet bread dough without kneading makes the shells light and delicious. Freshly brewed coffee and freshly baked gosen bread—it can hardly get better.

Dough temperature as cold as possible
Sits 1 hour in the refrigerator

For 33 pieces
625 grams (4½ cups) wheat flour high in
    protein
10 grams (2 teaspoons) baking powder

250 grams (1 cup) milk
50 grams (3 tablespoons) yeast
150 grams eggs (about 3 eggs)
75 grams (½ cup + 2 tablespoons) powdered sugar
5 grams (1 teaspoon) sea salt
300 grams (2⅔ sticks) regular salted butter   ➤

The photograph to the left: Saffron twist, light saffron Christmas cake, lussekatter

Hazelnut remonce

200 grams (1¾ sticks) regular salted butter, at room temperature

240 grams (1 cup + 3 tablespoons) farine sugar

100 grams (7 tablespoons) ground roasted hazelnuts

10 grams (1½ tablespoons) ground real cinnamon

Egg mixture

1 egg

1 egg yolk

a pinch of salt

1 doubled recipe Tosca paste (see Danish Tosca, page 194)

1. Keep all the ingredients for the dough at room temperature for 1 hour before mixing it.
2. Sift the flour with the baking powder. Mix the ingredients carefully into a dough, wrap it in plastic wrap, and put it in the refrigerator for 1 hour.
3. Make the remonce by stirring the butter until light and airy with sugar, nuts, and cinnamon.
4. Roll out the cold dough about 3½ millimeters (⅛ inch) thick and 28 centimeters (11 inches) wide with a rolling pin and a little wheat flour. Spread the remonce on the dough and roll it together into a firm long roll.
5. Cut 60-gram (2-ounce) shells with a sharp knife and put them on a tray with baking parchment. Brush them carefully all over with egg mixture.
6. Cook the Tosca paste and distribute it on top of the shells with a spoon. Let them rise for about 1 hour until doubled in size.
7. Preheat the oven to 230°C (446°F).
8. Bake the shells for about 10–12 minutes until golden brown.

Temptations

Frestelser

Delicious Swedish flavors that are good for parties with children and adults. This cold dough of Swedish origin is very moist and has a lovely butter taste. The buns should be light and airy and lightly baked.

For about 25 pieces

Butter filling

250 grams (2¼ sticks) regular salted butter

225 grams (2 cups) powdered sugar

25 grams (2 tablespoons) real vanilla sugar

Dough (Deg)

550 grams (4 cups) wheat flour high in protein, preferably stone ground

175 grams (¾ cup) cold water

50 grams (4 tablespoons) yeast

50 grams eggs (about 1 egg)

20 grams egg yolk (about 1 yolk)

40 grams (3 tablespoons) granulated sugar

5 grams (1 teaspoon) sea salt

225 grams (2 sticks) regular salted butter, at room temperature

Egg mixture

1 egg

1 egg yolk

a pinch of salt

almond shavings

1. First put the flour in the freezer for 1 hour. Stir the ingredients for the butter filling in a mixer until light and airy.
2. Dissolve the yeast in the water with a whisk. Add the other ingredients and knead for 13 minutes at lowest speed. Increase the speed and knead for another 7 minutes. Make a gluten test (see page 35). The dough should be soft and elastic.
3. Put the dough in a floured plastic bag and put it in the freezer for about 30 minutes until hard.
4. Roll out the dough 4 millimeters (⅛ inch) thick on a floured surface with a rolling pin, lifting it now and then to sprinkle flour underneath. Cut out squares, 8 x 8 centimeters (3 x 3 inches). Each piece should weigh 45–50 grams (1.6–1.8 ounces).
5. Pipe 20 grams (1½ tablespoons) of butter filling onto each piece, fold together from all sides, and push in the middle. Put them in pans, brush with the egg mixture, and let them rise for about 1 hour until doubled in size at no more than 28°C (82°F) or in a turned-off oven.
6. Preheat the oven to 230°C (446°F). Brush the buns with the egg mixture again, sprinkle with almond shavings, and bake for about 12–13 minutes until golden brown. Let cool on an oven rack.

Top: Temptation
Bottom: Gosen bread

Tarte au sucre

This French specialty is among the best with a cup of strong coffee. In Colmar in Alsace they used to make them at Pâtissérie Sitter. Neither Maître Pâtissiér Sitter or his lovely pastry shop are there anymore, but the memories live with those who bought their pastries there.

For 6 portions
Dough (Deg)
600 grams (2½ cups) milk, at room
    temperature
8 grams (2 teaspoons) yeast
175 grams (1¼ cups) enriched wheat flour
7 grams (1 teaspoon) sea salt
18 grams (1½ tablespoons) cassonade sugar
100 grams eggs (about 2 eggs)
80 grams (6 tablespoons) unsalted butter,
    at room temperature

Topping
120 grams (½ cup + 1 tablespoon)
    cassonade sugar
20 grams (1½ tablespoons) unsalted butter
20 centiliters (¾ cup + 2 tablespoons)
    crème fraiche

Egg mixture
1 egg
1 egg yolk
a pinch of salt

1. Dissolve the yeast in the milk with a whisk. Stir in the other ingredients except the butter. Knead at low speed for 5 minutes. Add 80 grams (6 tablespoons) of butter, increase the speed, and knead into a completely elastic dough. Make a gluten test (see page 35).
2. Put the dough in a lightly oiled plastic container covered with a lid and let it rest for 2 hours.
3. Push together the dough twice on a floured baking table and press out the air with your hands (see page 36). Fold it together like an envelope, put it back in the container, and let it rest for 2 hours.
4. Put the dough in plastic wrap in the refrigerator for 1 hour or overnight.
5. Divide the dough in half and tear into 2 tight buns. Flour them lightly on top, cover with a baking cloth, and let them relax 15 minutes.
6. Roll out the buns 24 centimeters (9½ inches) in diameter with a rolling pin and a little flour. Put them on a tray with baking parchment.
7. Brush with the egg mixture, sprinkle with the cassonade sugar, and let them rise at room temperature for 2 hours.
8. Preheat the oven to 240°C (464°F). Brown the butter for the topping until it starts to smell like hazelnut, add *crème fraiche*, and cook for 2 minutes. Spoon the mixture over the tarts and bake for about 15–20 minutes until golden brown. Let cool on an oven rack and serve with good coffee. You can also serve with strawberry jam and whipped cream.

Classic cinnamon buns

Klassiska kanelsnäckor

This delicacy is perhaps the most Swedish pastry there is. The first time I learned how to make cinnamon rolls, we only brushed the dough with melted butter and sprinkled generously with cinnamon sugar before we rolled it together. However, with almond remonce they become better and more moist, I think.

For 25 buns
1,000 grams (2 pounds 3.3 ounces) sweet
  bread dough

Almond remonce
2 parts (barely 350 grams/1½ cups) almond
  paste 50/50, at room temperature
1 part (barely 175 grams/1 cup) regular
  salted butter, at room temperature

Stir the almond paste until light and airy with the butter. Cover with plastic wrap and keep in the refrigerator. Keep the remonce at room temperature before using to make it easy to work with.

Cinnamon sugar (see page 158)

Egg mixture
1 egg
1 egg yolk
a pinch of salt

almond shavings, for decoration

1. Roll out the dough 3½ millimeters (⅛ inch) thick and 28 centimeters (11 inches) wide. Cover the dough with the almond remonce on top, sprinkle generously with the cinnamon sugar, and roll it together into a long firm roll.
2. Cut out 60-gram (2-ounce) buns with a sharp knife. Put them on a tray with baking parchment with the seam facing downward to keep them from opening while rising.
3. Brush them immediately with the egg mixture and sprinkle with almond shavings. Let them rise in a warm place for about 45 minutes until doubled in size.
4. Preheat the oven to 230°C (446°F).
5. Bake the buns for about 8–10 minutes until golden brown. Let cool on an oven rack.

See photograph on page 213.

Almond buns

Mandelbullar

Most ready-made almond paste contains preservatives and other things that do not belong there. Proper almond paste should only contain two ingredients, namely sugar and freshly peeled almonds, preferably Italian or Spanish macaroon almonds. They have a distinct taste, which Californian almonds do not have. The water content should be 10–12%. For a little bit more flavor, you can add 10% bitter almonds.

For about 40 buns
1,600 grams (3 pounds 8.4 ounces) sweet bread dough

Almond filling (cream paste, in jargon)
500 grams (2½ cups) almond paste 50/50, at room temperature
300 grams (1½ cups) vanilla cream (see page 211)

Almond paste
250 grams (1¾ cups) sweet almonds
250 grams (1¼ cups) granulated sugar

almond shavings, for decoration

Scald the almonds in boiling water for 1 minute, rinse them cold in a sieve, and remove the peels. Put them in a food processor with a jagged knife, add the sugar, and mix into a smooth paste. Put the paste in plastic wrap and let it swell at room temperature until the next day. Keep in the refrigerator.

1. Stir the almond paste into the vanilla cream a little at a time to create a smooth paste.
2. Tear the dough into round buns and cover them with a cloth. Let them relax for 10 minutes.
3. Roll the buns lightly and pipe 20 grams (1⅓ tablespoons) of almond filling onto each. Fold together the dough so that the almond filling is closed in and tear the buns lightly to make them round. Put them with the seam facing downward on trays with baking parchment, about 12 pieces on each tray. Let them rise in a warm place for about 45 minutes until doubled in volume.
4. Brush the buns carefully with the egg mixture and let them dry for 5 minutes.
5. Preheat the oven to 230°C (446°F). Brush one more time with the egg mixture. Cut a jack on top of the bun with scissors and sprinkle with almond shavings.
6. Bake the buns for about 8–10 minutes until beautifully golden brown. Let cool on an oven rack.

See photograph on page 213.

Cardamom buns

Kardemummaknutar

These buns became very popular in Scotland, where Peter Ljungkvist runs the bakery and cafe Peter's Yard in Edinburgh. At Olof Viktor's bakery these are also quick to sell out. Cardamom and cinnamon buns are very Swedish.

For about 25 buns
1,000 grams (2 pounds 3.3 ounces) sweet bread dough
500 grams (2 cups) almond remonce (see page 209)
20 grams (3½ tablespoons) coarsely ground cardamom

Egg mixture
1 egg
1 egg yolk
a pinch of salt

almond shavings, for decoration

1. Roll out the dough 4 millimeters (⅛ inch) thick and 30 centimeters (12 inches) long with a little wheat flour.
2. Spread half of the remonce over the dough and sprinkle generously with cardamom. Fold the dough together in 3 parts. Turn it upside down with the seam facing downward.
3. Cut 1½ centimeter (½ inch) wide strips, weighing 60 grams (2 ounces) each. Twist the strips on the table and fold them together like a knot. Put the buns in baking tins on a tray. Cover with baking cloths and let the buns rise for about 45 minutes until doubled in size.
4. Brush the buns with the egg mixture in 2 batches with 10 minutes in between to make them beautifully glossy. Sprinkle with almond shavings.
5. Preheat the oven to 230°C (446°F).
6. Bake the buns for about 8–10 minutes until golden brown. Let them cool on an oven rack.

See photograph on page 213.

Old-time sugar buns

Gammaldags sockerbullar

When I was a child I loved sugar buns. Behind the Catholic church in Malmö there was a bakery that made only sugar buns. Coming from school, we ate as many of them as the baker could make. There was always a line of people there.

This is how I think good sugar buns should taste. I do not think that cardamom goes in this dough. It should be airy and light and have a neutral taste to bring out the vanilla cream and butter. These days they pipe the cream directly into the buns before they are half baked, whereas we used to fold it into the buns in the old days, which tastes much better and gets more moist. Start by cooking the vanilla cream so that it is cold when it is time to fill the buns.

You can freeze these before they are brushed with butter and dipped in sugar. Thaw them carefully in a microwave oven.

Vanilla cream
The French call it *crème pâtissière*, or pastry cream. It is one of the cornerstones of good pastries and cakes.

½–1 vanilla bean, preferably Tahiti
500 grams (2 cups) milk
120 grams egg yolk (about 6 yolks)
125 grams (½ cup + 2 tablespoons) granulated sugar
40 grams (5 tablespoons) cornstarch
25 grams (1¾ tablespoons) butter

1. Divide the vanilla bean lengthwise, scrape out the seeds, and put them in a small pot with the milk. Cook, put the pot aside, put on a lid, and let the milk absorb the vanilla flavor.
2. Whisk the egg yolks and sugar lightly and add the flour. Pour in the milk over the mixture and mix everything thoroughly. Pour it back into the pot.
3. Cook the cream while constantly stirring; do not let it boil. Add the butter and whisk until melted. Strain the cream through a sieve and into a low pan to cool quickly. Cover with plastic wrap and cool the cream in cold water. Keep in the refrigerator until it is time to use it. Vanilla cream is perishable and keeps for no more than 2 days.

Melted butter
Cook 250 grams (2¼ sticks) butter in a pot and put it aside. After 20 minutes, pour the butter into a different bowl, without the sediment.

I always have clarified butter in my refrigerator for cooking meat and fish. This way you do not burn the butter.

Dough temperature 28°C (82°F)
Sits 30 minutes

For 37 buns
Pre-dough (Fördeg)
500 grams (2 cups) milk
75 grams (6 tablespoons) yeast
25 grams (2 tablespoons) granulated sugar
600 grams (4⅓ cups) wheat flour

Combining (Bortgörning)
200 grams (1¾ sticks) butter
150 grams (¾ cup) granulated sugar
25 grams (2 tablespoons) real vanilla sugar
100 grams egg yolk (about 5 yolks)
600 grams (4⅓ cups) wheat flour

The same preparation as for my classic sweet bread dough. The dough becomes a little bit lighter and smoother and softer because of the egg yolk.

1. Divide the dough into 4 equal pieces, using a scale. Roll them out into lengths and cut 10 60-gram (2-ounce) pieces from each length. Tear them into buns and cover with a baking cloth to not dry out the dough's surface.
2. Roll the buns out into the size of saucers. Pipe a ball of 20 grams (1⅓ tablespoons) of vanilla cream onto each, fold and pinch them together.
3. Put the buns on trays with baking parchment, about 12 buns per tray. Let them rise under a baking cloth at room temperature for about 45 minutes until doubled in size.
4. Preheat the oven to 250°C (482°F).
5. Bake the buns for about 9–10 minutes until beautifully and lightly golden brown, not too dark. Let them cool on an oven rack.
6. Brush the buns with the melted butter and roll them in granulated sugar.

See photograph on page 213.

Lundagård twist

Lundagårds specialkrans

Thure Collbring was a clever artisan who learned the pastry chef profession at Georg Fahlman's in Helsingborg. He had been the first baker at Thage Håkansson's classic pastry shop in Lund before he took over the Conditori Lundagård in Lund. They were the most famous for their "Japanese," made by the son, Boris. "Japanese" originates from Switzerland, and pastry chef Max Hämmerli took the recipe with him from there. Max eventually opened his own pastry shop Hämmerli in Malmö.

We filled this delicious twist with pistachio remonce. You should make it sometime when you feel ambitious, and make both sweet bread dough and Danish dough. Keep in mind that 50% of the dough weight should consist of the filling to make it moist and delicious.

For about 12 portions
a circular or long baking pan,
    26 centimeters (10 inches) in diameter
20 grams (1½ tablespoons) butter for
    the pan

250 grams (8.8 ounces) Danish dough
250 grams (8.8 ounces) sweet bread dough
250 grams (1⅔ cups) pistachio remonce
    (see page 176)

Egg mixture
1 egg
1 egg yolk
a pinch of salt

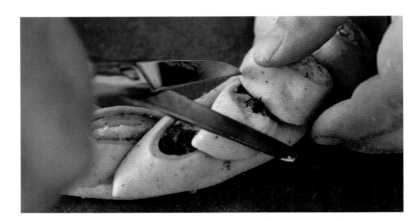

1. Fold the Danish dough in a piece of rolled-out sweet bread dough and roll it into a rectangle, 23 x 45 centimeters (9 x 18 inches).

2. Spread the remonce on the dough and roll it together into a twist. Cut it with scissors and put only 1 piece aside instead of 2, which is more common.
3. Put it in a greased cake pan or long baking pan. Brush with the egg mixture and let it rise in a warm place for about 45 minutes until doubled in size.
4. Preheat the oven to 190°C (374°F). Brush once more with the egg mixture.
5. Bake the twist for about 25–30 minutes.

Butter twists

Smörkringlor

This simple pastry is always good with a cup of strong coffee.

1. Tear a sweet bread dough with cardamom, saffron, or Karlsbader dough into 60-gram (2-ounce) pieces. Tear them into round buns, cover with cloth, and let them relax for 5 minutes.
2. Roll out the buns, about 12 centimeters (5 inches) long, and twirl into twists. Put them on a tray with baking parchment and let rise in a warm place for about 45

minutes until doubled in size.
3. Preheat the oven to 250°C (482°F).
4. Bake the twists for about 6–8 minutes until light and pretty. Immediately put them on a cold tray after baking so that they do not get dry.
5. Brush the twists with melted butter and turn them in granulated sugar.

Almond buns, butter buns, sugar buns
On the tray from the top: Cardamom buns, butter twists, cinnamon buns

Rolf's butter cake

Rolfs butterkaka

Rolf Augustsson ran the pastry shop Hollandia in Malmö and was a good friend and ingenious pastry chef who lived and died for his pastry shop. Until the very end of his life, he always called from Nybro and asked what we had on display in the window this month. Making beautiful and appetizing displays for his fine pastries was Rolf's specialty, and his wife Ingegärd minded the shop.

This good cake should be heavy with moisture and a lot of filling, then it is truly a world-class delicacy. Whether it is sweet bread dough or Danish dough does not matter, it will be delicious either way.

1 circular or long baking pan,
    26 centimeters (10 inches) in diameter
20 grams (1½ tablespoons) butter for the
    pan

For about 12 persons
Short dough (known by French bakers as pâte sucrée)
300 grams (2 cups) wheat flour
200 grams (14 tablespoons) unsalted butter
100 grams (¾ cup + 2 tablespoons)
    powdered sugar
2 grams (⅓ teaspoon) salt
50 grams eggs (about 1 egg)

Put the flour on the table and make a pit in the middle. Cut the butter into small pieces, put them in the pit, and work them with your fingertips until completely soft. Add the sugar and salt, mix well, and then add the egg. Mix and gradually work the flour into the dough. When all is mixed, work the dough a couple of times with your palm until smooth. Put the dough in the refrigerator for at least 1 hour wrapped in plastic wrap. Leftover dough can be frozen for another time.

50 grams (⅓ cup) raisins
50 grams (¼ cup) preserved chopped
    orange peel
20 grams (1½ tablespoons) dark rum
500 grams (1 pound 1.6 ounces) sweet bread
    dough with cardamom or Danish dough
250 grams (1⅔ cups) almond remonce
    (see page 209)

¼ recipe (200 grams/2 cups) vanilla cream (see page 211)
130 grams (½ cup) cream paste (see page 210)
coarsely ground cardamom and real ground cinnamon
20 grams (3 tablespoons) almond shavings
water glaze with lemon (see page 186, but exchange the rum
    for 25 grams / 1½ tablespoons lemon juice)

Egg mixture
1 egg
1 egg yolk
a pinch of salt

1. Marinate the raisins and the orange peel in the rum for at least 1 hour.
2. Roll out a short dough plate about 3 millimeters (⅛ inch) thick and 26 centimeters (10¼ inches) in diameter. Prick it well with a fork on a tray with baking parchment.
3. Butter the round or long baking pan.
4. Roll out the sweet bread or Danish dough into a rectangle, 28 x 45 centimeters (9 x 18 inches).
5. Spread the almond remonce on the dough with a palette, and pipe a string of cream paste with a piping bag. Sprinkle with the swelled raisins, orange peel, cardamom, and cinnamon. Roll the length together into a tight, long roll. Cut the roll into 12 pieces.
6. Put the buns first around and then toward the middle of the circle. Leave space in between for the dough to rise. Brush with the egg mixture and put them in a warm place to rise for about 45 minutes until doubled in size.
7. Brush once more with the egg mixture. Pour the vanilla cream into a plastic cornet and cut a hole in the front. Make a depression with your thumb in each bun and pipe a healthy pat of vanilla cream in each. Sprinkle with almond shavings.
8. Preheat the oven to 190°C (374°F).
9. Put the cake in the oven. Lower the temperature to 180°C (356°F) when it is a little bit browned.
10. Bake the cake beautifully light brown for about 25–30 minutes. Let cool in the pan and frost with lemon water glaze.

From the top: Cardamom twist, Rolf's butter cake, cinnamon twist

BRAIDED BREADS

The braided bread is known all over Europe. In Switzerland, Germany, and Austria, braided breads are important at holidays and on Sunday mornings. Jews also love braided breads (challah) for the Sabbath. The fact that braided bread stays fresh much longer than an ordinary loaf is less well known, however. Since the gluten strings break up during the braiding process, the crumb always gets softer than in regular bread. This is why pan-baked bread is often braided, or why you put buns in the pan instead; it is to break up the gluten strings.

Six-part braided French bread was a specialty in Malmö when I was a boy, and the bakers at Swedberg's bakery and Sundets Breads braided lots of 6-braids each day. Nowadays you only see 4-braided French bread. The other ones are considered to take too long to braid, but it is a question of habit; the more you make, the faster it goes.

The Viennese call this bread *Butterstriezel*, but they add raisins to the dough. Otherwise they braid it in the same way. Hofsuckerbäckerei Heiner in Vienna is considered to be the best in Austria at making this bread, but I have had even better at Kurcafé Oberla. The very best, however, is in Switzerland. We used to bake this Swiss Sunday bread at Honold Confiserie in Zürich by the thousands all Saturday night, and in the morning there was a line for them. Serve with good butter, proper strawberry jam, and good coffee.

Zürich is home to the world-famous Confiserie Sprüngli with its *Luxenburgerli* everywhere in their elegant shop in Paradeplats. Do not miss the café on the second floor, and order a *Zuger Kirschtorte* and a *café crème*. The cake is soaked with *kirsch* to the point that you will not be able to drive for an hour.

It is important when braiding that the dough is stiff and properly worked, and to always brush the bread with egg mixture just before baking to get the best possible gloss.

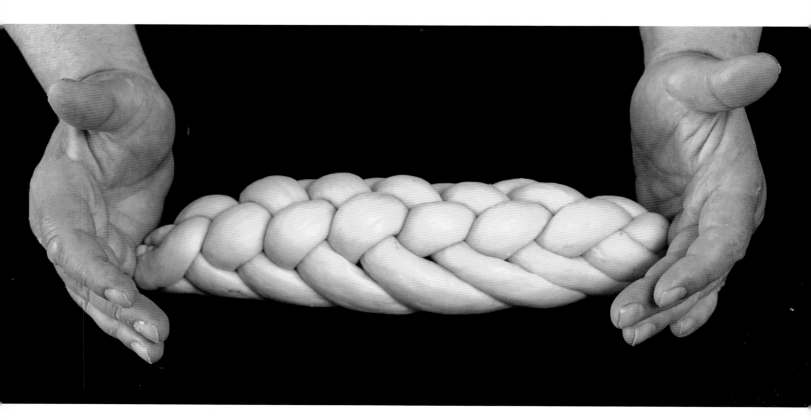

Practice makes the master

Braiding bread looks complicated, but once you know how to do it, nothing could be easier. Start with a 3-part braid, as it is the most simple. You do not have to cross your hands. You start crossing your hands for

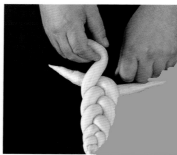

3-part braid

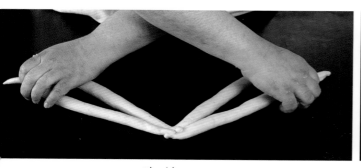

4-part braid

double 4-part braid

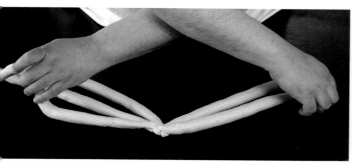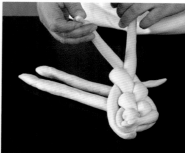

5-part braid

the other ones. Then you pick a string from the right and one from the left and put on opposite sides. Once you figure it out, it is like riding a bicycle— you never forget it.

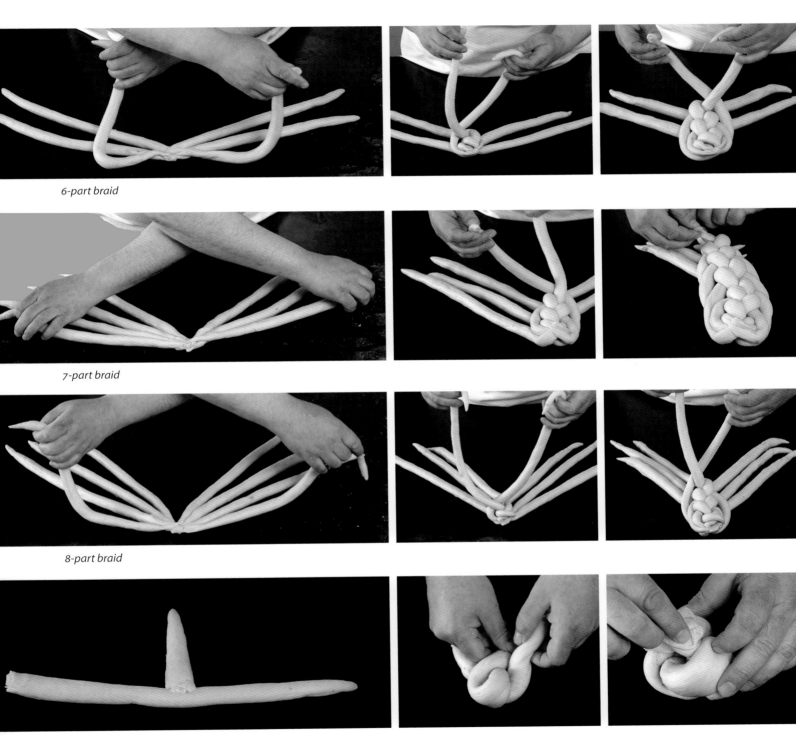

6-part braid

7-part braid

8-part braid

knot

Butter *zopf*

Smör-zopf

Ideal dough temperature 28°C (82°F)
Sits 30 minutes

Pre-dough (Fördeg)
500 grams (2 cups) milk
75 grams (6¼ tablespoons) yeast
750 grams (5½ cups) wheat flour high in
    protein, preferably stone ground

Dissolve the yeast in the milk and pour it
over the flour in a bowl. Knead at lowest
speed for 3–5 minutes. Put the dough in a
lightly oiled plastic container covered with
a lid and let it rise until doubled in size for
about 30 minutes, depending on the
temperature of the room.

Combining (Bortgörning)
1,325 grams (2 pounds 14.7 ounces)
    pre-dough
750 grams (5½ cups) wheat flour high in
    protein, preferably stone ground
150 grams (¾ cup) granulated sugar
200 grams eggs (about 4 eggs)
25 grams (1 tablespoon) honey
    or light malt
150 grams (10½ tablespoons) butter
18 grams (1 tablespoon) sea salt

1. Knead the pre-dough with the flour,
   sugar, eggs, and honey at lowest speed
   for about 3 minutes. Add the butter and
   work for another 5 minutes. Add the

salt, increase the speed, and work the stiff dough for another 10 minutes
until tough and elastic. Make a gluten test (see page 35) to make sure that
the dough is completely developed, otherwise knead it for a little bit longer.
2. Put the dough in a lightly oiled plastic container covered with a lid and let it
   rise for 30 minutes.
3. Push together the dough (see page 36), cover with a cloth, and let it relax
   for 10 minutes.
4. To make a pig shape, use 400 grams (14 ounces) of dough for the body, 2 x 5
   grams for the ears, and 5 grams for the tail and a raisin for an eye. For an
   Easter bunny: 350 grams (12 ounces) of dough for the body, 50 grams
   (1.8 ounces) for the head, and a raisin for an eye. For a knot, 300 grams (10.5
   ounces) (see photograph on page 219). For a 2-part braided zopf, roll 2 buns
   of 250 grams (8.8 ounces). For a 3-part braid, roll 3 buns of 100 grams (3.5
   ounces), for a 4-part braid, 4 buns of 100 grams (3.5 ounces), and so on up
   until an 8-part braided with 8 buns of 100 grams (3.5 ounces).
5. Let them relax under a cloth for 5 minutes.
6. Roll out and put together the braids with crossed hands like in the
   photographs on pages 218–219. Pinch the ends together properly so that
   they do not come apart. Let them rise in a warm place until doubled in size.
7. Cooling the leavened braids for 30 minutes in the refrigerator before baking
   makes them even prettier and the braided texture more apparent. Brush
   twice with egg mixture before baking.

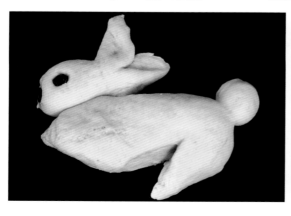

appetizers

entrees

desserts

A proper baker must also know how to make both sweet and savory dishes using different kinds of dough, such as butter dough. When *The Gentlemen's Cookbook (Herrarnas Kokbok)* was published at Christmas in 1968, everybody in the kitchen, cold-buffet, and pastry shop at the Savoy Hotel in Malmö was excited to see what their creations would look like. The book was created in the summer, and everybody participated in preparing the various meals. I was 18 years old at the time and entrusted to bake a Swiss onion tart, which was served at the buffet as a snack with beer and wine.

The pastry shop at the Savoy always baked blinis for an appetizer, which I also got to make, as well as small pancakes with rum ice cream under the supervision of master chef Einar Pettersson. I felt proud when chef pâtissiér Yngve Malmqvist said: "Let the kid make apple cookies and gooseberry cookies, too, he got the other ones right." Cookies with different berries and fruits were top sellers for lunch at the grill and cafe. After this I was also entrusted with making *Cointreau sufflé* and *Blanc manger aux prunes*. But when it was time to make the Savoy's famous *Coulibiac de Saumon*, chef pâtissiér Malmqvist stepped in. Rolling a perfect butter dough is not so easy when you are 18 years old.

French butter dough

Fransk smördeg

In France it is known as *pâte feuilletée inversée*. This type of dough is preferable for certain baked dishes, since it stays calmer than traditional butter dough. It becomes a little bit crispier than the classic. Rolling the butter on the outside of the dough makes it even richer. It sounds dramatic to roll the butter on the outside of the dough, but relax, you mix flour into the butter so it is not as strange as it seems. Do not buy margarine-rolled industrial butter dough, but take your time to make a proper butter dough, which tastes a million times better.

Baked dishes like Beef Wellington with truffle sauce, for which you always used this type of butter dough, were served often back in the day. This light-roasted tenderloin was made with ground veal with *duxelle* paste (finely chopped field mushrooms and onions) before being rolled in the butter dough.

Pheasant Souvaroff was another popular dish that we served often. Light-roasted pheasant was carved and put in a pot with light-roasted goose liver, slices of autumn truffles, and embossed roasted field mushrooms; flambéed in cognac; and covered with Madeira sauce. The lid was put on and the edge of the pot was covered with bread dough that was brushed with egg and cut with scissors, after which the pot baked in the oven for about 20 minutes until the dough was golden brown. The head waiter cut the lid open at the table, spreading the wonderful smell. This was often served with *pommes Anna*, thinly sliced potatoes layered in the pan with salt and pepper and covered in melted butter, which was baked in the oven until golden brown. The cake was cut open and the butter was drained. This delicious potato cake was then cut into pieces and served with the pheasant and good red wine at the table. It can hardly get much better.

Butter mixture
120 grams (1 cup) high quality wheat flour
320 grams (2⅞ sticks) unsalted cold butter

Work the flour into the butter and shape a plate, 2 centimeters (¾ inch) high and as big as the sheet of baking parchment (20 x 20 centimeters / 8 x 8 inches). Let it sit for 1 hour in the refrigerator.

Base dough (Grunddeg)
100 grams (7 tablespoons) butter
300 grams (2¼ cups) wheat flour
5 grams (1 teaspoon) white wine vinegar
   or pressed lemon juice
10 grams (½ tablespoon) *fleur de sel*
200 grams (1 cup) cold water

1. Melt the butter and put it aside.
2. Work all the ingredients together into a dough and knead for 5 minutes. Do not overwork the dough or it will shrink in the oven.
3. Knead the dough into a ball, wrap it in plastic wrap, and put it in the refrigerator for 2 hours to relax.
4. Roll out the dough slightly smaller than the butter plate.
5. Beat the butter plate with the rolling pin until softened. Put the dough on top and fold it into the butter like a package. Roll out the dough on a floured surface, preferably a marble plate, about 70 x 40 centimeters (27½ x 15¾ inches).
6. Brush excess flour off the dough. Fold it together in 3 parts (see photograph on page 183). Repeat the rolling and fold the dough again. Wrap it in plastic wrap and let the dough rest for 1 hour in the refrigerator.
7. Repeat the process twice. Wrap in plastic wrap and let rest for another hour in the refrigerator.
8. Repeat the process twice more. Now you have a classic butter dough folded 6 times.

Coulibiac de saumon

This classic Russian *pirogue* was often served as an appetizer at weddings and banquets at the Savoy Hotel in Malmö. They were taken straight out of the oven onto a cutting board where they were cut by skilled waiters at the table and served with melted butter and sour cream. This is served often in France at buffets and receptions. You can make it with Brioche dough or with French butter dough as we used to make it at the Savoy Hotel. It rises more evenly and goes better with butter-dough baked dishes.

When I passed my masters exam as a baker, I treated the censors and their wives to this dish and a glass of Chablis.

For 12 persons
1 recipe French butter dough

Rice pilaf
6 eggs
25 grams (1¾ tablespoons) butter
50 grams (3½ tablespoons) olive oil
150 grams (15 tablespoons) shallots, peeled and finely chopped
150 grams (¾ cup) Arborio rice
100 grams (½ cup) dry white wine, unoaked, such as Sancerre or Chablis
500 grams (2 cups + 3 tablespoons) chicken broth
400 grams (4 cups) fresh field mushrooms
25 grams (1¾ tablespoons) butter
250 grams (8⅓ cups) spinach
25 grams (½ cup) parsley
25 grams (3½ tablespoons) dill
15 grams (5 tablespoons) chives

fleur de sel
freshly ground white pepper
grated nutmeg

1,200 grams (2 pounds 10.3 ounces) fresh filet of big salmon
fleur de sel
freshly ground white pepper

100 grams (½ cup) dry white wine, unoaked, such as Sancerre or Chablis
1 lemon's pressed juice
100 grams (7 tablespoons) butter

Egg mixture
1 egg
2 egg yolks
a pinch of salt

DAY 1

Start by preparing the butter dough. Never buy industrial butter dough, which is made with margarine. If you find it troublesome to roll a butter dough, use a brioche dough that you have made yourself instead.

DAY 2

1. Cook the eggs for 8 minutes, run them under cold water, and peel and chop them coarsely.
2. Preheat the oven to 150°C (302°F).
3. Brown the onion in the butter and olive oil until golden yellow and transparent, for about 5 minutes. Add the rice grains and fry until glossy.
4. Add the wine and the broth and let the rice cook on low heat under a lid in the oven for 18 minutes. Add 25 grams (1¾ tablespoons) of butter and vent the rice with a fork.
5 Rinse and slice the field mushrooms, fry them in butter, and add the spinach. Season with the salt, white pepper, and nutmeg. Mix with the cooked rice pilaf and the chopped eggs, parsley, dill, and chives. Season carefully with salt and freshly ground white pepper, cover with plastic wrap, and let cool.

6. Preheat the oven to 150°C (302°F).

7. Cut the salmon into 100-gram (3.5-ounce) pieces, season with salt and white pepper, and put the pieces close together in a greased pan. Pour the wine, lemon juice, and the butter in pats and cover with baking parchment.

8. Put the pan in the oven for 5 minutes, until the salmon is still half raw inside. Let cool and drain on paper towels.

9. Roll out half of the butter dough about 2.5 millimeters (1/16 inch) thick with a rolling pin and a little wheat flour. Put it on a tray with baking parchment. Cut out the shape of a fish with a sharp knife (see the photograph).

10. Distribute half of the rice mixture on the dough, save 1 centimeter (1/4 inch) of the dough all the way around and brush it with the egg mixture. Cut the salmon on top and cover with the rest of the rice mixture.

11. Roll out the rest of the dough 2.5 millimeters (1/16 inch) thick and a little bigger than the other piece. Roll the dough onto the rolling pin and roll it out over the filling. Shape it as beautifully as you can with your hands. Cut off excess dough like in the photograph.

12. Brush the entire fish with the egg mixture. Mark the fins with a fork and the scales with a cutter. Add a sunflower seed for an eye. Let it rest in the refrigerator for at least 1 hour. Butter dough should always rest, or it will shrink in the oven.

13. Preheat the oven to 200°C (392°F).

14. Bake the fish for about 25–30 minutes until golden brown. Place it on a cutting board and let it rest for 10 minutes.

15. Serve in beautiful pieces with melted butter and sour cream (see page 229).

Swiss onion tart

Schweizisk löktårta

This onion tart can be served as an appetizer, like in Switzerland and Alsace, or for lunch.

For lunch, preferably serve with a mixed salad with Swiss dressing (see page 98). Brushing the dough inside with egg yolk makes the peel crispier after baking.

The best onion tart I ever had was at L'Auberge de l´Ill in Illhausern in Alsace between Colmar and Strasbourg. This fantastic 3-star restaurant leaves no customer feeling disappointed. If you have time, try to book a night at their hotel, too, when you are there.

For 8 portions
1 tart pan, 30 centimeters (12 inches) in
    diameter and 2 centimeters (¾ inch) high
25 grams (1¾ tablespoons) butter and a
    little wheat flour for the pan

For brushing the pan
2 egg yolks
a pinch of salt

Quiche dough (known as pâte à foncer in France)
250 grams (1¾ cups) wheat flour
125 grams (9 tablespoons) butter
5 grams (1 teaspoon) sea salt
50 grams (3 tablespoons) milk
40 grams egg yolk (about 2 yolks)

Onion paste
125 grams (4.2 ounces) bacon
50 grams (3½ tablespoons) butter
200 grams (2⅓ cups) sliced yellow onions
75 grams (¾ cup) Gruyère cheese, grated
75 grams (¾ cup) Emmenthaler cheese,
    grated

For baking the egg
200 grams (1 cup) milk
100 grams (½ cup) cream
30 grams (¼ cup) wheat flour
50 grams egg (about 1 egg)
40 grams egg yolk (about 2 yolks)
sea salt, freshly ground white pepper, *Maggi*
    aroma, grated nutmeg

1. The dough: Sift the wheat flour onto the baking table. Shape into a circle. Put the butter (at room temperature) and salt in the middle. Pinch together into a crumbly paste with your fingertips.
2. Add the egg yolks and milk. Work them with your hands into a dough (work the dough as little as possible). Wrap the dough in plastic wrap and keep for at least 1 hour in the refrigerator or 30 minutes in the freezer. (Naturally, you can mix the dough in a food processor too, but I prefer this old-fashioned method to make sure that the dough will not get overworked.)
3. Butter the pan with soft butter, flour it, and shake off excess flour.
4. Roll out the dough about 2½–3 millimeters (¹⁄₁₆–³⁄₃₂ inch) thick. Roll it onto the rolling pin, roll it out over the pan, and flour lightly on top.
5. Take a piece of dough and press it out in the pan. Prick the bottom with a fork. Roll on top to make excess dough fall off. Press up the edges carefully around and bend it a little bit over the edge. Brush with the egg mixture and mark a pattern around the pan with the back of a knife.
6. Put the pan in the refrigerator for at least 30 minutes to keep it from shrinking while baking.
7. Preheat the oven to 200°C (392°F). Put a baking parchment in the pan and fill with peas. Bake the dough for 20–25 minutes until golden brown. Let cool and take out the peas.
8. Make the onion paste: Cut the bacon in strips and let it cook until golden brown in the butter, add the onion, and fry until golden yellow. Stir in the cheese and take it off the stove.
9. Make the eggs for baking: Cook the milk and cream with the flour and pour it boiling over the beaten egg and egg yolks. Strain the batter through a *chinoise*, a fine-filtered sieve, and season carefully with the spices.
10. Brush the dough with the egg mixture and put it in the oven for about 5 minutes, until the egg yolk is golden brown.
11. Fill with the onion paste and the warm, baked egg. Bake the tart for about 30 minutes until golden brown. Let cool on an oven rack.

Swiss cheese cake–*Käsekuchen*

Schweizisk osttårta–Käsekuchen

We used to make this cake 2 different ways at Honold Confiserie in Zürich. For one of them, we added some butter-fried yellow onions, but it was the classic that sold the most. On Fridays we sold lots of them, since it was a cleaning day and no hot dinner was served.

The best *Käsekuchen* I ever had was as *amuse-bouche* at the 3-star chef Freddy Girardet's restaurant in Switzerland, where I have had some of my best dinners. The master Paul Bocuse once said that Freddy was one of the few chefs in the world who could surprise him with a new dish. His green pea terrine with duck liver counts as one of the great works in gastronomic history. Unfortunately, this restaurant no longer exists, but the memories live with those who were there.

For 12 portions
25 grams (1¾ tablespoons) butter and a
   little bit of wheat flour for the pan

Quiche dough
The same as for the onion tart on page 225
   and same method.

For brushing the pan
2 egg yolks
a pinch of salt

The same preparations as for onion tart.

For baking egg and cheese
50 grams eggs (about 1 egg)
40 grams egg yolk (about 2 yolks)
250 grams (1 cup) milk
125 grams (½ cup) cream
35 grams (¼ cup) wheat flour
125 grams (1 cup) grated Gruyère cheese
125 grams (1 cup) grated Emmenthaler
   cheese
sea salt, freshly ground white pepper, *Maggi*
   aroma, and a little bit of grated nutmeg

1. Beat the eggs and egg yolks. Cook the milk and cream with the flour, pour it boiling over the egg mixture, and whisk the paste until smooth. Strain through a *chinoise* or fine-filtered sieve over the grated cheese and stir until the cheese is melted. Season carefully with the spices.
2. Preheat the oven to 200°C (392°F).
3. Pour the cheese paste into the prepared quiche pan and bake the cake for about 30–35 minutes until golden brown. Spray a little bit of water in the oven with a squirt bottle; this will help melt the cheese better and keep the surface from getting burned.
4. Let the cake cool on an oven rack immediately when it comes out of the oven to make the dough crispy on the bottom. If it cools in the pan, it will get tough instead.
5. Cut the cake into pieces and serve warm for lunch with a green salad with Swiss dressing (see page 98), or in small pieces as an appetizer with a glass of wine.

Saucisson en Brioché de Lyon

Saucisson Lyonnaise is the name of the famous Lyon sausage that the chef Paul Bocuse always treats his guests to as *amuse-bouche* at his famous restaurant. The sausage is also served with lentils and cooked potatoes, and every pork butcher is proud of his own recipe. We do not have any similiar sausages in Sweden, but pick any other good sausage and make it the same way. It is great with a glass of wine and also good for a picnic.

For 10–12 portions as amuse-bouche,
5–6 portions as entrée
500 grams (1 pound 1.6 ounces) classic brioche dough (see page 148)
1 Lyon sausage weighing 1 kilogram (2 pounds 3 ounces) and 30 centimeters (12 inches) long (see recipe below)

Egg mixture
1 egg
1 egg yolk
a pinch of salt

1. Butter a 30-centimeter (12-inch) long cake pan with 25 grams (1¾ tablespoons) of butter. Flour the pan lightly and shake off excess flour.

2. Divide the dough in half, roll out one part, and put it at the bottom of the pan. Remove the sausage casing, put in the sausage with 1 centimeter (¼ inch) of space on each side, and brush it all over with the egg mixture.
3. Roll out the other half of the dough and put it on top. Brush with the egg mixture and press the dough down around the sausage. Possibly decorate with a pattern.
4. Let it rise in a warm place for 90 minutes until the dough has doubled in volume.
5. Preheat the oven to 220°C (428°F). Brush one more time with the egg mixture right before baking to get a pretty gloss.
6. Bake the sausage for about 25–30 minutes. Loosen it immediately from the pan and let cool for a few minutes on an oven rack.
7. Serve in slices with a glass of wine, preferably *Beaujolais*, or as an entrée with a classic *périgueux sauce* (truffle sauce).

Saucisson Lyonnaise

I got this this award-winning recipe from a pork butcher in Lyon.

Casing

1,500 grams (6⅔ cups) pork scraps
500 grams (2½ cups) fat
20 grams (3¼ teaspoons) nitrate salts
20 grams (3¼ teaspoons) sea salt
4 grams (1⅔ teaspoons) ground white pepper
1 gram (⅛ teaspoon) saltpeter
8 grams (2 teaspoons) granulated sugar
1 gram (½ teaspoon) grated nutmeg
40 grams (5¼ tablespoons) whole pistachio nuts
60 grams (¾ cup) chopped truffle
60 grams (¼ cup) cognac

1. Grind the meat and fat 3 times in a meat grinder with 8 millimeter (¼ inch) blade. Work the forcemeat heavily with all the ingredients, cover with plastic wrap, and let it sit cold for 48 hours.
2. Stuff the sausage in casings, 35–40 millimeters (1¼–1½ inches) in diameter.
3. Let the sausages dry on the surface and then simmer in salted water, 85–90°C (185–194°F). Prick them with a fork to keep them from bursting. Let them simmer for about 40 minutes and let them cool in the liquid.

Russian blinis

Ryska blinier

The pastry chefs always used to make these Russian yeast pancakes at the restaurants when I was a young pâtissière. Anything that contained yeast came from the pastry shops back then. You got caviar, onions, and proper sour cream from the cold-buffet, and the melted butter from the kitchen.

Personally I am very fond of blinis with a good rum, and I always order this masculine appetizer when in Finland. The Savoy, Nevski prospects, and Havis Amanda all serve excellent blinis in Helsinki. In January, when the burbot is the best, they serve it with roe instead of caviar. It is cheaper and almost as good. When I last guest-appeared on the Finnish ferry *Silja Symphony* I made chocolate blinis with *Smetana* ice cream and roe, which was also delicious.

Bake them in special stoneware pans—they have them in kitchenware stores—or use a regular pancake pan.

For 6 blinis
125 grams (½ cup) milk
125 grams (½ cup) beer, light lager
25 grams (6¼ teaspoons) yeast
100 grams (¾ cup) buckwheat flour
50 grams (⅓ cup) wheat flour
40 grams egg yolk (about 2 yolks)
15 grams (3 teaspoons) sour cream (see below)
60 grams egg white (about 2 whites)
5 grams (1 teaspoon) pressed lemon juice
6 grams (1½ teaspoons) *fleur de sel*

100 grams (½ cup) melted butter for frying

1. Heat the milk and beer to 35–37°C (95-99°F) and dissolve the yeast in the liquid with a whisk. Sift in both kinds of flour and whisk everything into a thick batter for about 1 minute. Cover with plastic wrap and let sit and swell for 2 hours at room temperature—24°C (75°F) is ideal. The batter has to be used within the hour, or the blinis will taste like yeast.

2. Melt the butter and pour the yellow part. The sediment, which is about 20% of the butter, gets thrown out.

3. Whisk the egg yolks and the sour cream into the batter and put it aside.

4. Whisk the egg whites with lemon juice into a stiff foam in an absolutely clean stainless bowl. When the foam is stiff, add the salt and whisk into a completely firm foam. Fold it into the batter with a spatula to make an airy batter.

5. Pour the melted butter into the pans. Pour in about 1 centimeter (½ inch) of batter and bake them at 125°C (257°F) in the oven until browning underneath. Or fry them on the stove in a griddle and put them one by one on a warm tray at 90°C (194°F) in the oven until all of them are ready.

6. Serve the blinis warm, brushed with melted butter, and put on a hearty spoonful of whitefish roe. If you are in the money, Iranian or Russian caviar are naturally the best. Serve with finely chopped red onion, *Smetana* or sour cream, and melted butter. Ice-cold vodka and cold pilsner go excellently with this meal.

Old-time sour cream
1 deciliter (½ cup) of sour cream and 7 deciliters (3 cups) of whipped cream are heated together at 37–40°C (99–104°F) and then covered with plastic wrap for 24 hours at room temperature, preferably on top of the refrigerator. Put the sour cream in the refrigerator to cool. It is much better than plain sour cream, I promise.

Basler *Mehlsuppe* and Shewbread

Basler Mehlsuppe and Skådebröd

A Swiss variation of classic French onion soup as it used to be served in the old Halls of Paris. It is baked in a gratin dish with bread and Gruyère cheese and is a classic in January for *Fastnacht* in Basel and Zürich with a glass of white Swiss Fendant wine or a red Dole. The soup is served in cups or in bread bowls. The cold cut leftovers and the roasted bread give the soup a pleasant character. I have made 3 simple Shewbreads with the same dough. It is a nice present to bring to a party.

Bread bowls to pour the soup into

For 8 bread bowls
Dough temperature 28°C (82°F)
Sits 1 hour

500 grams (2 cups) water
30 grams (2½ tablespoons) yeast
500 grams (5 cups) fine rye flour, preferably stone ground
150 grams (1¼ cups) coarse graham flour, preferably stone ground
200 grams (1½ cups) coarse rye flour, preferably stone ground
200 grams (1½ cups) wheat flour high in protein
30 grams (2¼ tablespoons) butter
20 grams (3¼ teaspoons) sea salt

1. Pour all the ingredients except the butter and salt in a baking bowl. Work for about 20 minutes until the dough is smooth. Add the salt and butter after 10 minutes.
2. Put the dough in a lightly oiled plastic container covered with a lid and let it rest for 1 hour.
3. Put the dough on a floured baking table and cut 200-gram (7-ounce) pieces. Tear them into round buns and dust with fine rye flour. Put them on a floured cloth and let them rise until doubled in size.
4. Cut around the bread with a sharp knife.
5. Preheat the oven to 250°C (482°F) and place a baking stone or tray inside.
6. Lift the bread with a baker's peel onto the stone or tray, spray in a little bit of water with a squirt bottle, and bake the bread for about 20 minutes until golden brown. Check with a thermometer that their internal temperature is 98°C (208°F) and immediately put them on an oven rack to cool.
7. Cut a lid off the bread with a bread knife and hollow the inside with a fork to create a bread bowl.

Soup

For 6 portions
125 grams (1 cup) wheat flour
1 day-old baguette
60 grams (4¼ tablespoons) butter
200 grams (1 cup) smoked beef, or ideally Bündnerfleisch from Switzerland and a little bit of Italian salami or coppa, finely chopped
1,000 grams (7⅔ cups) yellow onions, peeled and thinly sliced
25 grams (3 tablespoons) garlic, crushed
1,250 grams (5¼ cups) dark broth from veal or beef
250 grams (1 cup) dry white wine
20 grams (3 tablespoons) caraway
5 grams (3½ teaspoons) thyme
2 bay leaves
200 grams (2 cups) Gruyère cheese, grated

1. Preheat the oven to 200°C (392°F). Pour the wheat flour onto a sheet of baking parchment and roast for about 10 minutes until brown.
2. Cut the baguette in slices and roast in the oven for about 10–15 minutes until golden brown.
3. Melt the butter in a pot, and put in the finely chopped cold cuts. Add the onions and garlic and fry carefully for 15–20 minutes until dark golden brown.
4. Add the roasted flour and let it brown a little bit. Pour in the broth, wine, and spices and let the soup simmer for 20 minutes.
5. Pour the soup into 6 *koppar* or baked bread bowls as in the photograph. Put the bread on and top with the cheese in the cups or bread. Put them in the oven until the cheese is melted and golden brown.

Shewbread

Skådebröd

Grape bunches are a classic motif when making Shewbread. I have made a round bottom plate with the dough, cut it all the way around with scissors, brushed it with water, and shaped small dough balls like a grape bunch. Then I rolled out the same dough, about 3 millimeters (¹/₁₆ inch) thick, cut out a leaf and marked the leaf veins with the back of a knife. Finally, I rolled out a few spirals of thin dough, then dusted lightly with a little bit of fine rye flour using a sieve.

The second bread is also cut along the edges with scissors. I have arranged stems and leaves on the dough and cut them out, shaped a bowtie of rolled-out dough, and then rolled out the dough thinly and turned it into rose shapes and cut-out leaves. Dust with fine rye flour using a sieve.

I finally made a heart-shaped bread, decorated it with roses and leaves with the dough, and then dusted with fine rye flour.

Let the bread rise for about 45 minutes. Preheat the oven to 250°C (482°F). Put the bread in the oven and spray generously with water using a squirt bottle. Lower the temperature to 200°C (392°F) after 5 minutes. Bake about 45 minutes until golden brown for and let cool on an oven rack.

Belgian yeast waffles

Belgiska jästvåfflor

Perfect for a book on bread as they have a nice taste of yeast. These should be served freshly baked with powdered sugar and lightly whipped, sugared cream and a good jam, or with fresh berries. The tartness makes them especially delicious. They bake them around Grand Place and Place de Sablon in Brussels, where there is also a lovely antique market on Saturdays. You can also bake them in advance and heat them in the oven when it is time to serve them, to make it less stressful.

For 9 waffles
250 grams (1 cup) milk
12 grams (3 teaspoons) yeast
250 grams (2 cups) wheat flour
5 grams (1¼ teaspoons) granulated sugar
19 centiliters (¾ cup) lukewarm water
1 vanilla bean
125 grams eggs (about 2½ eggs)
1 tiny pinch *fleur de sel*
150 grams (10½ tablespoons) melted
    butter

butter for baking
powdered sugar
lightly whipped cream with sugar
raspberry or strawberry jam, or
    fresh red berries

1. Dissolve the yeast with a whisk in the milk, whisk in the flour, sugar, and water, and whisk into a thick batter. Let it sit and swell, covered in plastic wrap, for about 30 minutes until doubled in volume.
2. Divide the vanilla bean lengthwise, scrape out the seeds, put them in the batter, and whisk in the eggs and salt and finally the melted butter.
3. Brush the waffle iron with butter and bake waffles until golden brown. Dust with powdered sugar and serve with lightly whipped, sugared cream (about 60 grams / ½ cup of sugar per liter [2 pints] of whipped cream) and a good red jam or fresh red berries.

English Summer Pudding

This classic English bread pudding should be served with mixed red berries. It is also often served with lightly whipped cream, or a vanilla sauce, *crème anglaise*. It is both delicious and beautiful, and a wonderful way to make use of old white bread. Remember not to use strawberries, as they contain too much juice and become sticky.

The best Summer Pudding I ever had was at the Riverside Restaurant at the famous Hotel Savoy in London, which opened in the 19th century with the great Auguste Escoffier as their first head chef along with the legendary Caesar Ritz. The old baking oven from the 19th century is still in the kitchen.

For 6 portions

750 grams (5–6 cups) mixed red berries, for example raspberries, wild strawberries, blueberries, red currant, and blackberries

90 grams (½ cup) granulated sugar

8 slices of dry white pan-baked bread, cut edges

1 1½-liter (3-pint) pudding pan

1. Clean and rinse the berries in water. Mix the wet berries with the sugar in a pot and simmer while stirring. Let them simmer for 5 minutes and cool.
2. Dress the pan with the bread slices, which have been cut to fit without gaps. Cut out a lid with a cookie cutter that fits in the bottom of the pan.
3. Put in the berries and enough juice to soak the bread thoroughly, and save the rest of the juice.
4. Cut out a lid that fits. Put it on top of the pudding and drown with liquid.
5. Wrap the pudding in plastic wrap, put a weight on top, and let it sit in the refrigerator for at least 24 hours.
6. For serving, put the pudding on a plate and brush with the rest of the liquid. Garnish beautifully with fresh berries and powder with powdered sugar. Serve with whipped cream or vanilla sauce.

Baba au rhum

This yeast dessert is a historic pastry that I love. It was created at the famous Pâtissérie Stroher at Les Halles in Paris, and when I am in Paris I like to go to the restaurant La Coupole and have a plate of fresh oysters followed by one of my favorite dishes, *Sole Meunière* with lemon, and a *baba au rhum* afterwards. After this dessert you should not drive.

    We used this recipe at Confiserie Zoo in Basel, which was the famous Coba school's pastry shop where I got my education when I was young. You can freeze them, dipped or undipped, and they last for a long time.

Dough temperature 28°C (82°F)
Sits 1 hour

For about 15 40-gram (1.4-ounce) baba
Pre-dough (Fördeg)
50 grams (3 tablespoons + 1 teaspoon) water
10 grams (2½ teaspoons) yeast
60 grams (½ cup) wheat flour

Dissolve the yeast in the water with a whisk. Pour it over the flour, knead until the dough is elastic, and put it in a plastic container covered with a lid to rise for 1 hour until doubled in volume.

Combining (Bortgörning)
120 grams (4.2 ounces) pre-dough
180 grams (1⅓ cups) wheat flour, extra strong
250 grams eggs (about 5 eggs)
4 grams (⅔ teaspoon) *fleur de sel* or sea salt
15 grams (2 teaspoons) honey
50 grams (3½ tablespoons) butter

15 baba forms 5 x 5 centimeters (2 x 2 inches) in diameter
   (you can also use muffin tins)
butter for the pans

1. Put the pre-dough in a bowl with the flour, eggs, salt, and honey. Work the dough at medium speed.
2. Melt the butter and add it (it should not be too warm, no warmer than 35°C / 95°F). Work into a smooth and pipable dough. It should be elastic and shiny. Let the dough rest for 5 minutes.
3. Butter the pans with the soft butter using a brush. Pour the dough into a piping bag and distribute it in the pans (fill up to half; about 40 grams (1.4 ounces) in each form). Put them in a warm place until the dough has risen up to the edge of the pan. Ideal heat is at 30–35°C (86–95°F), or in a turned-off oven.
4. Preheat the oven to 175°C (347°F).
5. Bake for about 20 minutes, until beautifully light brown as in the photograph. Turn them out of the pans and let cool on an oven rack.

Syrup
1 orange
1 lemon
½ vanilla bean
1,000 grams (4 cups + 3 tablespoons) water
500 grams (2½ cups) granulated sugar

If you are a professional, or want to become one, measure the syrup with a sugar scale, or Baumé scale. The liquid should be at 16 Baumé. If it is too thick, the pastries will be too sweet and shrink. If the sugar content is too low they will collapse instead, but take it easy—you do not need a sugar scale, I know the recipe is correct.

Wash the orange and lemon and cut them into slices. Cut the vanilla bean lengthwise, put it in a pot with the sliced citrus fruits, and pour in the water and sugar. Cook everything, take it off the heat when the sugar is dissolved, and let it sit and brew for 30 minutes.

Apricoture (see page 153)

Crème Chantilly
½ vanilla bean
350 grams (6 cups) whipped cream
30 grams (2½ tablespoons) granulated sugar

Scrape the seeds out of the vanilla bean and put them in a cold stainless bowl. Add the cold cream and sugar and whisk until it becomes a soft foam.

150 grams (⅔ cup) *rhum vieux* (aged dark rum), for brushing

1. Strain the syrup and cook it again. Put 5 babas at a time in the simmering liquid and let them brew. Put them on an oven rack to drain, and repeat the process and twice more. (*Puncher* is the French term for drowning babas and *savarins*.)
2. Brush the baba with the rum until completely absorbed.
3. Brush with the apricoture.
4. Put the pastries on a plate with a bottle of rum next to it, so that you can season with more rum if you wish. Serve with the whipped cream.

index